Inside the New Mexico Senate

INSIDE THE NEW MEXICO SENATE

Boots, Suits, and Citizens

DEDE FELDMAN

For Beth —
Thank you for all
your efforts to
preserve fresh water
& the environment.
It's making a difference.
Best —
Dede Feldman

University of New Mexico Press | Albuquerque

© 2014 by the University of New Mexico Press
All rights reserved. Published 2014
Printed in the United States of America
19 18 17 16 15 14   1 2 3 4 5 6

LIBRARY OF CONGRESS CATALOGING-IN-PUBLICATION DATA

Feldman, Dede.
  Inside the New Mexico Senate : boots, suits, and citizens / Dede Feldman.
     pages cm
  Includes bibliographical references and index.
  ISBN 978-0-8263-5438-9 (pbk. : alk. paper) — ISBN 978-0-8263-5439-6 (electronic)
  1. New Mexico. Legislature. Senate. 2. New Mexico—Politics and government.
  I. Title.
  JK8066.F45 2014
  328.789'071—dc23
                              2013029208

Book design and composition by Lila Sanchez
  Adobe Garamond Pro 10.75/14
  Display type is Adobe Garamond Pro

CONTENTS

Introduction and Acknowledgments

With an exotic landscape and a majority-minority population, New Mexicans consider their state to be different from all others. There's even a column in *New Mexico Magazine* called "One of Our Fifty is Missing"—meaning New Mexico. The column features stories about hapless outsiders who want to know whether you need a passport and shots to visit, or extra postage to send something here, since it's a foreign land. But when it comes to the state legislature, New Mexico's is not that different from other statehouses where legislators try each year to balance revenues and expenditures and struggle with spiking health care costs, education reform, and economic development. Whether they are from Mississippi, Maine, or New Mexico, lawmakers tangle with the National Rifle Association (NRA) and tobacco and pharmaceutical lobbyists. They struggle with redistricting and campaign finance reform; they come up with solutions to air pollution, drunk driving, and chronic disease that later find their way into federal law after they've been road tested on the highways of various states. During times of national gridlock, state legislatures keep going, balancing their budgets, electing their leaders, and doing battle with their governors—or not— depending on the political divisions within each state.

But in many ways, New Mexico's legislature is unique. For years it was the only reliably Democratic statehouse in the West outside of California (Colorado's legislative chambers have flip-flopped over a dozen times in recent years). It was organized as a part-time citizen legislature, where members receive no salary and cannot count on personal staff. Spanish might be spoken in the halls of the capitol as often as English, and Native American issues are often pivotal. Personal loyalty and regional identity make political outcomes unpredictable and, for most of the past few decades, New Mexico has been a swing state in national elections.

As you will see, the New Mexico legislature is a conglomeration of the new, the old, the rural, the urban, the "boots and the suits." It is no less partisan than other legislatures, but its small size and family feeling create a different style for dealing with some of the big issues present in every state.

At the heart of the process are the legislators. Every other year, hundreds of them are elected from around the country to serve for the first time in their state legislature. In January 2013, as I was completing this book, sixteen hundred new legislators took their seats. It was a record number; there was a much higher turnover than usual.

Whether Democrats or Republicans, candidates who get elected to public office for the first time often feel they have been sent to their capitols to do big things—especially if they ran on a reform platform to either "throw the bums out" or take on the establishment. In 1996, I was elected to the New Mexico Senate from one of its most liberal districts as an avowed progressive—but I was not naïve enough to think I could make a change overnight. I was optimistic, though, that once I learned the system I could find enough allies to advance an agenda of affordable health care for all, protection for New Mexico's breathtaking landscapes, and a system of financing campaigns to reduce the influence of special interests.

I didn't anticipate how tricky it would be to navigate the choppy waters of the New Mexico Senate, a forty-two-member chamber dominated by peculiar personalities, strange alliances between men I didn't know, and lobbyists I couldn't identify. I wasn't sure I could master the moves needed to succeed in what many of my fellow members seemed to treat as some kind of sporting event.

My first session in 1997 convinced me that the Roundhouse, as the New Mexico capitol is called, was a crazy, unpredictable place. Our leadership team, for example, was an odd couple composed of mercurial Manny Aragon, the president pro tempore, and a seeming country bumpkin named Tim Jennings, then majority leader. Often, during that first session, I couldn't understand what they were talking about or what their real motivations were. I assumed they were in favor of the well-being of New Mexicans and the defeat of archrival Republican Gov. Gary Johnson. But then Senator Jennings would start talking about elk wandering onto his ranch and eating his crops, or Senator Aragon would erupt into a tirade against "rich people" from Four Hills or the North Valley of Albuquerque who had it all, while his constituents in the South Valley were smelling shit (yes, shit is what he said) from the city's wastewater treatment plant. Meanwhile Sen. Shannon Robinson, from Albuquerque's Southeast Heights, might, at any time, burst into an Irish ballad or even appear in costume.

The first bill that I voted on was rushed to the floor as if there was a fire going on. Under the bill, New York companies would automatically become resident New Mexico companies, even though their base of operations was in the Empire State. Written at the behest of eastside legislators to accommodate a New York bus manufacturer considering locating in Roswell, the bill didn't make sense—but it passed unanimously.

There didn't seem to be a method to the madness. Yet I needed to figure it out before I could get down to business.

The lack of progress on a coherent budget that year, the failure of the Senate to do much of anything on the floor of the chamber for weeks on end—much less take substantive action on the pressing issues of the day—was really puzzling.

But what did I know? I was just off the boat, so to speak. When I asked the old timers, they said cheerfully, "Don't worry; everything will work out in the end."

Hmm—here was a problem. I had work to do. My bills were not moving the way they should in order to pass out of each committee and come to the floor for a vote. And the end of the session was fast approaching. The chairman of the Public Affairs Committee, Sen. Shannon Robinson, seemed nice enough as he smoked cigarettes and joked with a circle of buddies I later found out was the committee's staff. Yet somehow my bills didn't get scheduled. He was particularly noncommittal about when he would schedule a bill I was sponsoring with the help of then attorney general Tom Udall to license the retail sellers of tobacco products so a licensee could be fined if the retailer sold cigarettes to minors (which is illegal under federal law). His method of hearing bills seemed haphazard, and it was only after repeated entreaties that he finally heard mine.

Sen. Fernando Macias, the handsome chairman of the Senate Judiciary Committee (also called "Fernando's Hideaway"), to which my bill to limit campaign contributions was assigned, at least told me he had some reservations and suggested that I prepare an amendment if I wanted to get the bill through. But I was still clueless about the logjam of bills that had passed committees but were not being debated on the floor.

Was there a plan? Were people working on a behind-the-scenes deal between the parties or the two chambers? Why did the sessions start two, even three hours late with all the time taken up with ceremonial introductions and confirmations of the governor's appointments to the Game Commission or the board of the Farm and Ranch Heritage Museum? I didn't know. But I did know that debate on the important bills, if it came at all, occurred late at night when everyone was tired and tense. Then, as if lying in wait all day, bill opponents would talk in a tedious and time-consuming fashion, asking endless detailed questions about the minutiae of boll weevil control or load limitations for garbage trucks. These opponents of any given bill, almost always Republicans, would introduce amendment after amendment designed to divide the bill's supporters or damage key pieces of the legislation. Sen. Leonard Lee Rawson, the minority whip, in particular, seemed to be an expert in this technique. "It's starting again," Democratic colleagues would say, shaking their heads, when I asked about this line of questioning.

"Don't worry, it's just a game," some of them told me.

"It," I found out, was a slowdown tactic used by the minority party (there were seventeen Republican and twenty-five Democrat senators at that time) to avoid passing bills that could regulate business or enlarge government. That year saw the ultimate use of the slowdown, a marathon filibuster by Sen. Bill Davis, a Republican from Albuquerque. Davis, a portly lawyer with a silver tongue, knew that the rules of the Senate allowed him to talk up to two hours if he did not relinquish the floor, and talk he did, lecturing on the differences among communism, socialism, and Marxism. His filibuster came on the last day of the session, and since most of the bills had been delayed, they all died without a vote as the clock struck twelve noon—the hour of adjournment. One of the bills that the filibuster killed was the all-important capital outlay, or "pork" bill, which legislators use to fund projects they designate in their districts (see fig. 1).

As the floor session melted down that day, I wondered if it would ever be possible to understand this Alice-in-Wonderland spectacle, complete with kings, queens, mad hatters, rabbit holes, fading smiles, and abrupt about-faces. I was particularly dubious because much of the confusion seemed to be emanating from my own party.

Why, for example, was Sen. Manny Aragon switching his position on the key issue of private prisons from one of vehement opposition to silent support—or at least what seemed like support? Why couldn't the Democrats prevail upon him to make a deal with the Republicans to let a few of their priorities pass (see fig. 2)? Maybe if that happened Senator Davis would quit droning on about communism and allow the capital outlay bill to pass.

Why did the Democrats allow themselves to be led like sheep down the path to slaughter? What was the role of the governor in all this? Was he putting the Republicans up to it because of his well-known feud with Manny and Ray (Raymond Sanchez, the Speaker of the House), as he called them?

It suddenly occurred to me that no amount of hard work, expertise, good intentions, positive media coverage, or powerful allies could help advance a progressive agenda unless I understood the process.

That's what this eyewitness account of the strange-but-true events that occurred during my sixteen years in the New Mexico Senate is all about. Yes, there is a method to the madness, and I will try to pass on some of the lessons I learned—without letting go of the madness. After all, that's what makes the process New Mexican.

The first chapters of this book are about the players in a high-stakes political game that allocates resources and money and creates economic winners and losers out of hundreds of thousands of New Mexicans. The players include powerful lobbyists and Roundhouse leaders whose interplay determines the outcome of important issues. At the center are citizen legislators who struggle, first to get elected and, once in office, to pursue a wide variety of goals from simply bringing home the bacon to pushing a specific agenda. Some are there to do big things like stamp out driving while intoxicated or help people with mental illness. Others want the prestige and power that comes with being a senator and hope only to get reelected or, with luck, to climb toward a higher office. Still others are there to stop what they see as bad things from happening.

If the objectives of the legislators are sometimes unclear, the objectives of the other major players are not. Special interests have a powerful grip on the New Mexico legislature; those interests are fronted by well-liked lobbyists in tasteful suits who have the time, expertise, money, and charm that many legislators lack. A huge number are former legislators. They know how to raise campaign cash, endear themselves to committee chairs with food and drink, and kill bills they don't like. Their influence is tough to surmount even when there is public demand for health care, public safety, or consumer protection measures. Their power will be made clear in several different chapters focused on legislative dances with pharmaceutical companies, fireworks manufacturers, tobacco companies, and the gun lobby.

But laws can actually be enacted with the right ingredients, some of which are simply a matter of luck. The job gets done with supportive and even inspired leadership, good timing, divided opposition, media and grassroots support, and willingness to compromise. When these elements come together, the results can be life changing for New Mexicans. Opportunities can open, disease can diminish, and lives can improve. Several of the stories in this book illustrate those few-and-far-between victories.

Keeping up with the fast and furious interplay of clashing personalities, diverse interests, and conflicting loyalties made me crazy that first session. After I got home I told the Democratic Women of Bernalillo County in a speech that it was a little like "riding a motorcycle in a thunderstorm in the nude."

Gradually I learned how to move legislation through the storm. Sometimes I won and the issues I cared about advanced, albeit in unanticipated ways. Other times I lost in the face of overwhelming pressure from special interests, failures of leadership, or simply because the reforms I wanted were too big, too threatening, or too difficult for a chamber that had changed little since its establishment in 1912.

Here are lessons I learned at ground zero of the New Mexico Senate, not only from special interests but also from senators themselves. Successful legislators from around the country have learned their own lessons, allowing them to address similar problems and advance their bills through a maze of special interests and partisan leaders. They do it using skills adapted to their particular political landscape, whether it is through the Albany handshake (see chapter 3) or the independent politics of New England (see chapter 9). In New Mexico the political landscape—just like the physical landscape—is slightly different. The basic rules of the game are the same but—true to our state nickname (the Land of Enchantment)—the process is, well, enchanted. It is pretty to look at in its colorful finery and opening pledge to the Zia symbol of perfect friendship and harmony among united cultures. But, like a fine Southwestern painting, it has shadows and undertones that a casual observer may not notice at first, but which make the difference between victory and defeat.

Part 1 describes the basis of "La Vida Política" (political life) for New Mexico senators, including its mariachis, its *matanzas* (traditional Hispanic barbeques), and its accessible, retail-style of politics. Chapter 1 gives an overview of the legislature as it swings into action on a typical opening day, with a few snapshots of the citizen legislators who are at the center of the process. Chapter 2 describes the process of getting elected to the New Mexico Senate—past and present—using my own campaign as an example. Part 2, "Boots, Suits, Leaders, and Lobbyists," examines the roles of some of the major players who operate inside the New Mexico Senate—the leaders (chapter 3) and the lobbyists who represent various special interests (chapter 4). The behavior of both reflects a national pattern, but with a distinctly New Mexican flavor.

Part 3, "Dances with Wolves," recounts several different struggles with some of the biggest special interest groups in the nation: Big Tobacco, Big Pharma, and the NRA. I also describe one battle with a well-connected local industry, the fireworks vendors. The David and Goliath showdowns all had different outcomes. Part 4, "Patients and Patience: Turning Around the Battleship," takes on the question of how citizen advocates can reform huge systems and what can get in the way. Other states have reformed their schools or prisons with various degrees of success. Here we also examine New Mexico's struggle to improve health care. Chapter 9 describes successes, failures, and some "near misses" in health policy over twenty-five years. Chapter 10 takes us beyond the smokescreen to reveal patients, heroes, and mavericks along the road to marijuana reform. Part 5, "By Grit and Grace," covers two case studies—cockfighting (chapter 11) and the death penalty (chapter 12). Both efforts resulted in landmark legislation through successful advocacy. In the case of the death penalty, state advocacy efforts were intertwined with a bigger, national network—the National Coalition to Abolish the Death Penalty—just as local efforts to combat the ravages of tobacco in New Mexico were connected to a national lawsuit and a national group, Tobacco Free Kids. The struggle to ban cockfighting was also part of a national campaign waged by animal rights activists like TV star Pamela Anderson and movie actress Ali MacGraw.

Part 6 covers ethics, transparency, and campaign finance reform. These are areas in which New Mexico trails other states, but they are all keystone issues that will bring change. At the end of this book I offer some common-sense solutions: ways to rescue good people caught in a bad political system, and ways to restore public trust in state government.

A word about my bias. I am a liberal Democrat from an urban district, a woman, and a migrant to New Mexico in 1976. I'm passionate about equal opportunity; good education; affordable, accessible health care; and preserving New Mexico's unique environment. I am anti-gun and pro-choice. I admit it. I believe unchecked special interests, unlimited campaign contributions, secretive political leaders, and opaque government are threats to democracy here and everywhere. I hope after you read this book you will see how these things work in New Mexico and gain some ideas on how to get out of the fix we're in.

Throughout my legislative career, I took copious notes in committees, caucuses, task forces, and conferences. These notes, drawn from my own experience, are the basis for this book, along with official documents, media accounts, and interviews with staff, advocates, lobbyists, legislators, and many others. I have also used data from the secretary of state's office, the Legislative Council Service, followthemoney.org, and other campaign finance reports. Tracey Kimball, the Legislative Council Service's librarian, honored my many requests for information with patience and good cheer. Media reports from the men and women of the capital press corps served to confirm my memory and keep me honest. And I could not have soldiered on without the editing and encouragement of Beth Hadas, a longtime constituent who went above and beyond to help me in this endeavor.

This book was completed at the end of 2012. History marches on in the New Mexico Senate, of course, rendering some of the tales told here less current. I have tried to update where possible, but I leave it to the reader to continue the story.

Special thanks go to numerous colleagues directly involved in the episodes recounted here who shared their stories. The following took the time to read the relevant chapters for accuracy: Sandra Adondakis, Stuart Bluestone, Matt Brix, Nathan Bush, Rep. Gail Chasey, RubyAnn Esquibel, Mary Jane Garcia, John Gastil, Jessica Gelay, Viki Harrison, John Heaton, Ruth Hoffman, Jim Jackson, Bill Jordan, Emily Kaltenbach, Roxanne Knight, Ellen Leitzer, Sen. Cisco McSorley, Sen. Bill O'Neill, Sen. Jerry Ortiz y Pino, Ellen Pinnes, Cliff Rees, Richard Romero, Rep. Ed Sandoval, Cynthia Serna, Cindy Simmons, Reena Szczepansi, Steve Terrell, Joe Thompson, Karen Wells, and Barak Wolff. I am also indebted to three interns, Consuelito Martinez, Kendra Tully, and Jonas Armstrong, who helped with footnotes and other details. And my hat is off to New Mexico librarians who helped me retrieve tiny details.

My husband, Mark M. Feldman, deserves the most credit of all—for putting up with me during my sixteen years in the Senate and holding my hand during the writing of this book.

PART I *La Vida Política* in the New Mexico Senate

MOST WESTERN LEGISLATURES ARE OF THE PART-TIME, CITIZENS' variety. Like Hollywood westerns they spring from each state's history at the turn of the last century. In New Mexico, modern-day cowboys, ranchers, Hispanics, and Native Americans occupy important positions, as they did in 1912 when New Mexico became a state. But now they scramble along with their urban counterparts to keep up with more sophisticated constituents, complex issues, the demands of fundraising, and the twenty-four-hour news cycle. They have no full-time staff or regular salary. Getting elected is more and more expensive and technological. But things get done—New Mexico style, with mariachis, matanzas, and buffalo dancers all playing a role (see figs. 3 and 7). Chapter 1 sets the scene for the boots, suits, and citizen legislators who define the state's legislative culture. They are together again on the opening day of the 2003 session. In chapter 2 we hit the campaign trail and follow in the footsteps of Senate candidates—like me—who struggle to engage voters and retain a personal touch as they hunt for votes from ordinary citizens and contributions from far and wide. In New Mexico, more than in other states, ethnic politics plays a major role in campaigns, and local traditions—whether urban or rural—are at the forefront.

CHAPTER I

Cue the Mariachis
and Put On Your Cowboy Hat

The New Mexico Legislature Is in Session

OPENING DAY, JANUARY 21, 2003

IT WAS THE UMPTEENTH TIME WE HAD CLAPPED FOR YET ANOTHER county commissioner, a pueblo governor, a district court judge, the daughter of the Speaker, and the husband of the lieutenant governor. Enthusiasm was waning a bit, and it was hard to keep smiling. But here we were again, carnations pinned to our lapels: the full Senate and House along with a rostrum full of dignitaries, former governors, and Democratic and Republican Party officials, assembled on the floor of the New Mexico House of Representatives, awaiting the governor's entrance. The first session of the 46th legislature was getting under way.

New Mexico's unique political culture is on display in all its finery on opening day of every session of the state legislature. New Mexico finery, that is, where squash-blossom necklaces from the Navajo Nation mix with the latest in upscale business attire and pinstriped suits sit next to Sikh turbans and black cowboy hats. We have our own style here, drawn from the diversity of a state where Native Americans and Hispanics—with a few African and Asian Americans thrown in for balance—form a majority. The remaining 41 percent of the population is classified as "Anglo," whether they are hard-bitten ranchers from Little Texas on the east side of the state, high-tech scientists from Los Alamos, or Midwestern transplants from Albuquerque's Northeast Heights.

Opening day is the real show, and the introductions are part of the package. As those introduced stand up and wave, showing off their fine concho belts (cell phone firmly attached), their leather jackets, broomstick skirts, or bolo ties, they smile, knowing that they are part of the colorful tapestry of New Mexico political life (see fig. 4). And they are close to the center of power. Some have weathered tough campaigns; others are there because of who they know or who their relatives are. "Así es Nuevo Mexico," as the state song goes, from the Zuni war chief to the Doña Ana County sheriff. Here they are, defending their territory, seeing what they can get, plotting and scheming, paying tribute to the governor and the legislative leaders.

High above the floor of the House, the gallery is packed with well-wishers, lobbyists, state employees, union members, and state policemen. All are friendly, upbeat, and on the hunt.

In the press gallery, the familiar faces of the capitol press corps are visible, with pens poised and notebooks at the ready. The cameras are already rolling, some of them from national news outlets, since this is the debut of Gov. Bill Richardson, a familiar face on the national scene.

But it's been almost forty-five minutes since the introductions began. Smiling and clapping for that long takes its toll and, with the heavy jewelry and tight clothing, some of the women are beginning to feel weary.

Finally, Gilbert Baca, the sergeant at arms, comes to the door. The governor of the great state of New Mexico, he bellows, Bill Richardson and his wife Barbara Richardson, the First Lady of the state of New Mexico. Escorted by selected senators, the governor makes his way to the podium amid cheering and applause, shaking hands as he goes, cameras flashing, staff members scurrying to the front bench where they frame him as he gives his State of the State address, scheduled to begin at noon, a full hour and a half ago (see fig. 5).

The ceremony is typical of opening days in many legislatures around the country, but New Mexico does it with the pride of a small state gone big time. And the state's new Democratic governor, Bill Richardson, who is now approaching the lectern, has big ideas, bold policies, and a larger-than-life personality. Under his leadership New Mexico will become *bigger*, for better or worse, shaking off its image as a poor, outlier state with little relevance to the national scene, both politically and economically.

"Give me the tools to jump on our problems," the new governor asks the assembled legislators, in what turns out to be the longest, and most forceful, speech that we have heard in years. "And I will give you results, putting our state on a path to progress."

Using a teleprompter, Richardson declares that he will not move slowly, nor will he settle for second best in his quest for economic development.

Quoting Bob Dylan, he says he will not let anyone stand in the doorway or block up the hall. "We will not be impeded," he says in closing.

As we applauded the speech, I was optimistic about my chances for moving legislation I had long sought through the 2003 legislature. In the six years that I had been a Democratic state senator from the North Valley, I had learned to navigate the system, or at least know what pitfalls to avoid. Although I was on the opposite team from triathlete Republican Gary Johnson, the former governor had not run over me personally and had even signed a number of my important bills. I had weathered what was one of the most significant developments in the Senate in over a decade—the overthrow of Sen. Manny Aragon as president pro tempore. I had become somewhat of an expert in health and human services issues. In the process, I was promoted to chair the Senate Public Affairs Committee, which handled health care, gambling, local government, pensions, tobacco, alcohol, and firearms.

In the months leading up to the session, the new governor had called for a ceasefire between the loyal supporters of Manny Aragon, who was now the majority leader, and Richard Romero, who, with the help of all the chamber's Republicans and three Democrats, had ousted him in 2001. The ceasefire between the two Albuquerque Democrats held. A new day was dawning in the politics of the New Mexico Senate. For Bill Richardson, the sky was the limit and, as we soon found out, the presidency was within his sights. The winner of a landslide election (Richardson got 55.5 percent, his Republican opponent, John Sanchez, got 39 percent, and the Green Party candidate David Bacon, 5.5 percent), the former UN ambassador, who had negotiated with Saddam Hussein and freed prisoners around the globe, Richardson was a national figure. For someone of his caliber, dealing with the New Mexico legislature would be a piece of cake. Or such was the conventional wisdom.

The New Mexico legislature is a part-time "citizens" legislature, which meets in Santa Fe starting in January each year. Since 1933, the Senate has been controlled by the Democrats, except for a one-year interlude in 1986. Beyond the one-party dominance lays a tangle of sectional and personal loyalties, which often cross party lines. With a mixture of car dealers, realtors, lawyers, insurance agents, and many other professions, the Senate is difficult to understand, and hard to manage—especially for governors, and even its own leaders. Floor debate is by turns solemn, raucous, formal, outrageous, boring, and nonsensical (see fig. 6). Votes often follow sectional lines, with division between rural and urban legislators pronounced. Coalitions have become common, delays and filibusters routine.

During my first session here in 1997, before I understood the lay of the land, I felt a little like Alice in Wonderland—wondering what new surprise would pop up as I circled the third-floor balcony and discovered the travertine nooks and crannies of the unique Roundhouse that houses New Mexico's legislature, the governor, and their staff.

As the first Anglo and the first woman elected senator from Albuquerque's near North Valley, I was eager to contribute to the team I had joined—which was then engaged in a pitched battle with Gov. Gary Johnson over private prisons, tuition vouchers, and more. Our team's larger-than-life leader, Sen. Manny Aragon, didn't give me many clues as to what was going on. When I asked him to seat me beside someone who would help me decipher what the party line was, he put me between the chamber's two Navajo members, Sen. Leonard Tsosie of Crownpoint and John Pinto of Tohatchi. They were not exactly forthcoming with details—except for one. Senator Pinto, a former WWII code talker who is somewhat of a legend, advised me that I could duck under my desk and sleep during the long night sessions. And I should always point my chair to the south so that the media cameras, to which he was now pointing, wouldn't see me sleeping or eating.

My new seat was at the very center of the forty-two-member chamber. It was literally at ground zero, equidistant from the Republicans on the right, the Democrats on the left, the lieutenant governor in the front, and the public gallery to the rear. It was from there that I pieced together the method to the seeming madness of the New Mexico Senate and figured out how to pass legislation, take on special interests, create alliances, and start to reform a system that is often subject to conflict of interest and corruption. On January 21, 2003, I thought I had a new ally in the governor.

When New Mexico's founding fathers wrote the state constitution in 1912 they set up a legislature that met only two months every other year during the winter, when there wasn't much work to do on the farm or ranch. They believed in a "citizen" legislature, where ordinary people served without a salary, relying instead for their income—as well as their identity—on the work they did in their home communities during the balance of the year. A short session of the legislature, which meets for only thirty days in even-numbered years, was later added. But even then, the forty-two elected volunteers in the Senate and the seventy in the House were incapable of doing too much "damage," especially since they had little professional staff to help them until the Legislative Council Service started to draft bills in 1951, and the Senate chief clerk began to help with constituent relations in 1964.

If you were designing a system to limit government's ability to tax, spend money, and respond to urgent year-round issues, you could not have done better. But in the modern world of complex budgets and twenty-four-hour news cycles, the system comes up a little short. And it is very difficult to change, since the constitution does not provide for initiative, recall, or referendum, the usual methods of reform. The only recourse for reformers are constitutional amendments, which are formulated by the legislature, then ratified at the ballot box—a difficult path. To appear on the ballot, a measure must garner a majority of all elected senators and representatives (not just a majority of those present), and then win a majority at the ballot box. Some constitutional changes even require a two-thirds majority in each county! A constitutional convention proposed a new, updated constitution in 1969, but it was narrowly defeated at the polls.

So, the largely archaic setup has remained, making New Mexico one of the few states where legislators serve without compensation except for mileage and a per-diem reimbursement for time spent in session or committee. The per diem was pegged at $75 per day for decades, only changing when a rather deceptive constitutional amendment won approval in 1996, which "limited" per diem to the federal rate. Actually, that meant an increase in per diem—something legislators themselves were afraid to vote for. Colorado, Arizona, and a host of nearby states' legislatures meet longer and many chambers provide legislators with personal staff year round.

With these constraints you might think that no one in their right mind would want to be a New Mexico legislator. You'd be wrong. Elections for both the House, held every two years, and the Senate, held every four years, are hotly contested. By 2012 key Senate races in swing districts cost $200,000–$375,000.[1]

And, now, on opening day, 2003, the winners were all around me in their finery—twenty-four Democrats and eighteen Republicans in all. Here they were: real estate agents, lawyers, insurance people, doctors, retired judges, and consultants of all stripes. The number of oil and gas men was down from previous years, but two of the most senior members identified themselves (almost daily) as farmers or ranchers.

The theory is that with all this diversity and personal knowledge of various fields, good policy will emerge—with a common touch.

But the professional diversity of the citizen legislators is overblown, and the professions represented here don't look much like New Mexico's working stiffs or even its middle class. For example, in 2012 there were about five educators in the Senate, but three were retired or current administrators, one a counselor, leaving only one classroom teacher. Even those who identified themselves as businesspeople (the most common way senators describe themselves in their yearly financial disclosure statement) were the independent types, entrepreneurs, not people who worked from nine to five and let the boss worry about the rest. At least seven were consultants, hustling for contracts to write proposals, provide advice, or work with Indian tribes or other branches of government. In 2012, there were approximately eight senators who were really retired, or semiretired, although many would not admit it. (In a state with a young population, 60 percent of legislators are fifty plus, 28 percent are over 65.) There were five real estate professionals, two insurance salesmen, five attorneys, with one senator from the nonprofit sector and two others employed by other branches of government.

A reformer friend of mine from the advocacy group Common Cause used to say that legislators fall into three categories, the three Rs, as he called them: rich, retired, or resourceful. And he's largely right.

The truth is that it's difficult to make a living while being a legislator, and most people can't afford it. I could never have served but for my husband, a homebuilder, who, in effect, subsidized my service. And so it is for many others, whose spouses strain or who draw on savings from previous endeavors. For younger members, the financial burden is often very stressful and the opportunity costs high. For anyone who needs to make ends meet, it requires either a very sympathetic employer or constant hustling for new contracts, new business, and new leads.

Here's where a number of legislators have been a little too resourceful, opening themselves to charges of using their office to benefit themselves financially, something we swear on opening day not to do.

In 2011 there were ten women senators, out of forty-two.[2] The proportion is about typical for chambers around the country, but far from reflective of the world outside the Roundhouse. The women who serve tend to be experienced, paid-their-dues types, many of them veterans of other offices. Sen. Nancy Rodriguez, for example, was a Santa Fe County commissioner; Cynthia Nava was a school superintendent from the Gadsden District; and Diana Duran, who served through 2010, was the Otero County Clerk. The women often find themselves mixing it up with younger, ambitious men— an interesting combination that can be frustrating on both sides.

Despite their economic status, the idea that legislators are ordinary people whom you might meet in Furr's Cafeteria or at the supermarket is true. New Mexico is such a sparsely populated state. People tend to know one another, with only a few degrees of separation. Former governor Bruce King was famous for knowing almost everyone by name and even asking you about your uncle or cousin.

Sen. John Pinto, from the remote Navajo reservation, loved to tell the story of his first day in the New Mexico Senate in 1975. Low on funds, Pinto was hitchhiking the 230 miles to the session from his home in Tohatchi. A big Cadillac pulled up on the side of I-25 and skidded to an abrupt stop, pebbles flying.

"Where are you going?" asks the young, well-dressed driver.

"Santa Fe," says Pinto.

"Get in. I'm going there too."

"I've just been elected to the New Mexico Senate," Pinto grunts, throwing his bag in the back.

Amazed, the driver says, "Really? I've just been elected to the Senate, too."

The two men stared at each other in disbelief, which soon turned into laughter and thence to a loyal friendship that lasted thirty-five years.

It turns out that the driver was young Manny Aragon, who had no fear of mixing it up with scruffy hitchhikers, or anyone else for that matter. A young lawyer from Albuquerque, Aragon would soon become the most powerful force in the New Mexico Senate.

Outgoing and omnipresent in local cafes, supermarkets, and on the highway, New Mexico legislators are out there, available to constituents, lobbyists, or anyone else who makes an effort to contact them. The personal touch has been replaced somewhat by Facebook, Twitter, and e-mail, but still, compared to most states, like Pennsylvania, where I lived until 1975, legislators are remarkably accessible. Even after 9/11 and later, throughout a decade when Tea Party people on the right and antiwar protesters on the left assembled almost daily in front of the capitol—some of them carrying guns—anyone can walk into the Roundhouse and have direct access to committees and offices.

Among senators themselves there is a special bond, with personal loyalty a key virtue. This value is especially strong among the chamber's Hispanic senators.

In 2011, fifteen of the chamber's members were Hispanic (36 percent), all of them Democrats. (The one Republican Hispanic senator, Diana Duran, from Alamogordo, became secretary of state in 2011.) In the legislature as a whole, there were four Garcías, three Chávezes, three Martínezes, two Lujans, and two Griegos. The percentage of Hispanics has never risen above 50 percent, but the power of Hispanic senators is disproportionately large due to their geographic concentration in safe Democratic seats in both the north and south, which makes them almost invulnerable in general elections. Primaries are their real challenge, and most are enthusiastic participants in the Democratic Party statewide.

This status, along with the fact that there are no term limits in New Mexico, allows Hispanics to accrue a lot of seniority and positions them for leadership posts controlled by the majority party, the Democrats. And Democratic political power—and that of its elected officials—has grown with the increase in Hispanic population here and nationwide in the first decade of the twenty-first century. A swing state in 2008, and a bellwether for many years, the growing proportion of Hispanics (now 46 percent) put the state in the "safe" column for Obama in 2012. Popular Hispanic legislators campaigned vigorously for the president and sometimes he rode on *their* coattails to victory.

During the sixteen years I served in the Senate (1997–2012), for the most part, Hispanic males occupied the office of the president pro tempore, which is elected by the entire body. First Manny Aragon, then Richard Romero and Ben Altamirano, who was replaced by the office's first Anglo in years—Sen. Tim Jennings. Jennings was also the majority leader from 1997 through 2001, but since that time Hispanics (Aragon and Michael Sanchez) have occupied that post.

Although I am not Hispanic (people tell me I could have counted on more Hispanic votes if my name was Dede Fernández rather than Dede Feldman), I've always been proud of the Senate's Hispanic leadership as it has brought with it a passion to protect the rights of all minorities and provide economic and educational opportunities for people who, by accident of birth, don't always have them. In the early 1970s, the New Mexico legislature was one of the first to pass the Equal Rights Amendment (the ERA) for women. Its Hispanic leadership was a key reason. The Mama Lucy Gang, an earlier Democratic coalition composed of northern Hispanics and liberal Albuquerque representatives (named after a Las Vegas, New Mexico, restaurant where they met) had brought many needed reforms to the state during the 1970s and set the pace for educational and environmental issues in the following decades.

I've always chuckled when out-of-state organizers come to New Mexico with the intention of empowering Hispanics. They are thinking California or Arizona. Here Hispanics have long been pillars of the political establishment, and they have a history of eager political participation. In my largely Hispanic district in Albuquerque, folks have an excellent record of voter turnout and take real pride in Hispanic political leaders, who have been influential at every level since statehood.

Hispanic pride is on display daily in the Senate as we cue the endless mariachis from high schools around the state, sing "Las Mañanitas" when someone has a birthday, and joke about the chupacabra (see fig. 7). Sometimes this goes overboard. Every year the Hispanic Roundtable gives an award to a Hispanic leader called the "Flor de las Flores." The awards are lavish, with various lobbyists and their clients donating a Navajo rug, airline tickets, Nambé ware, Pendleton coats, and other expensive gifts later banned by the long overdue Gift Act passed in 2007.

Native Americans have their own special day at the Roundhouse, with speeches by Pueblo, Navajo, and Apache leaders, dancing, Indian food, and festivities. But the numbers of Native Americans are low in the legislature (only two in the Senate) and tribal sovereignty has placed the tribes in a far different position than Hispanics. According to that doctrine, tribes are sovereign nations, above the level of mere states, with whom they have had a checkered relationship. Still, the New Mexico legislature has got to be one of the few statehouses where Native American vendors throw out a blanket and sell their pottery and jewelry to anyone passing by. And where else can you hear an eighty-eight-year-old WWII code talker, Sen. John Pinto, sing the traditional potato song in Navajo, as senators and staff gather round, clapping and using their desks as drums.

Cowboys, farmers, and ranchers from the oil patch continue to exert a huge influence in the Roundhouse even though rural domination was moderated by two landmark U.S. Supreme Court decisions in the 1960s (*Baker v. Carr* and *Reynolds v. Sims*). Until then, each county in New Mexico was represented by one senator, with large urban counties like Bernalillo (where Albuquerque is located) getting the same number of votes as rural Harding County in northeastern New Mexico where there are still more cattle than people. After the Supreme Court rulings, legislatures around the country were required in the late 1960s to redistrict their chambers based on one person, one vote, which cut down drastically on the number of rural representatives. But every time redistricting occurs, rural senators fly in the face of demographic trends, striving to maintain districts with diminishing populations. They often succeed. Legislators from the safe Republican districts in the oil patch or on the ranch stick around a long time, as do those from safe Democratic seats in the north, accumulating seniority, making change difficult, and disproportionately affecting the tone and the outcome of many debates.

On any given day, the halls of the Roundhouse are full of cowboy hats, worn by lobbyists for the New Mexico Cattle Growers Association, land grant colleges, dairy farms, *acequia parcientes*, and even proponents of cockfighting. Elk hunting, other game and fish proposals, and especially water bills draw huge crowds. One of my lobbyist friends from the New Mexico

Association of Counties calls these bills "hat bills," and I learned very quickly to identify the issues based on the number of cowboy hats on the rack outside the hearing room (see fig. 8).

Usually the rural interests in the New Mexico legislature, from the eastern and southern parts of the state, stick together and vote as a bloc, often in opposition to those from Albuquerque and Santa Fe. The country folk have lots of jokes about the Emerald City (Albuquerque) and the City Different (Santa Fe) and the effete snobs who live there. Mostly they boil down to a resentment of the resources devoted to the flagship University of New Mexico, the newly constructed "Taj Mahal" of a Metropolitan Courthouse in Albuquerque, and the antichrist: the New Mexico Rail Runner, a commuter train between Belen and Santa Fe, which they feel diverts money from rural road projects. Divided between Republicans and Democrats, legislators from Bernalillo County are much less apt to stick together, although they represent about one-third of the seats in both the Senate and the House. These rural alignments and urban heterogeneity give the legislature a rural tilt far beyond what the raw numbers might indicate.

Whether rural, urban, Hispanic, Native American, or Anglo, senators in New Mexico are proud of their chamber, their independence from both the House and the governor, and their service to the state. New members are encouraged to act like a senator and show the colors. Shortly after I was elected in 1996, at my first Democratic caucus in the Senate lounge, Sen. Roman Maes, from Santa Fe, congratulated me. "This is the best, most exclusive club in the state," he said, "There is nothing like it. You're going to love it," he added as he stood next to a lavish buffet provided to the senators by lobbyists always eager to please the majority party.

I didn't know what to say, and frankly I still don't know how to react when I listen to my chamber's leaders wax poetic on the greatness of the New Mexico Senate. Longtime Sen. Tim Jennings, president pro tem in 2012, was the chamber's best booster, and his boosts got bigger and bigger as we neared the end of each session, often ending in a tearful crescendo of praise for fellow members as the moment of adjournment arrived.

"We can do anything we want in this Senate," said Jennings in early March 2011 as he eulogized a former senator who passed away during the session. "We just have to come together . . . and look at each other. We don't need people from the far right or the far left. We can work together for the best interest of the people of New Mexico."

"Our actions have always been on behalf of the people of New Mexico," he said as his discussion rambled from the yearly House-Senate basketball game, to the foibles of governors, and back to former senator Charlie Lee, who pretty much exemplified the greatness of the New Mexico Senate. "When I was a sheepherder, he was just about the most progressive cowboy I ever met," he ended.

Jennings's ramblings reflect the general notion that the Senate, with fewer members and longer terms than the House, is the deliberative body— for better and worse. "The Upper House," as it is called, has also been more evenly divided between Democrats and Republicans, which has forced compromise, given rise to coalitions, and lent a more conservative cast to both budgets and policies. It tends to move at a slower pace, with freewheeling debate and less discipline than the House.

The pride that senators display in themselves contrasts sharply with public impression. During the time I was there, the public approval rating for the legislature as a whole never reached 50 percent, as measured by various surveys of registered voters taken by Research and Polling, Inc.; the University of New Mexico (UNM) Institute for Public Policy; and the *Albuquerque Journal*.

A December 2011 poll of registered voters taken for the Democratic Party pegged legislative favorability at 40 percent.[3] Past surveys reflected approval ratings ranging from a high of 44 percent in 2006 to a low of 26 percent in 2000.[4] In a national study of state governments, the Truman School of Public Affairs at the University of Missouri pegged New Mexico's rating at 40 percent in 2008. The Truman School calculated the nationwide average that year as 35 percent, so New Mexico doesn't look as bad comparatively.[5]

Satisfaction is a tricky measurement because it reflects the economy, scandals, and other factors. But certainly the approval level doesn't fit the self-image. For one thing, legislators don't think the rating extends to them personally—and they are right. When pollsters ask whether people like their own senator, they say "yes"—but citizens do not respond in similar fashion when asked their feelings about the legislature as a whole. Is there some sort of strange psychological phenomenon going on here? Usually, when the self-image does not fit the reality, there are consequences, but legislators and voters seem to roll along, seeing no contradiction.

Beyond the approval ratings, there was one poll that really upset me, propelling me down a rocky path through the New Mexico legislature. It was taken in 1999 by the well-respected Albuquerque firm Research and Polling, Inc. for New Mexicans for Campaign Reform. It indicated that 47 percent of New Mexico registered voters thought that special interest contributions to legislators' campaigns affected their vote "a lot" and 35 percent said it affected their vote "some." A more recent poll showed that 60 percent believed that state government was corrupt.[6]

That kind of cynical view has the potential to discourage participation in the process, depress voter turnout, and make idealistic candidates think twice about running for office. It also tars all office holders who are trying to make the best decisions they can—based on their conscience, their constituents, or the evidence—with a brush of corruption and self-interest. The perception—much less the reality—eats away at the core of democracy and the ideal of public service, to which many of us in the state's legislative branch are dedicated. But, as we will see, it's easy for good people to get caught up in a bad system.

The opening morning of the 46th Legislature was drawing to a close. Legislators, their families, and constituents drifted off for lunch at the India Palace (offered free every year by the followers of Yogi Bhajan), the nearby Pink Adobe, or the Rio Chama. Sixty full days stretched ahead. A flurry of bill introductions would start immediately after lunch. Confirmation hearings for the governor's new cabinet secretaries would begin in the Rules Committee the following week. Looking back, the 2003 session was one of the most active and productive sessions ever. With Democrats in control of both the legislature and the governor's office, 520 bills passed both houses and were sent to the fourth floor (where the governor's offices are located). Richardson vetoed far fewer than the previous governor, Gary Johnson, who had become known as "Governor No." It was like a dam had burst, changing the landscape for the next decade.

Significantly, the legislature gave the highly popular governor his major campaign promise—a reduction in personal income taxes that in five years would cut the rate in the top bracket from 8.2 percent to 4.9 percent. The cut, passed early in the session, was something that the previous governor had long sought, and for Richardson, the victory was sweet. It would become a major boast on the 2007 presidential campaign trail, for which he was saddling up even then.

But the tax cut would become a major problem for the state when a recession hit in the later part of the decade, and revenues from declining sales decreased dramatically. In 2003, House members wanted to put a circuit breaker in the bill that would stall the cuts in future years if the economy declined. But the Senate went along with the governor, who wanted the whole enchilada. It was a failure of leadership on our part. The result was that in 2008 and beyond, programs were cut and educators and state employees saw a reduction in take-home pay, since legislators facing reelection were not willing to reinstate taxes for those in the top income brackets.

The structural deficit that was created by the Richardson tax cut is with us still. It serves as a potent reminder to lawmakers. Politically, it's much harder to reinstate a tax than it is to cut it, so caution is called for.

One senator who foresaw the problem was Sen. John Arthur Smith, who would later become the chairman of the Senate Finance Committee.

"This is faith-based economics," Smith said repeatedly, as a succession of tax cuts and incentives sponsored by the administration were brought before the committee in the name of economic development. "I sure hope it works."

Several other measures that were set in motion that session would have long lasting effects. A long overdue education reform package that included a three-tiered salary plan for teachers who achieved higher professional standards was set in motion to bring the state's teachers' salaries up to regional levels. A constitutional amendment was placed on the ballot for citizens to decide whether to allow a portion of one of the state's piggybank funds (the land grant permanent fund) to be used for educational salaries and improvements. The voters approved the reform (narrowly), after a high-profile campaign waged by U.S. Sens. Jeff Bingaman and Pete Domenici, who joined the governor to push the measure.

The 2003–2004 budget bill weighed in at $4.1 million, about a 5 percent increase from the year before. Artful dancing was used to cover a shortfall in Medicaid through a temporary raid on the tobacco settlement fund, a premium tax on Medicaid providers that would be matched by federal funds, and an increase in cigarette taxes. All were fought bitterly by Republicans (see fig. 9).

The optimism I felt at the start of the session for my own measures was, for once, justified. Several measures I had sponsored for years finally became law, including the state's first venture into public campaign financing, a do-not-call law to protect consumers from unwanted telephone solicitations,[7] and an anti-spam bill to curb unwanted faxes and e-mail. A statewide water plan, sponsored by Albuquerque Rep. Mimi Stewart and me, set in motion regional planning efforts in this drought-prone state. And I finally got a measure to require discounts on outlandish prescription drug prices for seniors, a victory in my never-ending battle with the pharmaceutical industry.

After years of struggle, the legislature that year finally passed a hate-crimes bill, bringing tougher penalties to criminals motivated by hatred of the victim's race, religion, disability, gender, or sexual orientation. We also outlawed discrimination based on sexual preference. Both bills were signed in an emotional ceremony attended by tearful members of the LGBT community and other minorities at Temple Albert in Albuquerque.

In years to come, the first starry-eyed months of the Richardson administration became a distant memory replaced by conflicts between the executive
and the legislature, and increased rancor between conservatives, resentful of
the strongest governor the state had ever seen, and liberal legislators who were
benefiting from increased state funding and Democratic popularity.

CHAPTER 2

Campaigning and Getting Elected

Vámonos a la Matanza

¡VÁMONOS A LA MATANZA! FOR YEARS, THE MATANZA HAS BEEN THE signature item of the New Mexico political campaign, particularly on the Democratic side. Presidential candidates visiting from other parts of the country have enjoyed this popular Hispanic celebration, which has its roots in local tradition. Originally, matanzas often included a rodeo, but today they are more likely to feature mariachis, especially as part of large community celebrations like the one held regularly in Valencia County, which draws thousands (see figs. 10 and 11).

The event is centered on the butchering of a pig, goat, or sheep seasoned with red chile or otherwise prepared by the hosts, then slowly cooked in a pit on a bed of hot coals. The roasting goes on overnight so the partying starts early. Preparing the fixings and the various side dishes is labor intensive (not to mention digging the hole) and the whole process takes a few days, reaching a crescendo as the *chicharrones*, or pork rinds, are fried over an open fire in the family's biggest black pot. For many aficionados, chicharrones are the best part of the outdoor feast. Unfortunately, at the matanza organized in November 1999 by my campaign committee, Friends of Feldman, the chicharrones fell a little short.

"Not crispy enough," said some of the old-timers from the neighborhood who had helped cut the onions, warm the tortillas, and serve up the pork and chile as constituents filed through my newly neatened garage, plates in hand. These people knew chicharrones.

Here in Senate District 13, in the North Valley of Albuquerque, Hispanic families named Armijo, García, and Lovato trace their roots back to the eighteenth century. Ever since then, farmers in the district have been irrigating their fields with river water delivered through an elaborate ditch network. The neighborhoods are still known by their old names—Los Duranes, Los Candelarias, Los Griegos, and Los Poblanos—all within the sound of the church bells of Our Lady of Guadalupe, San Felipe de Neri, or St. Therese Catholic churches.

They were probably right about my chicharrones, but my New Mexico cooking was not bad at all for a first-term Anglo state senator. After all, my husband was a Jew and most of my friends were vegetarians. Pork was not on their menu. Yet here they were, sitting under one tent, at tables borrowed from the North Valley Senior Center, listening to the Garfield Middle School Spanish band and signing up for the raffle right alongside old-time Democratic regulars. Here were young families, independent-minded Anglos, and adventurous do-it-yourselfers, drawn to the area for its ethnic mix and semirural lifestyle right in the middle of a big city. And of course here were my Hispanic neighbors who had adopted me and my husband back in the 1970s as we mixed mud and laid adobes in the hot sun, adding a solar green house to our small home, which looked a lot like theirs.

In 1996, I struggled successfully to bring these two groups together on election day to allow me—a woman and an Anglo—to represent Senate District 13, the land of white wine and tortillas, as I had started to call it when I was a Democratic ward chair in the 1980s. Now, facing my 2000 re-election campaign, I was pulling out all the stops to keep the coalition together and honor the Hispanic traditions of our area. Of course, it wouldn't hurt if word of the well-attended and joyous event spread to any potential primary election opponents either.

The greatest challenge to most incumbents in the 112-member New Mexico legislature comes not from the opposite party, but from challengers from within their own. In the Senate, this is true because approximately thirty-five out of the forty-two seats up for election every four years are "safe" seats, containing a hefty majority for one party or another. The majority is usually so hefty that a general election challenge is almost pointless, barring extraordinary circumstances. Most incumbents don't face a November challenge—a fact of political life born of a redistricting system that, every ten years, has incumbents redrawing their own district lines to eliminate opposition.

In the decades before I was elected to a Senate seat in the heavily Democratic North Valley, there were few contested primaries in the area, and incumbents tended to stay in place for a long time. My predecessor, Sen. Tito Chavez, was there twenty years. Rep. Ed Sandoval has served for over thirty. City Councilor Vince Griego was at city hall so long (twenty-four years) that they named the council chambers after him. With few open seats, it was extremely difficult for challengers to break into the system at any level, and the Democratic Party didn't really reach out to the growing stream of newcomers to the area.

It took me years to find out when and where ward and precinct meetings were held and how the party worked (or didn't work) in my own area. What I found, with some very important exceptions, was a rather rusty machine, operated by what seemed like an extended family, with squabbling members and great enthusiasm but little effective organization. A number of disgruntled old-timers seemed to be in charge, even if they were not the elected officials, and they spent their time over coffee complaining mightily about how the North Valley was taken for granted by larger campaigns, or how this candidate or that one was totally wrong. I was not immediately accepted into this structure, except by my neighbors Joe and Esther Ramírez, who became lifelong friends. They were desperate for other precinct volunteers who would walk—and not just talk.

In spite of some initial opposition from local ward chairs I finally fell in with the group, especially the perennial players, Tom Castillo and Sam García. These guys loved politics, loved talking about issues and speculating about who was going to win or lose. They had a steadfast belief that the secret of success was walking the neighborhoods, knocking on doors, and making personal contact with voters.

In that respect the North Valley ward heelers were typical New Mexicans. Former Republican governor Dave Cargo, no stranger to grassroots campaigning himself, famously remarked, "New Mexicans hate government, but love politics." And Emilio Naranjo, longtime Rio Arriba County chairman, asked, "If it weren't for politics what kind of government would we have?"

Politics as a sporting event is still with us, but old-style *patrón* politics like that practiced in the 1960s by Emilio Naranjo is fading, mainly because there just aren't the jobs or the "pork" (in the form of capital outlay funds for local projects) to dole out any more. Over the years Naranjo held almost every Democratic party post in Rio Arriba County (including state senator and sheriff). He was best known as a big daddy county chairman who endorsed candidates and then, using his organization, his family, and those who owed him favors, turned out the vote. He inspired loyalty from his followers, who often were the beneficiaries of state and local jobs given by various administrations in recompense for Naranjo's efforts.

County chairs still wield power in New Mexico, especially during the primary season, as any statewide candidate will tell you, and some still call the shots in rural counties. One longtime county chair, Fidelio Sedillo in Valencia County, would just have a meeting and say who would be running for what, recalled Sen. David Ulibarrí. The slate went down to sheriff and county clerk. Sometimes someone would say, "But I don't want to run for sheriff, I want to run for state rep," and Fidelio would say, "Too bad, it's not your turn."

In the North Valley there was no such boss, but, as a candidate, I found out there were families that could not be ignored. The Garcías, it was said, controlled hundreds of votes, as did the Gabaldóns. One had to talk to Fidel García and Henry Gabaldón or risk losing the election. A candidate's campaign sign in the yard of either was a signal of sure triumph. And the same is still true for many districts where large, extended families regularly turn out for their favorite son. As Sen. Peter Wirth of Santa Fe says, "Part of my district includes Cañada de Santa Fe, a small Hispanic hamlet, and when you have your sign in the yard of Terrie Rivera, where the road passes, you've got the whole village."

For me, a sure example of the family's influence was whether they had a road or a section of the North Valley named after them. The extended Griegos family, for example, had hundreds of members stretching from Old Town to Los Griegos, an area surrounding Griegos Road. This became painfully obvious to me when I ran for City Council in 1995 against Vince Griego, losing by nine votes. Likewise, the Candelarias were all around me in my neighborhood on Meadow View Drive, just south of an area called Los Candelarias.

These and other local families are active participants in the game of politics. They wait for someone to ask for their support. Remarkably, they still feel their personal support can swing an election and determine the face of government. It's a far cry from the kind of cynicism and lack of political participation that characterize minority groups elsewhere. And it makes running for office here—mixing it up with the old-timers—a lot of fun. If they embrace you, they rarely let you go. A sense of personal loyalty to a winning candidate whom they supported from the start takes hold, creating a special relationship. These relationships are fundamental in New Mexico politics and they work two ways. The supporters who elatedly return from the polling places, results in hand, yelling, "Ganamos!" (We won!), later appear to ask for favors and assistance that is difficult to provide from a state government where most jobs are now civil service and capital outlay projects are not as plentiful as the pork served at the matanza.

Still the personal is the political, which is why door-to-door campaigning and personal endorsements are so important in the North Valley. The first step in both my city council (1995) and my Senate campaigns in this heavily Hispanic area, was to meet people where they lived and let them know that Dede Feldman (a.k.a. "not a Hispanic") was not a threat to their way of life. Every voter I met at the door during both of these campaigns received a handwritten thank you note to show my appreciation for sharing their concerns with me. Even today, sixteen years later, people still remember that personal gesture (see fig. 12).

In rural parts of New Mexico it's not easy to go door-to-door, but candidates find ways to extend the personal touch. "My father, who homesteaded in the area, went ranch-to-ranch and little-bitty-town-to-little-bitty-town with me, from Clovis to Tucumcari," recalls former senator Clint Harden, who won the District 7 Senate seat in 2002. Even though they stopped at every house, they ended up visiting only a few families, because each lived at the end of a long dirt road.

Harden's district, the largest in the state, encompassed roughly 14,000 square miles and all or part of seven New Mexico Counties, including Quay, Curry, Harding, Taos, Colfax, Union, and San Miguel. It is the size of Belgium.

"I had to log a lot of windshield time," Harden says, "going from where I live in Clovis, to Angel Fire, to Raton, and to Nara Vista, which is actually on Texas time."

Harden relied on special events like parades (sometimes with horse-drawn wagons), rodeos, and pie auctions to meet people in the district's many small towns. District 7 leans Republican, although it is still competitive, and Harden spent a fair amount of time at large churches in Clovis like Central Baptist and Faith Christian. He also relied on events sponsored by the New Mexico Cattle Growers' Association or the Farm and Livestock Bureau to meet rural families. "If I could get to the right family in a little town, I was in good shape" he says.

Harden practiced one-by-one "retail" politics, going door-to-door in his Clovis precincts ("If I carry my base in Curry County, I'm hard to beat," he says) and standing outside the post office in Raton, near the Colorado border. "It's a little secret I picked up," he told me. "Most rural folk have post office boxes, not home delivery, so if you want to meet 'em, go to the post office between 8:30 and 11:00 a.m. when they pick up their mail."

Like other rural candidates, Harden, once the owner of a burger restaurant in Clovis, used mailings and cable TV to get his message out in the far-flung district, but he still feels that the most important thing is to be authentic. "Although I wear a cowboy hat, I'm not actually a rancher," he says, recalling his closest race with the genuine article, Bob Frost, a cattleman whom he beat by only thirty-eight votes in 2004. "But when people meet me, they see I'm dashing and debonair," he jokes.

In heavily Democratic Senate District 13, an endorsement from the New Mexico Cattle Growers' Association would probably be the kiss of death. And I never held my breath waiting for the kind of help from the Democratic Party that Clint Harden could expect from the Republicans. Unlike Harden, who had never been challenged in a primary and fought for his swing seat in the general election, my serious challenges arose in primaries, where many groups were reluctant to take a stand. Besides, some of the major players in this urban area are neighborhood organizations, which are nonprofit and nonpartisan. Catholic churches do play a role in local politics, even though there is supposed to be a firewall between church and state. This is especially true during their annual fiestas, where an introduction before the assembled crowd is a great opportunity for name recognition and the candidate's presence—or absence—is duly noted by parishioners. The weekend before the election is another crucial time in church parking lots as freelance campaigners often plaster car windshields with anti-abortion literature directed at pro-choice candidates.

In primary campaigns, ambitious candidates cannot count on groups, but must build their own organizations, starting with their Christmas card lists, their contacts from professional groups, their families, networks of friends, and associates. Because I did not grow up in the neighborhood, or attend high school or college in New Mexico, this was a fairly daunting task. To make matters worse, I had only three people in my family, and I was not personally wealthy. But as a former newspaper reporter and an activist on various issues, I had the beginnings of a network. And I was willing to ask for help, which is not easy to do.

Women and progressives were the first to respond, and within a month I had a core of loyalists who were willing to work. Most were from the North Valley and motivated by the idea of preserving this unique area. I capitalized on the community-building aspect of the group endeavor and encouraged folks to have fun, make new friends, and be the "deciders," not just the worker bees. Some of these volunteers were veterans of national campaigns, dating from the 1960s, like that of Sens. Gene McCarthy and Robert Kennedy; others had worked for local environmentalists like Land Commissioner candidates Brant Calkin or Jim Baca, or pioneering women like former state representative Judy Pratt, the first woman to run for the U.S. Senate in New Mexico.

For many of us, campaigns were where we had met our best friends, our husbands, where we decided what we wanted to do with our lives, what we believed in, or whether to go back to school or move to another town. Campaigns were where we formed a support system, a network, long before the word became trendy. Now, within the context of a contained area and an achievable goal, it was not a hard sell to convince volunteers that walking some of the fascinating, beautiful, and historic neighborhoods of the North Valley would be a lot of fun. And, I emphasized, you might even lose weight.

I personally knocked on six to seven thousand doors that year, often walking with a group of energized volunteers. Our opener was always, "what are some of your concerns about state government?" We listened and recorded the answers. Together we discovered amazing things about the area and the people who lived there. Practicing this kind of street-level politics changes your perspective. You never know what can happen out there when you open yourself to it—to danger, to dog bites, to arguments, to peoples' incredible personal struggles and unbelievable kindness. This kind of campaign takes sustained energy and commitment, and buoying the spirits of volunteers is job one. I made sure to never violate what Grace Williams, a longtime Albuquerque American Civil Liberties Union director, told me was most essential in the care and feeding of volunteers—never running out of toilet paper. And when we gathered, we shared stories about our top moments at the door, like the time when

› You arrived at the same time as a life insurance salesman
› You were distracted by a pig in the yard and didn't know how to proceed
› A young couple greeted you at the door, you asked for Alfred Martinez and Lydia Brown, and the woman said, "Who's Lydia Brown," and the man said, "Oh, I forgot to tell you—she's my former wife."
› You accidentally drooled on your nominating petition right where they were supposed to sign
› You knocked on the door of a Jehovah's Witness and came away with more literature than you dropped off.

Until the Obama campaign of 2008, door-to-door campaigning was fading rapidly throughout the country. Candidates in legislative districts have found other, more efficient ways to contact voters using Facebook, text messages, and precisely targeted direct mail. Busy, transient families are scattered, and the thousands of advertising messages they are exposed to everyday have sapped their attention span. More important, voters are cynical and distrustful, worn down by incessant "robo calls" and negative TV advertising designed to make opponents look like crooks or child molesters.

In 1984 the median cost of a Senate campaign was $2,541. Twelve years later, in 1996, I considered it to be a small triumph to raise and spend about $26,000 in the primary and $25,000 in the general election. But now, even in New Mexico, where the cost of campaigns is cheap by national standards, things have changed dramatically.

In 2008, Sen. Tim Eichenberg, running as a Democratic challenger for a mid-Albuquerque swing seat, spent a combined total of $291,000 for both the primary and the general elections (much of it was his own money). His Republican opponent, incumbent Diane Snyder, spent $170,000 for the general election—and lost. Another "hot" race that year between Democrat Steve Fishman and incumbent Republican Sen. Lee Rawson in Las Cruces cost a combined total of $420,000. Both were outliers. The median contribution level for Senate candidates (for the primary and the general election) that year was $44,121. But the figure doesn't tell the whole story. For the winners (mostly incumbents) the median amount raised was $58,335; for the losers, the median was around $15,000—a gap of over $40,000.[1]

In 2012 the prices went haywire. Candidates for the legislature (both Senate and House) raised an average of $31,540 according to data from the secretary of state's office.[2] But that's an average, and in the Senate, the contested races were even more expensive. Incumbent Democratic senator Tim Jennings, of Roswell, raised $411,251 to keep his seat in the face of an onslaught from Reform New Mexico Now, a super PAC (political action committee) associated with Republican governor Susana Martinez, who was then seeking to topple Senate leaders and recapture the House. Jennings lost. Sen. Michael Sanchez, another Senate leader in a swing district, raised $312,114—and won. Incumbent Democratic senator Lisa Curtis raised $342,521 (90 percent of it from her own funds)—and lost.[3] With TV advertising financed by super PACs now aimed by the governor at the legislature, the campaigns entered a whole new realm.

Inevitably, fundraising takes center stage in these modern campaigns, and endless phone calls and fundraisers replace door-to-door solicitation. Candidates still use their Christmas card lists, but without the big-dollar donations they can't compete. And where does the big money come from? The website of the National Institute for Money and Politics follows the flow of contributions into New Mexico Senate districts and the conclusions are clear.

In the 2008 general elections, special interests and lobbyists financed 81 percent of the cost of campaigns, with the Republican Party, Democratic Party, or leadership PACs, as well as other kindred candidates, kicking in 9 percent. Self-financing accounted for another 10 percent.[4] Incumbents get the lion's share of this loot, with Democrats hauling in more because they are in the majority, controlling committee chairmanships and leadership positions—and hence, the overall agenda.

Major contributors on the Democratic side come from the trial lawyers and the unions, with the president pro tem and the majority leader operating their own funds to protect the majority and score points with successful candidates whom they support. Majority Leader Michael Sanchez's Committee to Elect Senate Democrats contributed $58,000 in 2008 to key challengers to Republican incumbents. In the House, the Democratic Legislative Campaign Committee (DLCC), composed of House members, collects contributions from industry groups and committee chairs. It then coordinates mail and polling efforts for promising challengers or at-risk Democrats. Single-issue groups like the New Mexico Conservation Voters Alliance are also players on the Democratic side, contributing cash, in-kind donations, and volunteer hours.

Republicans rely on party organizations and fellow legislators. Senate Minority Leader Stuart Ingle collects contributions and passes them on to his members. Special interests that mainly support Republicans include the oil and gas industry, realtors, builders, agriculture and dairy producers, and insurance companies.[5]

Of course special interests swing both ways. In 2010 businesses gave both Democratic and Republican candidates about $1 million for their campaigns. The health care industry gave about $640,000 to Democrats and $590,000 to their Republican rivals. The restaurant industry gave about $180,000 to Democrats and $140,000 to Republicans; the gambling and lodging industry gave $160,000 to Democrats and $140,000 to Republicans. The tobacco industry was relatively even handed as well, giving $41,000 to Democrats and $40,000 to Republicans.[6]

Most often, these contributions come in response to direct appeals from candidates who are provided a list of lobbyists or frequent donors, along with their phone numbers. "Call time" is now a requirement, with candidates coached by their fundraising chair or campaign manager (who is often standing right by them) to ask for a specific amount by a specific date for a certain purpose.

One common fundraiser is the golf tournament, arranged by a friendly lobbyist who invites all of his or her lobbyist friends to the Santa Ana Star or the Isleta Eagle Golf Course to benefit the president pro tem's fund or an individual senator's campaign committee. Donors can sponsor a hole for $500, sign up for a raffle, or simply play a round ($100) to benefit the cause. Sometimes these events can net as much as $60,000, leaving the candidate with little need to attend time-consuming house parties and community matanzas.

Fundraising became more complicated in 2012 when the contribution limits adopted in 2009 (see chapter 15) went into effect. Candidates and committees could no longer receive contributions from PACs greater than $5,000 or from individuals greater than $2,300 for each election cycle. This meant that leadership PACs and organizations like the DLCC, which coordinated campaigns for each chamber, would have less money to work with. In response, senators got creative. The Democrats set up six different PACs, each controlled by a senator who did not have an opponent. Each could receive contributions under the limit, which was then pooled and used to support colleagues in competitive races.

Aside from fundraising, one of the first moves of a candidate running a modern campaign is to develop a research- and data-driven strategy. Most often this requires hiring a consultant who will develop a plan and a schedule based on the composition of the district, the strengths of the candidate, and information about how voters feel about the issues and personalities of the day. An experienced consultant can cost from $3,000 to $6,000 a month.

Neri Holguín, who worked with Soltari, one of the original progressive consulting firms in New Mexico, in the early 2000s, says that the first step is to do background research on both the candidate and the opposition. She often hires a private investigator to search public records for anything hidden about the candidate that may come out later in negative advertisements. And she encourages candidates to take a poll of their district or at the very least to consult other polls taken by the party, news organizations, or special interest groups.

Information from pollsters on the Democratic side, like Celinda Lake or the firm of Greenberg Quinlan Rosner, can tell you many things, not just who is ahead in the district horserace. It can tell you what messages resonate with voters, what the hot-button issues are, exactly who is predisposed to vote for you—or your opponent—and who is undecided. With polling data in hand, candidates can determine a theme for the campaign, to be carried through in brochures, letters, and direct mail. Depending on the size of the sample and the number of questions, polling costs can run from $3,500 to $20,000, or more.

Once the message is defined (and the candidate pledges to keep "on mes-sage" no matter what distractions may appear), the next step is to figure out how to deliver it to the right voters, at the right time, and within budget. In Senate campaigns, the message is usually delivered via direct mail, dropped on the doorstep, or communicated over the phone to voters most likely to vote. It is delivered, and delivered, and delivered over and over again in as many different media as possible. (Consultants say it takes seven or eight attempts to cut through the clutter.)

Long gone are the days when candidates can do one or two mailings to a broad swath of registered voters in their area, cut a radio ad or two, and stand outside the polling place on election day to give one last pitch. Now the mes-sage must be tailored to the interests of distinct audiences making up the district and delivered via e-blasts, Facebook, or by videos posted on the can-didate's website. And the number of "hits" needed in each medium keeps going up. TV is rarely used since it is expensive and the audience is too broad. Direct mail is still the favored medium. However, where six or seven mailings were once thought sufficient, now it takes twelve or more pieces, timed over a longer period, since the polling places are not just open on elec-tion day, but voting occurs over a month-long period—thanks to absentee and early voting.

"For my 2010 general election campaign, I sent ten mailers at a cost of $45,000," recalls Democratic Rep. Mimi Stewart, whose district is in the mid-Heights of Albuquerque. "My Republican opponent sent thirteen, ten of which were negative and arrived during the last week of the campaign."

In the 2012 campaign there were even more mailings, since the candi-dates' mailers were supplemented by pieces from independent groups. With larger budgets, the independent mailings often dwarfed the candidates' more modest efforts.

Legislative campaigns are now based on sophisticated databases, which include registered voters, contributors, volunteers, and other information that can be organized into walk lists, mailing labels, and phone sheets. The data bases include all kinds of information on voters, including their past voting habits, whether they typically vote absentee or early, their party affil-iation, age, and household composition. Much of this information was not available for purchase from the county clerk when I first ran for the city council in 1995. I had to compile it the hard way by lugging my computer down to the city records center, pulling up the signature rosters from past elections, and creating my own record of frequent voters. Now you can obtain all that information from the Democratic party voter file and the New Mexico secretary of state. And, if you have the money and the computer capability, you can buy e-mail addresses and modeling information that shows buying habits and reading preferences of voters down to the zip code and even by the block. Even more information on voters can be collected by workers at the door, bar-coded and scanned into campaign databases for later use. And field workers—often paid, rather than volunteer—now have precise information on target voters as they go door-to-door. It's all available on their hand-held devices—smart phones or iPads.

But the name of the game is still targeting the right people with the right message—and not wasting postage or energy on those unlikely to come through for you. It's Political Science or Marketing 101, and it can cost big money. But in 1996 it was still doable on a human scale.

"A victory for social science! A victory for social science?" my campaign manager John Gastil kept yelling from his seat at the computer on election night in 1996. Using projections based on voter returns, Gastil knew we had won the primary when the first few precincts reported. And he was right. Our targeted and door-to-door program had worked. I won with 56 percent, more than both of my opponents, Virginia Trujillo and Charles Sanchez, combined. Gastil, an academic political scientist then working at the University of New Mexico, loved applying his skills to the real world. He went on to become a professor at the University of Washington and Penn State.

The only problem with the "social science" approach is that the other side is doing the same thing, using the same tools, repeating to their voters the messages their consultants told them to use.

In a competitive campaign, voters are getting carpet bombed by literature, phone calls, and e-mails from both sides. Undecided voters have a bull's-eye painted on their backs. And then come the negative mail pieces with unflattering photos, or the phone calls that start by saying, "If you knew that Sen. Dede Feldman ate live children for breakfast, how likely would you be to vote for her—very likely, likely, unlikely, or very unlikely?"

The last two weeks of a campaign, which, appropriately, coincide with the Halloween season, can be scary. Taught by consultants to contrast themselves sharply with their opponents, candidates resort to wedge issues, out-of-context voting records, or outright character assassination. North Valley Democratic candidates have been accused of condoning child pornography, rape, and juvenile violence. Incumbents, we are told, are naturally corrupt politicians who take out-of-state junkets, vote for pay raises for themselves, and serve special interests behind closed doors. Some may have even forgotten to vote in a minor election twenty years ago!

Often the most negative mailings are paid for by party organizations or independent PACs, acting on information they collect about certain key votes. Sometimes these votes are even engineered during the prior legislative session for that very purpose. In 2012 the Republican super PAC, Reform New Mexico Now, sent ominous black-and-white postcards with hooded figures asking, "Should we stand with the victims or the child killers?" The Democratic candidates, it was alleged, stood with the killers. Democratic leaders Michael Sanchez and Tim Jennings were targeted again and again for their votes against a bill to increase penalties for suspected criminals. They were also hit for voting against repealing drivers' licenses for illegal immigrants, a signature issue for Governor Martinez. Democratic mailers are not much better, depicting sad school children or sick seniors affected by Republican budget cuts. There's little honest discussion of the issues during the whole process, and the public inevitably feels they are voting for the lesser of two evils.

But the issues are what brought us here, both as voters and as candidates. They should be front and center in any campaign. A campaign is not the time to shy away from controversy, but an opportunity to engage in direct political discourse with voters, both supporters and opponents. It's a time to search out common values, which often exist over party lines. In a local, grassroots campaign, it can even be a time to increase whatever sense of community still exists in the area.

If you love your area, this community-building task will be a labor of love, connecting you with local "characters," allowing you to hear personal stories of hardship and success, taking you to events you never dreamed of attending. And you will be a better public official for it.

In Albuquerque's North Valley, an area made up of historic neighborhoods, my campaign slogan was, "A Good Neighbor, a Great Senator," which Murray Fischel, a progressive political consultant, thought might give me a sort of folksy charm. I was relentless in engaging neighbors in conversation, even incoherent conversation, at their doors, outside the John Brooks supermarket at 12th and Candelaria, or over modest meals at the North Valley Senior Center. Listening—not always easy to do—became an important task.

I drew on my earlier campaign for the city council, which had brought me into contact with dozens of neighborhood organizations, most of them focused on a major, unifying North Valley issue—the campaign to stop the

construction of a North Valley bridge through our common treasured re-
source, the bosque. The bosque, a cottonwood forest that lines either side of
the Rio Grande in Albuquerque, is a local gem used by hikers, bicyclists,
birdwatchers, and wildlife lovers.

Hundreds were involved in the struggle to save the feature that gave the
North Valley its sense of place, and, even though the effort failed, people
learned that their efforts counted—an idea that I kept repeating in an effort
to inspire and empower. At times I felt like a cheerleader, constantly hammering the idea that real power comes from the grass roots and, if we worked hard
enough, we could make a difference. My supporters could see that it was
true. A political campaign is the one area in which personal efforts—walking
another precinct, calling another one hundred voters—yield tangible results
that are recorded in the history books. Where else can you get that kind of
satisfaction?

Soon, the campaign began to grow organically, with one success building on another, with people connecting, and the fun factor flowing. We had
a frijoles fiesta at the home of Penny Rembe, featuring a 1964 Mercury
Marquee studded with over 350,000 pinto beans and rhinestones, an event
that sparked opposition from the Hispanic Roundtable for being racist. I
often quoted Bob Dylan as part of my stump speech—"Let us not talk
falsely now, the hour is getting late"—much to the surprise of baby boom-
ers, who had never heard a local politician do that. Our final flyer featured
a pair of tattered, stinky tennis shoes that were testament to my hard work
and personal efforts to connect with thousands of people.

Humor was an intrinsic part of my campaign plan as it was for Minnesota
Sen. Paul Wellstone, whose grass-roots tactics inspired campaign schools
for progressives in the decades after his unexpected death in 2002.

"A campaign is a journey we are on together," Wellstone said. And that includes the electorate, supporters, contributors, and the community at large.
Dialogue, honesty, and respect for diverse opinions during a campaign—
whether in conversations at the door or by constituent surveys—all build an
atmosphere of public spirit and civic engagement. In the North Valley you
can actually feel this community of active, informed voters—sometimes I
even thought you could feel them *too* much, judging by the volume and detail
of calls, e-mails, and letters that I later got.

But community building is secondary when special interests, consultants, sound bites, and fundraising replace door-to-door efforts, nuanced
conversations, and serious candidate forums. Gone is the assumption that
voters are adults with good ideas that they might even modify if presented

with the facts, the tradeoffs, or the conflicting values that are part and parcel of public policy choices. For most candidates, it's too risky to tell the truth about controversial issues and explain real feelings. Instead, the first piece of advice they receive is to tell people what they want to hear—the magic message that will not offend any big contributors but push the hot buttons of fear, division, and self-interest.

A serious candidate tries to differentiate him or herself as much as possible from the opposition, embrace the symbols of his or her party, and simplify complex questions into one appealing, folksy phrase or image. Increasingly, candidates themselves join in the refrain that all politicians are crooks and Santa Fe or Washington is the source of the problem.

The trouble is, it's a self-fulfilling prophecy. Candidates who win using these techniques are ill-equipped to actually serve in a legislative body where you need to find common ground, listen, and be tolerant of each other's positions in order to solve the state's problems. Politicians are less likely to compromise when the other side will accuse them of flip-flopping or worse. And they are less likely to take a stand that threatens their ability to raise campaign funds from special interests for the next campaign. Courage, in short, is not rewarded on the campaign trail, and consequently it is in short supply among elected officials.

It used to be that candidates needed to convince voters that they would work hard to understand the complexity of public issues, tell the unvarnished truth, and solve problems in education, health care, or economic development, even if it meant compromise with the "enemy."

Former governor Bruce King, in his book *Cowboy in the Roundhouse*, expressed it in his own folksy way: "If candidates couldn't afford consultants they'd spend more time getting out to people with their own messages, and they would be more responsive to the needs of voters."[7] King was a supporter of a campaign fund limit. So am I. Limits on contributions to state campaigns were finally adopted by the legislature in 2009 after more than a decade of intense struggle with legislative leaders in both parties who were reluctant to change the rules of a game they had won (see chapter 15). But they didn't go into effect for the 2010 election (otherwise we could never have gotten them through), and when limits did kick in for the 2012 elections they had unforeseen consequences. And they were not good.

Everyone knew contribution limits were an imperfect solution since they do not limit the total amount of cash spent on these contests and do nothing to reduce spending from independent groups or wealthy individuals. But we did not foresee the following year's Supreme Court decision in Citizens

United, which unleashed a huge wave of independent spending by super PACs and nonprofit groups. The decision effectively struck down existing national limits set by the McCain-Feingold law on spending by PACs, and it was based on the idea that spending money is equivalent to free speech.

In 2012, spending on legislative races by super PACs reached over $3.6 million. Reform New Mexico Now, a super PAC operated by Jay McClesky, a political advisor to Gov. Susana Martinez, spent $2 million to influence the outcome of statehouse races, especially in the House, where Republicans thought they could gain control for the first time since 1954. Much of Reform New Mexico's contributions came from out of state, including $415,000 from the Republican State Leadership Committee and two $100,000 contributions from oil companies.

Patriot Majority New Mexico, a Democratic super PAC, spent more than $1.3 million, with most of its money coming from out-of-state labor unions like the American Federation of Teachers and the American Federation of State, County and Municipal Employees.[8] Verde Voters, a super PAC affiliated with Conservation Voters New Mexico, spent $329,000.[9]

The outside money was spent on an avalanche of negative mailers and, for the first time, TV ads, largely directed at two Senate leaders who were accused of thwarting the governor's agenda. Viewers statewide saw Reform New Mexico's attack ads and the senators' responses (Sen. Tim Jennings's featured him in wader boots struggling through a sea of mud). The wedge issues were now aired statewide, hitting viewers upside the head with partisan vitriol, even though most of them lived outside the affected districts. Candidates and consultants had rejected this kind of shotgun approach in the past as too much bang for the buck—and the absence of TV was one factor that kept the costs of legislative races down. Now, with vast amounts of cash flowing freely, the sky was once again the limit.

Some candidates (both Republicans and Democrats) asked the outsiders to "butt out" of their races—but they had no power over the groups, which had been ordered by law not to coordinate with individual campaigns. And so, the onslaught continued. A whole new type of election was emerging, where individual candidates, the quality of their characters, their positions on the issues, or their districts mattered little in comparison to the priorities of ideologically driven super PACs determined to win majorities at any cost.

The flood of money created by Citizens United drowned the hard-fought campaign reforms we passed in New Mexico designed to reduce the dollars spent in state races. To stem the tide, we need more reform to solve problems created by the momentous Supreme Court decision. Nationwide, citizens are mobilizing to pass a constitutional amendment to nullify the disastrous idea that money is the same as speech and should be allowed to blast out those who can only afford smaller megaphones.

Elsewhere, citizens have long known that a more comprehensive approach is needed. Back in 1998 Arizonans endorsed a statewide initiative starting a voluntary public financing system. The "Clean Elections" system awarded a set stipend to participating candidates who agreed to limit spending to a certain amount based on what similar campaigns have cost in the past. The system was used by Janet Napolitano (former secretary of homeland security) when she ran for governor in 2001, as well as by scores of both Republican and Democratic candidates eager to put down the phone, stop "dialing for dollars," and begin contacting voters the old-fashioned way. Until a backlash developed during the Bush years, the system was hugely popular with the public at large, as it is in New Mexico.

Even though New Mexico has no statewide initiative mechanism to start the system at the ballot box, the legislature has begun publicly financing some campaigns. But Republicans have successfully challenged some of the system's provisions in the courts, requiring yet more modifications.

Campaign finance reform in New Mexico is a never-ending struggle. No other bills in the legislature guarantee bipartisan opposition right out of the chute. But for those who think that the way we finance and run campaigns is the reason we can't solve political and economic problems at any level—it's worth the fight. And for those who yearn for old-fashioned matanzas and retail politics instead of endless e-blasts, hate mail, and negative commercials that even the candidates can't control—it's our only hope. Without it, the deep pockets of some of the interest groups you will read about in the following chapters will call even more of the shots in legislatures around the country.

PART II Boots, Suits, Leaders, and Lobbyists

T HERE'S A ROAD SIGN THAT POPS UP REGULARLY ALONG NEW Mexico's interstate highways, proclaiming, "Caution: Gusty Winds May Exist." The signs, which are often accompanied by wind socks, are placed in usually tranquil spots that can suddenly become turbulent and dangerous for unsuspecting travelers—just like the New Mexico Senate, with its wild mix of mavericks from all over the state. The following chapters examine the major players operating inside the New Mexico Senate and how they interact with citizen legislators at the center of the process. These players are the leaders (chapter 3) and lobbyists (chapter 4). The personalities and relationships between these individuals set the climate for each session and determine the success or failure of many a bill. Sometimes gusty winds blow from the basement where the leaders have their offices; other times everything is done behind the scenes. The roles played by individuals in each group overlap—leaders make recommendations to special interest groups on which lobbyists to hire; former legislators become lobbyists; lobbyists give gifts, make contributions, and determine winners and losers. There's lots of drama and lots of history when the boots, suits, and ordinary citizens interact on the Senate floor.

CHAPTER 3

Leadership Styles in the Senate

Caution: Gusty Winds May Exist

O VER THE PAST FEW DECADES, THE MEN (ONLY MEN UNTIL 2013) who have held the top leadership posts in the New Mexico Senate have been at the center of power—setting a policy agenda, writing budgets, and, with their fellow senators, making decisions that have a huge impact on citizens throughout the Land of Enchantment. Some have seen themselves as partisan warriors, ready to do battle with the governor or the opposing party, willing to ride roughshod over the rules for the sake of a cherished value or the right outcome. Others have seen themselves as great compromisers and consensus builders, reaching across party lines to build coalitions, solve problems, and get things done. Some operate behind closed doors, doing their best to block measures with which they disagree, even if the votes are there for passage. Others take pride in their down-to-earth background and common sense.

Each of the Senate leaders I knew during my time there had his own unique style, the product of personality and background. One was a grocer, another raised sheep. Two were unmistakably lawyers, with whom you feared to tangle. One was a retired high school principal. Most of them have been mavericks—often at odds with their party, their governor, and even the law. The atmosphere that each created by their interaction with fellow members, special interests, and other branches of government has shaped major issues: the level of state funding for education and health care and the amount of income and gross receipts taxes we pay.

Some have said that, with 112 members, the legislature is ill equipped to lead on policy, slow to innovate and reform, and—with the exception of appropriating the money—is mostly reactive to other branches, especially the executive. However, much depends on the character of the Senate leaders and how they wield their power to solve problems, move an agenda, or block change.

Here are some examples of how the styles of top elected leaders in the New Mexico Senate changed our policies—and our history.

POWER COMES WITH A TITLE

The leaders' power starts with the Senate's rules. The New Mexico Senate, like similar bodies across the country, is organized on a partisan basis with the majority party calling most of the shots. The leader of the majority party (which in New Mexico has been the Democrats since 1933, save for one year) is the majority floor leader, now Sen. Michael Sanchez of Los Lunas. Elected every two years by his fellow party members, he directs the flow of business on the floor of the Senate, assigning bills to committees and choosing which bills to put on final passage for debate and a vote yea or nay. The Senate leaders who have held the post have made it into a powerhouse almost equal to the Speaker's role in the House, especially in the final days of the session, when the majority leader decides—sometimes without consulting his own members or the minority—which bills get heard and which are left to die upon adjournment.

The other partisan leaders in the Senate include the majority whip, a position that Doña Ana County's Sen. Mary Jane Garcia held from 1996–2012, and the caucus chair. The whip is charged with rounding up the votes for the bills that the majority caucus prioritizes, if it does prioritize—a rare occasion in the unruly Democratic family. The caucus chair calls meetings (if they happen at all) and helps the majority leader set a direction for the session, a tough job.

The president of the Senate is identified by the constitution as the lieutenant governor, who wields the gavel when the forty-two-member body meets. However, the real leader is the president pro tempore (the pro tem, for short). Elected by the entire body, he presides "pro tempore," that is, for a time, when the lieutenant governor is absent. His real power, however, is his ability to appoint standing and interim committee members, hire staff, and make decisions for the whole body during the interim. The selection of committee chairs, who can act either as key lieutenants or independent agents, is a crucial component of the pro tem's power and ability to see his agenda through to completion.

Unlike the House of Representatives, where the Speaker is supreme, the pro tem shares his power with the Committee on Committees, which he appoints at the start of each session. This committee declares bills "germane" (and eligible for a hearing) or "non-germane" during short (thirty-day) sessions of the legislature. It takes care of many important housekeeping details like the assignment of offices. In the Senate, under Pro Tem Manny Aragon, the Committee on Committees fell into disuse, making the office of the pro tem almost as powerful as the Speaker of the House, who singlehandedly appoints committee members, assigns bills, and runs floor sessions in the House.

The minority party is organized in the same way, with a minority leader, a whip, and a caucus chair. Sen. Stuart Ingle of Portales has been minority leader for years. His relationship with Sen. Tim Jennings, a Democrat who, until he was defeated in 2012, was in leadership for decades, either as pro tem, majority leader, or majority whip, extended his power and the influence of the Republicans.

When I arrived in the New Mexico Senate in 1997 the pro tem was Sen. Manny Aragon of Albuquerque, and, although I didn't understand it at the time, the chaotic events happening all around me (filibusters, special sessions, frequent "calls" of the Senate that required all senators to be present in the chambers) grew out of the body's turbulent history in the 1970s and 1980s. "It was a time when icons like conservative Democratic senators Ike Smalley and Aubrey Dunn controlled the Senate," recalled former senator Joe Carraro, who represented the west side of Albuquerque from 1985–1988 and 1993–2008. Carraro, and others who experienced the leadership of Ike Smalley of Deming (pro tem from 1972–1984 and again from 1986–1987), said that the rank and file had little say in the budget and retribution was the rule. "The Bear," as Smalley was called, and Finance Committee Chair Aubrey Dunn, of Alamogordo, tightly controlled information. Fiscal impact reports, which explain the impact of bills and are now distributed for every bill, were not even shared with the Finance Committee members working on the budget. Individual bills were not considered on their own merits—if at all. Senator Dunn once passed twenty-one bills on the floor of the Senate with a single motion, an action that was later ruled unconstitutional by the New Mexico Supreme Court.

There was a huge generation gap between young senators like Manny Aragon and Tom Rutherford, both lawyers from Albuquerque, and the old bulls. Rutherford, elected in 1973 at age twenty-five (the youngest you can be a senator) had long hair, owned a "head shop," and worked as a DJ. Now a lobbyist, Rutherford recalls late night sessions in the Senate Finance

Committee when budget decisions were made after the crowds had left the building. "I just hung around in the audience, making coffee, sharpening pencils, and giving apples to committee members," he said. "Once in a while I'd get a crumb . . . It was very conservative."

By the 1980s discord disrupted almost every session. Leadership changed often. Neither party held a decisive majority. Coalitions shifted and long-standing rules like seniority were abandoned. Smalley was overthrown in 1985 by then Democratic senator Les Houston, who formed a coalition with Republicans and a few Democrats. The next year, however, Smalley returned as pro tem and ousted Houston, who had changed his party registration from Democrat to Republican. But the Bear's return was short lived. In the chaos created by the even split between Democrats and Republicans in the Senate (twenty-one each), Manny Aragon was able to assemble a coalition of eighteen Republicans and five Democrats to elect him pro tem in 1988.

The Republicans recognized the young lawyer's courage, ambition, and talents, recalled Carraro, even if they didn't always agree with him. "Who else would go into the enemy camp and challenge Caesar (i.e., Smalley) knowing that he would be at Smalley's mercy if he lost?" he asked. Aragon rewarded the Republicans with several committee chairmanships and the coalition lasted until the following year, when the Democrats, who had by then increased their majority to twenty-six, elected Aragon.

Aragon would remain in the top position until 2001, but turmoil in the Senate would last, with petty vendettas, frequent roll call votes, late-night sessions, premature adjournments, and procedural moves designed to delay bills or punish opponents. Some chalked it up to a power vacuum caused by the departure of Smalley. Others said it was because loose Senate rules, designed to create a deliberative body, gave each quirky member permission to go on and on both in committee and on the floor without much decorum or respect for others.

But a lot had to do with leadership.

MANNY ARAGON
Charisma and Confrontation

March 1997. Sen. Manny Aragon had a solution to the budget problem. It would solve the prison problem, the Medicaid crisis, and use revenue from the state's new gambling compacts with the Native American tribes. It would also raise revenue and satisfy the unmet needs of New Mexicans. It was all contained on a scrap of paper, which the swashbuckling senator kept in the pocket of his double-breasted blazer. Manny, as I was encouraged to call him even though I was a mere freshman, had rattled off the plan from memory many times in the Democratic caucus. Now he was passionately presenting it to the entire Senate, with a flow chart and arrows connecting the revenues to the spending. As usual, Aragon had stayed up late modifying the plan with the help of his faithful staff, led by boyhood friend Bobby Giannini. The plan was his, composed in his basement office rather than on the third floor of the capitol by members of the Senate Finance Committee, who normally were charged with handling the key legislation. It was pure Manny.

The Democrats—even those on the Finance Committee—were willing to go along with Manny's plan, although the Republicans, including Gov. Gary Johnson (with his veto pen) were bitterly opposed. As a newcomer to the Senate, I was beginning to grasp the Democratic consensus on Manny: he was brilliant on the budget and knew how, as Las Cruces Sen. Fernando Macias used to say, "to pull rabbits out of the hat." He worked harder than anyone, knew the minutia of state government, and had the right instincts, especially when it came to protecting the sick, the young, the poor, and the elderly. He also knew how to stick it to the Republican governor—and for all this he deserved, and got, our undying loyalty.

The Republican consensus was quite different. Gov. Gary Johnson called him a "tyrant" and an "emperor." Republican Party Chairman John Dendahl blamed every ill in the state on what he called the "Raymond and Manny show" (Raymond Sanchez was then Speaker of the House). Many of us felt the epithet was racist, lumping together two very different leaders based largely on their race, not their positions.

Manny Aragon grew up in the Barelas neighborhood of Albuquerque and attended St. Mary's school downtown. Upon graduation he attended the University of Albuquerque on a baseball scholarship, later transferring to the University of New Mexico where he completed a Bachelor of Arts degree and a Juris Doctorate at UNM School of Law. He entered the legislature in 1975 as a senator from the South Valley a few years after graduating from UNM School of Law. His father, Mel Aragon, was a barber and a local political leader who later became an Albuquerque city councilor. Manny soon developed a passion for politics, attending the 1968 Democratic Convention in Chicago. As a young legislator, he took on controversial causes. He defended the Equal Rights Amendment, and he tried to legalize marijuana, repeal the death penalty, increase the minimum wage, provide health care for all, institute collective bargaining for state employees, and reform the penal system. His fiery speeches and quick wit made him popular with his constituents in

Senate District 14 and with older Democratic senators like Ben Altamirano and Joe Fidel, who had watched him grow up in the Senate (see fig. 13). Others were equally inspired by him.

His social heart was "stunning," says Lorene Mills, a Santa Fe broadcaster whose husband Ernie was a longtime legislative reporter. "He could bring tears to your eyes."

"He was passionate about things," said tobacco lobbyist and former senator Bobby McBride, who died in 2012. "He inspired people with his intellect and his speeches." McBride, a close friend of Manny's even though Manny often led the charge for increased tobacco taxes, said his charisma earned him followers. These followers allowed him to advance his agenda and get things done. In the 1990s some of the things that got done included expanding Medicaid and increasing services for people with developmental disabilities and mental illness.

But it was his facility with the complicated New Mexico budget that gave him the most power. "There wasn't a smarter guy when it came to the budget," says Legislative Finance Committee (LFC) Director David Abbey, who assumed his position in 1997—the same year as Manny's scrap-of-paper budget and my arrival. "He could have been LFC director in a cinch." Abbey's first years at the LFC were an adventure. "One year I drew up seven budgets," he said. Mostly, the final budgets passed on a strictly partisan basis, with Manny bringing his followers on board through the goodies he handed out. Trouble was the budgets were later vetoed by the governor, triggering one or more special sessions every year.

Over time, Manny took over the entire budget process, says David Harris, a former LFC director who then became the department of finance and administration secretary for Governor Johnson during those years. At first it was invisible, but then he took over the process whereby the Senate amended the House budget as it passed between the chambers.

He appointed himself to both the LFC (which produces the legislature's budget proposal during the interim) and the Senate Finance Committee. He ultimately dominated both with detailed questions and lengthy diatribes. Sen. Ben Altamirano, the chair of the Finance Committee, finally admitted that he could do nothing without Manny's approval. The House Appropriations and Finance Committee, led by Rep. Max Coll, was often at odds with the Senate budget—forcing the formation of a Conference Committee to iron out the differences. But Manny appointed the Senate conferees, held the meetings late at night, and simply wore down any opposition to the changes and budget provisions he relentlessly unveiled at the eleventh hour.

The frenzied backroom process led to tension between the House and the Senate, the governor and the legislature. Manny plowed ahead, with his troops willing to support him even when he changed directions. In 1997, Manny was zigging and zagging from one plan to another. After we had all voted for his budget plan, which included a tax increase, he suddenly abandoned it. The unexpected change in his position on another heated issue—the construction of new prisons—left us in the lurch on the last day of the session. A photo on the front page of the *Santa Fe New Mexican* depicted puzzled senators questioning Manny, fearful that a last-minute filibuster by Republican Sen. Bill Davis, of Albuquerque, would prevent the passage of the omnibus capital outlay bill, which had funds for each member's district (see fig. 2).[1] Davis had used the delaying tactic to make Manny withdraw his prison bill, which Manny refused to do despite pleas from his caucus. Minutes after the photo was taken, the session cratered, taking with it the funding for capital projects that everyone (both Republicans and Democrats) wanted. Manny didn't seem to mind.

Despite the surprises, almost all of the Senate Democrats stuck with him. "It left us dangling," Sen. Roman Maes, of Santa Fe, said of the 1997 debacle, "but Manny—you have got to rely on him."[2] "This guy had it all," said Republican Sen. Joe Carraro, who had returned to the Senate in 1993 after a four-year absence. "He was a one-man political machine. He was thinking many steps ahead. He was a chess master. The others were still playing checkers, but Manny was brilliant, and I loved him." Carraro says he always ended his speeches, especially those diametrically opposed to Manny's position, with the phrase, "and I love you, man." But soon Manny lost his smile and Carraro noticed a change in tone.

He often bullied people who testified before committees—even legislators themselves—whom he felt he could intimidate by challenging the values or projects they held most dear. In 1997, he led the Senate in refusing to confirm Johnson's nominee for corrections secretary, Donna Wilpolt. He publicly and heatedly humiliated her on the floor of the Senate. When criticized for his combative behavior, he said coldly, "*así es,*" which in English means, "that's the way it is."[3] Manny always insisted that none of his speeches were personal attacks. "Sometimes I have a tendency to take it a little far," he once admitted to the *Albuquerque Journal*.[4] But, for me anyway, it was hard not to take his attacks seriously, particularly since his control of the process was almost complete. And there was always something that you thought was secure, that Manny now wanted to place on the table. For me, in 1997, it was the very existence of the Rio Grande State Park, which ran like a green ribbon through my riverside district.[5] For others it was their capital outlay, or a program they had established years ago that now just might be eliminated.

"The nuclear option was always on the table," says Carraro.

Here was the secret of this leader's success: Manny knew where to go to assemble the votes on any given measure. He knew what was important to almost every member, whether it be a favorite facility back home, a family member with a health problem who needed help, or a cause near and dear to a member's heart. And he knew how to use that information to bind members to him on a personal basis and punish those who crossed him.

"I used to kid him that he would know the technical issues better if he didn't spend so much time doing favors and getting somebody's nephew hired," said Les Houston, lobbyist and former pro tem from Albuquerque. But relationships were an important part of the package and Manny's friends were loyal.

So was "hostage taking," a tactic used by many leaders. It came into focus a little too clearly during my first session when Manny abruptly tabled seven bills that had passed the House. The sponsors had voted against a bill sponsored by one of Manny's key allies (Sen. Phil Maloof, scion of a prominent Albuquerque family and later a congressional candidate) to place large advertisements on school buses. He announced the impoundment boldly and said the bills would be released when the House reconsidered—which it promptly did, passing the school bus bill. The *Albuquerque Journal* called it a *movida*, a classic political move, and used it as an example of the concentration of power in the hands of one man.[6] Others did not take it too seriously, since for Manny picking fights was business as usual.

In 1997, Manny was at the height of his power. He personally selected almost all of the Senate staff, from attendants and analysts to the cleaning crew. He had a personal retinue, which included some of the best and the brightest minds stolen from the LFC, other agencies, or even other senators (yes, he stole my Harvard-educated attendant). He seemed to be everywhere, dominating every committee and every caucus. He introduced fifty-seven bills that year. "He just sucked all the oxygen out of the room," one lawyer recalled.

Like Ike Smalley during much of the 1970s and 1980s, Manny had become the dominant leader of the Senate during the 1990s. With the Democrats locked in mortal combat with libertarian Gary Johnson, Manny played the partisan card to a tee. And he had the *caballos*, or the horses, to move his agenda down the field. As a fellow liberal, his goals were the same as mine, but as time went on the means he used to further his ends gave me pause—even before he entered into a controversial contract with the private prison operator Wackenhut in 1998 (a clear conflict of interest, I thought) and long before his indictment in 2007.

Manny was overthrown in 2001 by a coalition of three Democrats and eighteen Republicans. For the two years that followed, Senate Democrats were engulfed in bitterness and division, with Manny's loyal followers never fully cooperating with the new president pro tem, Richard Romero of Albuquerque. In 2004, Gov. Bill Richardson appointed Manny as president of Highlands University. He had always wanted to be president of the northern New Mexico college, whose primary mission is to serve Hispanics. His tenure there was cut short by an investigation into the diversion of state funds during the construction of the Metropolitan Courthouse in Albuquerque. Manny Aragon, the legislature's most dominant figure in decades, ultimately pled guilty to siphoning off $600,000 from $4.2 million in courthouse construction funds, which he had sponsored while in the legislature. He is now finishing a five-and-a-half-year sentence in a federal penitentiary in Florence, Colorado.

"He thought he could have it all," said Carraro. "In the end his loyalty to his constituents and his own beliefs played second fiddle to his own ambition and private interests."

RICHARD ROMERO
One Man with Courage Makes a Majority

January 17 2001. Downstairs in the Senate lounge, amid the oversized leather couches lining the perimeter of the handsomely paneled room, the Democratic senators were beginning to gather, but without the friendly banter— or the food—that usually accompanied caucus meetings. I made it there shortly after the meeting had begun, and I was let in by the sergeant of arms who controlled the door. He was as tense as the rest of us with the prospect that longtime president pro tem Manny Aragon could be replaced by a coalition headed by Sen. Richard Romero or, maybe, Sen. Joe Carraro.

The Democratic caucus chair, Sen. Linda Lopez, who had tried to use her skills as a facilitator to run meetings in an orderly fashion, was absent. The Albuquerque senator had just given birth to a son and was still in the hospital after a difficult birth (see fig. 14). Given the situation, there was confusion as to who should actually be running the meeting. The senators were still reeling from the events of the day before when two renegade Democrats, Sen. Cisco McSorley, of Albuquerque, and Sen. Leonard Tsosie, of

Crownpoint, nominated Sen. Richard Romero for pro tem. It suddenly became obvious that, with Lopez's absence, Manny did not have the votes to hold on. Some senators thought it was futile to even have a meeting because the die had been cast—a deal had been struck between the Republicans and Richard Romero. We all knew that this was our last chance to come together as Democrats.

"Can't we just all get together and be a family, in spite of our differences," asked Majority Whip Mary Jane Garcia, in what was to become a familiar refrain.

Richard Romero, Leonard Tsosie, and Cisco McSorley sat stonily silent.

"Well, have you made a deal with the R's," someone asked. "Are they going to be running the place?"

"So, Richard, which Republicans are going to become committee chairs?" Still silence.

"Do you have the votes?" asked another senator.

"Yes, I have the votes," Romero nodded, knowing that earlier in the day the Republicans had made their decision, encouraged by Gov. Gary Johnson and Sen. Joe Carraro, who by then had withdrawn his bid.

Manny sat silent, fiddling with his water bottle, staring straight ahead as if in a trance. Now there were none of the long harangues, none of the exhausting tirades that wandered far from the point and left members too tired to focus.

But the point was crystal clear.

"Well, is there anything we can do to make you change your mind," I asked Richard Romero.

"What if we were all to agree on another D to run for pro tem; then we could at least maintain our majority."

Sen. Nancy Rodriguez, of Santa Fe, and others were becoming more insistent as time was running short before the floor session was due to convene at 3:00 p.m.

"Benny, would you be willing to run for pro tem," Rodriguez asked Sen. Ben Altamirano, the much-loved chairman of the Senate Finance Committee from Silver City and one of the Senate's longest serving members.

"Well maybe I should," said Benny. "I know I should, but I promised Manny, and I'm loyal to him. I know I shouldn't be, but he's done a lot for me and my family, so I can't . . . I'm not running."

"This is all useless anyway," Sen. Shannon Robinson, who had arrived late, jumped in. "If you've got the votes you can do anything you want. You can run roughshod over the Democratic Party, you can depose chairs, you can kick people out of their offices, anything."

"Wait," I said, "let me just ask both of you one more time—Richard, would you step aside if we could agree on another candidate besides Manny?"

"Yes," he nodded, "I would."

"Manny, would you?" I asked, turning toward the sulking figure.

"No, I'm not stepping aside," he said. "I'd rather die on my feet than live on my knees. This caucus is over."

He strode from the room and we followed him into the Senate chambers, where the crowd gathered in the gallery fell silent. Moments later, Richard Romero defeated Manny Aragon for pro tem, twenty-one to twenty, with all eighteen Republicans and three Democrats voting for him. It was a vote that sent shockwaves around the state, with angry supporters of Manny shortly holding rallies outside the Roundhouse and praying the rosary in front of Romero's Albuquerque home. It was clearly the most dramatic development I experienced in the New Mexico Senate, and I learned more about leadership, loyalty, courage, and group dynamics on those opening days than I wanted to.

My immediate reaction to the caucus was that it was Romero who was actually the loyal Democrat and it was Manny who was obsessed with his own power and not the good of the group. Naïvely, I thought everyone who was there would see it that way, given Manny's dramatic declaration, taken from a quote by Emilio Zapata, the Mexican revolutionary, which, earlier, I had seen carved into the floor of his remarkable adobe castle in the South Valley.

But I was very wrong. Most of the Democratic caucus remained fiercely loyal, joining in a pitched battle waged daily to tear the new leader down, humiliate him personally, and sabotage his agenda. Most observers thought Romero would not last beyond the first weekend. Few believed that he could pass a budget or deal with redistricting, slated for action that year, since it was the year immediately following the census.

Like Manny, Richard Romero was born in the barrio of Barelas, a Hispanic community south of downtown Albuquerque that sprang up around the rail yards. Romero and Manny knew each other in their youth, playing baseball and flag football. Like Manny, Romero was athletic and competitive, a characteristic hidden by his mild manner. Romero spent most of his life as an educator, becoming the principal of two Albuquerque high schools, Sandia and Albuquerque High. He entered the Senate in 1993; most people took him as an expert in public education and little more (see fig. 15).

As an administrator who knew how to use staff and delegate authority, Romero had become increasingly disenchanted with Manny's leadership style. He had a favorite analogy for it, and it revolved around basketball.

"Why should one person be the one who controls the ball, makes all the passes, and takes all the shots?" he asked. "There's a whole team out there with talents, but they never get to use them."

From the very start of his term as pro tem, Romero was determined to empower capable senators to do their jobs, make their own decisions, and not continually defer to one brilliant leader. It was a vision that resonated with Republicans who had been shut out, but the Democrats were wary, thinking that the idea was just a ruse to gain power.

Contrary to popular belief, Romero's deal with the Republicans was not based on giving Republicans committee chairmanships. It was based on the promise that he would allow the system to work fairly. Committees would hear all bills and vote them up or down. The Committee on Committees would meet and actually function to appoint committee members. There would be fewer last minute surprises and, most important, the Senate Finance Committee would formulate the budget.

But the old regime would not go down easily. Romero was finding out how difficult it was to dismantle a system built over the previous thirteen years, constructed with a slew of patronage positions and the personal loyalty of budget analysts, attendants, and temporary clerks. There was general outrage on the first floor in 2001 when Richard got rid of approximately fifty-three staffers, some of whose duties and salaries were laughable. It was only because of the conciliatory remarks of Sen. Joe Fidel, of Grants, that Romero, Tsosie, and McSorley were not barred from the Democratic caucus. And it was a constant daily struggle on the floor of the Senate as Manny's loyalists threw verbal grenades and mounted personal attacks. Sen. Shannon Robinson was particularly outspoken, his face reddening and his arms waving wildly as he circled his prey, who sat directly in front of him on the floor of the Senate. When, after days of being called Judas and Benedict Arnold, Romero refused to turn and acknowledge the abusive remarks, Robinson took to calling him "the invisible man."

Aragon and other Democrats would chime in. Even noncontroversial matters, committee reports and routine motions, were contentious. Everyone had his or her rulebook at the ready. Very little got done—and that was the point. Aragon and his loyalists knew that if they could exhaust and divide the chamber there would be less chance of passing the budget. Coming up with the blueprint for state spending was the major job of the session and the mark of success for its leader.

From day one, Romero had said his goal was a small one: to let the Senate Finance Committee do its job. And it did, coming up with a spending blueprint for $3.9 billion, which included an 8 percent pay raise for teachers, a number of health care expansions, and a $72 million income-tax cut. The Republicans, for the first time, were included in the negotiations.

"It was the first time my chairman had been able to craft a budget," said Senate Finance Committee Vice-Chair Sen. Joe Fidel.

"We finally got the budget out of the basement," recalls David Abbey.

It wasn't easy. Committee members were not used to formulating a budget on their own, and the staff had been depleted. Maralyn Budke, a well-respected advisor to former governor Garrey Carruthers, who had worked with both the Department of Finance and Administration (DFA) and the LFC, volunteered to help her old friend Sen. Ben Altamirano. Working together, the committee voted to pass the bill out, and now it was time to report to the floor and ask for approval.

The fireworks that followed during that long night featured an endless stream of amendments introduced by Aragon and Robinson, designed to pick off votes and clutter up the document so it wouldn't balance. But the members of the Finance Committee stood strong, along with the Republicans and a few others (like me). One by one the amendments were defeated, and finally the budget, HB 2, passed the Senate twenty-three to thirteen.

Richard Romero had sat silent during the four-and-one-half-hour debate, not wishing to prolong what he knew was an attempt to wear down wavering senators. Typically, Romero resisted what other senators could not—the opportunity to talk on every single subject. Now he was exhausted, but he knew he had won an important round. The budget eventually passed the entire legislature on a bipartisan basis, for the first time in years. It was not vetoed by the governor, although an accompanying tax cut that Johnson had long sought was (amazingly) rejected. A number of controversial bills got bipartisan support, including bills to restore the vote to felons, to repeal a law against cohabitation, and a requirement that insurance companies cover contraceptives.

In the two years that followed there would be greater victories for Romero's leadership style. Although the special redistricting session was a disaster, with almost every plan passed by legislators landing in court, Romero was able to snatch victory out of the jaws of defeat. After the governor vetoed the take-no-prisoners Senate plan favored by Manny, Romero appointed a committee with an equal number of Republicans and Democrats. Naturally, they came up with an incumbent protection plan, but it was popular enough to garner the votes needed to pass in the 2002 session. The governor did not veto it.

There were still choppy waters all around. Romero survived a backroom counter coup staged at the Santa Ana Pueblo's resort, Tamaya, by loyalist Democrats in November 2001, shortly after the special session. Tim Jennings and Linda Lopez did not. Jennings was replaced by Manny as majority leader and Lopez as caucus chair by Phil Griego, of San Jose. Lopez and Jennings, trying to keep the peace, had worked too closely with the new pro tem.

The following year, Romero responded by removing one of Aragon's biggest allies, Sen. Shannon Robinson, from his post as chairman of the Public Affairs Committee, and naming someone he knew he could trust to actually hear both Republican and Democratic bills, convene the committee regularly, and refrain from burying controversial measures without even a hearing. That someone was me. I tried to run the committee in a respectful and predictable way for the next ten years. It fit in with Romero's emphasis on fairness and his desire to give rank and file committee members more power. Sometimes the process allowed passage of bills the liberal Democrat in me hated. But that was the idea: the ends no longer justified the means.

Gradually Romero was reestablishing the process, ending the chaos, and stimulating members to take every issue on its own merits. For many senators, thinking on their own, without a strong leader to give them the cue, was difficult.

"Loyalty makes people stop thinking," one lobbyist told me. "There are so many people that can't tell you their position on an issue until they check with the pro tem or the Speaker."

Another lobbyist called it, "Loyalty, unencumbered by the thought process."

Eric Lane, a professor at Hofstra Law School who spent six years as counsel to the Democrats in the New York Senate in the 1980s, describes the syndrome as the "Albany Handshake."[7] Followers affected by the syndrome don't have to do much work; they leave it to the leaders who dole out capital outlay, campaign funds, trips, and other benefits so that senators retain honor and prestige. Preoccupied with affairs in their districts, most are happy to leave the heavy lifting to the leaders. Voting is usually in lockstep, along party lines.

Former Arizona Republican senator Randall Gnant, who was elected by a coalition unhappy with the former Senate leader there, was going through the same struggle as Romero. I visited with him in the fall of 2001. "It's hard to get members to think on their own after years of being eunuchs who have settled for scraps and said 'go ahead and cut off my nuts,'" he said.

Month after month, as senators realized Romero was not going away, the new pro tem was making followers into leaders.

Romero's biggest victory came in 2002 in the wake of Johnson's vetoes of two budgets and a threatened shutdown of state government. Romero worked with Minority Leader Stuart Ingle and Speaker Ben Lujan to do what no other New Mexico legislature had ever done: call itself back into an extraordinary session. Usually a governor must call a special session, but legislators may call themselves back in if they get three-fifths of each chamber to request one. That is exactly what they did—and more. Meeting a tight deadline, the legislative leaders lassoed seventy-seven far-flung legislators, got them to sign on the dotted line, and convened a one-day session. During the session they passed an alternative budget, drawn up by a bipartisan committee. And when the governor vetoed it, the House overrode the veto, 62–2, and the Senate swamped it 36–4. The leadership had built a consensus, which included Republicans who had overridden only one of their governor's seven hundred–plus vetoes. Ironically, former pro tem Manny Aragon, Governor Johnson's nemesis, was one of the few senators who did not vote for the override.

"It was a watershed," recalled David Harris, who then was working for Governor Johnson. "It vindicated the separation of powers and was a high-point for the legislature."

The "invisible man"—whom critics said lacked charisma and communications skills—had a huge role in the historic accomplishment.

"It's easy to abdicate and retreat into your own little niche, when you're a legislator," said lobbyist and former representative Tom Horan. Those words sometimes applied to me, but not to Richard Romero, who could have stuck to education. He ventured forth and changed the system.

"How did you do it?" I once asked Romero. "I don't really know," he admitted. "I was just fed up and felt like I had nothing to lose."

SEN. TIM JENNINGS
The Wisdom of the Clock

March 2007. Roswell's Sen. Tim Jennings and Deming's Sen. John Arthur Smith, two of the Senate's most conservative Democrats, stood in the House chamber goading the representatives to go home. "Sine die," they yelled, the signal to adjourn without a date for reconvening. Exhausted by several all-night sessions, the House Democrats could have been a receptive audience, but Speaker Ben Lujan was able to maintain order. Banging his gavel, he ruled the senators out of order and kept his exhausted troops in session long enough to take care of business and wrap up the special session without a major breakdown.

A major breakdown was exactly what Jennings, the Republicans, and a handful of angry Democrats were trying to foment. Fuming at Governor Richardson's presidential campaign travels and his simultaneous call for a special session, they were out for blood. To sabotage the special session, Jennings and the Republicans had taken extraordinary measures. The unusual meddling with House floor action was just one. Twice, they had succeeded in getting the votes to adjourn the special session that the governor had called to pass several of his priorities, which had stalled earlier in the Senate. After the vote to adjourn, senators had returned to their homes around the state, relieved of the burdensome business of discussing an ethics commission, campaign finance reform, road funding, or whether to legalize domestic partnerships. Trouble was, the House, which was much more aligned with Richardson, stayed in session. That meant that, according to the rules, senators had to reconvene within seventy-two hours—which we did, only to vote to adjourn sine die again. Score another blow to big Bill Richardson.

The senators did finally return for good, voting on some of the governor's initiatives, passing public financing for statewide judicial elections and pared down funding for his roads package. All of the measures had originated in the House, where they had labored long and hard on an ethics commission, in particular. I was ashamed that the Senate was thumbing their noses at the more liberal House and upset that we had now lost our last best chance for a bill to legalize domestic partnerships.

But for Jennings, who was later elected pro tem by a coalition of Republicans and nine Democrats in 2009, it was a source of pride. The Senate had been supreme (see fig. 16).

"There is such a thing as the wisdom of the clock," Senator Jennings told me when I asked for his view on leadership. "Sine die allows people to go home and feel like they've done their job—otherwise we'd be up here all the time."

"What about the pressing issues of the day?" I asked.

"In a democracy there is supposed to be less, rather than more, government," the maverick Democrat responded. "If we stay up here we pass more laws and take away peoples' freedom."

Sen. Aubrey Dunn, whom Jennings called a mentor and one of the finest public servants New Mexico ever had, also held this viewpoint.

In an article Dunn wrote in 1981 for the *Albuquerque Tribune*, the powerful chair of the Senate Finance Committee compared the legislature to his apple orchard in Alamogordo. "Raising apples is just like the legislative session; if you don't have too many, you have nice, big ones and they are healthy.

In the legislature if you don't pass too many laws in the session, the better the session."[8]

A small government with short legislative meetings in January of each year was what the framers of the New Mexico constitution had in mind in 1912. And the constitution suits conservative eastsiders like Jennings and his friend Republican Minority Leader Stuart Ingle just fine. The "East Side Twins," as some called them, regularly traded floor speeches filled with farm and ranch analogies, the virtues of dry land farming (for Ingle), and the greatness of the New Mexico Military Institute. The rural ribaldry could sometimes take hours, with Jennings taking us "down the road a piece," and Ingle, whose sense of timing was superb, often deadpanning the role of a country bumpkin. During redistricting debates, both resisted a reduction of seats in eastern New Mexico, in spite of a population decline. At committee hearings, Jennings often waved the state constitution, warning the captive audience about bureaucrats who would make you put an extra drain in your swimming pool and University of New Mexico administrators who would reject all eastern New Mexicans (like his daughter) from the medical school just because they were from that part of the state.

The rural, antigovernment approach is usually a Republican one, and although Jennings is loyal to the Democratic Party, his constituents in Chavez, Lincoln, Eddy, and Otero counties are largely Republican—a fact that finally caused his defeat in 2012. Jennings was the last Democrat left on the east side, which resembles West Texas more than New Mexico. As such, he was ideally positioned in the center of the conservative chamber and in 2009 won election as pro tem even though the majority of the Democratic caucus did not support him.

Often at odds with his own party and the governor, Jennings relied on his many years of experience in the Senate (he came in 1979, and held virtually every post) and the personal relationships his family has built throughout the state. Jennings was not afraid to side with his Republican friends, especially when he believed it was a matter of fairness. During the 2009 campaign, he recorded robo calls to voters in defense of Sen. Leonard Lee Rawson, the Republican whip from Las Cruces. Democrats were outraged, but somehow Jennings survived and was reelected pro tem at the height of the Democratic tide.

"Loyalty, respect, and friendship" were the first words to come to his lips when I asked about leadership. And it was on those qualities that Jennings depended to find a middle path through the maze of controversial issues that faced the body. "You try to get people to listen to one another, even if they are on opposite sides. People on the right and left will mellow, if you just ask for help and explain your position. We have to live with one another here and get along," he said.

Ever the peacemaker, Jennings was always trying to patch things up between his members and negotiate a settlement acceptable to most. He truly believes that "those of us in the middle will always take this state forward."[9] In part, his optimistic belief traces back to the things that he and his wife, Patty Ikard Jennings, were able to accomplish in the face of partisan gridlock in the 1980s.

Before Senator Jennings and Patty Ikard were married, they played on the legislative stage together, advocating for opportunities for people with developmental disabilities, like Ikard's daughter Courtney. In the early 1980s, during the tightfisted heyday of the "Cowboy Coalition" in the House of Representatives, Ikard and a rag-tag bunch of parents of kids with Down syndrome and other disabilities were able—with the help of Jennings—to pass a bill that mandated early special education for three- and four-year-olds. In the early 1990s the couple, then married, established the New Mexico Medical Insurance Pool to guarantee insurance coverage for families whose members had serious or chronic conditions. The Pool, as it is called, continues to provide coverage to people turned down by insurance companies because of preexisting conditions. Much later, in 2008, as Patty Jennings was dying from inflammatory breast cancer, the legislature, without much discussion, appropriated $1 million for a joint program with University of New Mexico and MD Anderson cancer centers to combat the disease. The Jennings's personal story (romance, tragedy, and all) engendered a personal connection and compassion that became a part of the fabric of the institution.

In 2004, as the Richardson administration was picking up speed, the senator from Roswell blew a gasket. Over the next few years, he became convinced that the governor was out only for short-term political gain and would do anything to further his career. Jennings would take to the floor again and again to denounce the governor as a bully, a crook, and a liar. The kicker was a meeting the governor held with pharmaceutical lobbyists where his wife witnessed profanity and strong-arm tactics, not unusual in the Roundhouse. Jennings took it as an affront to the Senate itself. He felt that the Democrats were giving away the store to their strong governor, yielding to his increased spending and enlarged share of capital outlay projects. The personal again became the political.

"I am going to tell you that if this body and this legislature doesn't stand up on its feet and defend this institution, this governor is going to take us straight to hell," the red-faced senator blasted from his seat in the chamber, demanding an apology for the alleged insult to pharmaceutical lobbyists.[10]

Taking umbrage at what he perceived as the governor's lack of integrity, Jennings brought up every hint of corruption, whether it was pay-for-play contracts with Richardson's contributors or cronies appointed to high paid positions within the administration. While the Republicans cheered, many Democrats were dismayed. Majority Whip Mary Jane Garcia said, "Some people just have personal agendas and if they don't get their little proposals they go berserk."[11]

The *Santa Fe New Mexican* said that Jennings was creating a soap-opera atmosphere. Others blew it off as hot air. Gusty winds were always present in the Senate, after all. Whatever it was, it had a cascading effect. Richardson vetoed $750,000 in capital outlay for Jennings's district that year. He would veto more in the years to come, increasing the stature of the maverick senator in the eyes of Republicans and others who admired his courage and forthrightness. In the years that followed, Jennings and his ally John Arthur Smith, of Deming, would succeed in blocking much of the governor's agenda, from health care reform in 2008 (see chapter 9) to domestic partnerships, ethics, and campaign finance reform (which Jennings thought, for Richardson, was the height of hypocrisy).

The blocking action was part of Jennings's idea of leadership, and he is not alone. Many applauded his actions and those of Sen. John Arthur Smith—who consolidated his position as chairman of the Senate Finance Committee once Jennings became pro tem—as the state fell into recession in 2009. Both Jennings and Smith maintained that the Richardson administration had lied to them about the growing revenue crisis and had kept spending money when it knew better. Jennings and Smith quickly put on the brakes, cutting almost $1 billion in school funding and state government while steadfastly refusing to raise taxes.

Many, especially the Republicans who would capture the governor's mansion in 2010, applauded the forced departure from Richardson's policies. Jennings and Smith got credit for crossing party lines and upholding the institution—a mark of leadership in many books. That should have earned Jennings the support of the new Republican governor, Susana Martinez. Instead the governor's PAC poured in hundreds of thousands to defeat him in 2012. With demographics in their favor, they succeeded.

SEN. YES AND DR. NO

Ben Altamirano, whose term as pro tem was cut short by his untimely death in December 2007, was loved by members of the Senate for his caring, respectful demeanor. I liked to joke with him about how he could never say no to most requests, which often put him in the situation of sponsoring eighty or ninety bills per session. A former grocery store operator from Silver City, Altamirano chaired the Senate Finance Committee for seventeen years, where he wielded more power than he did as pro tem, although he often abdicated to Aragon. He was the natural choice for pro tem after the departure of both Manny Aragon and Richard Romero. His laid back, collaborative style did not create waves, and he was a more ceremonial leader than an active one. His good relationship with Governor Richardson allowed for the passage of many of the governor's priorities, which did not sit well with the two men who stepped in to fill the vacuum after his death.

Just as Pro Tem Ike Smalley teamed up with Senate Finance Chair Aubrey Dunn in the 1970s, Pro Tem Jennings relied on the current Senate Finance Chair John Arthur Smith, of Deming. A real estate appraiser by trade, Smith has boosted the power of the interim Legislative Finance Committee (LFC) and its staff, extending its reach into every policy area considered by the body. New Mexico is one of the few states where the legislature formulates a budget proposal before the session convenes in January, which gives it more power than legislatures that simply react to executive proposals. The LFC, composed of both House and Senate members, is the entity that comes up with that proposal. In recent years it has become larger, pushing its agenda through newsletters and frequent publications. In times of economic crisis, the power of the budgeteers has increased, and the budget document has become more difficult for rank and file members to change.

Critics of Smith say that the Senate finance chair has concentrated power in the committee among rural, conservative senators (appointed by Jennings) and used it to block initiatives from both Democrats and governors without adequate consultation with the rank and file. Indeed, Smith's fiscal conservatism and gruff demeanor have earned him the moniker of Dr. No —although anyone who has served with him can vouch for his humor and wit on the floor.

Health and education advocates are particularly disappointed in Smith and the way bills that have widespread support consistently go down either without a hearing or upon a tabling motion supported by Smith, the Republicans, and conservative Democrat Mary Kay Papen, of Las Cruces. (Papen replaced Jennings as pro tem in 2013, with the support of all the chamber's Republicans.) In 2012, a constitutional amendment to allow voters to decide whether to use a small fraction of the state's permanent fund for early childhood education was tabled in that manner. In 2013 a similar constitutional amendment, passed by the House, did not even receive a hearing. In 2008, a compromise bill establishing a Health Care Authority was not heard, although it too passed the House overwhelmingly and was poised for passage.

"Here's one man, from one of the smallest, most rural districts of New Mexico, dictating to the rest of the state," Allen Sánchez, a lobbyist for the New Mexico Conference of Catholic Bishops, complained.

For others, Smith's fiscal conservatism is the height of responsibility, a saving grace in a time of economic crisis. David Abbey, director of the LFC, feels that one of the greatest accomplishments of the legislature in recent years was how well it weathered the "great recession," when the state lost 20 percent of its revenues. Throughout the period, he says, Senator Smith and Rep. Kiki Saavedra, the chair of the House Appropriations and Finance Committee from Albuquerque, put together budgets that passed with wide bipartisan majorities. In his view, they saved the state from layoffs and major economic damage. "Just holding the ship afloat was a big accomplishment," said Abbey.

"Even in ordinary times, just passing the budget is a big deal," says Dick Minzner, a lobbyist who is a former representative and secretary of taxation and revenue. "In this partisan environment it is doubly difficult." Minzner points to budget gridlock at the federal level and pines for the day when "people were more interested in doing what the arithmetic demanded." Getting everyone on board, getting the liberals to give up their priorities and the conservatives to spend a little more, is a big challenge. And writing the two-hundred-plus page document in a way that it has a little something for everyone and cannot be altered dramatically by line item vetoes (whereby the governor can simply cancel an appropriation or program) is almost an art form. Budgeteering may not be sexy or heroic, but it is the key accomplishment of any legislative session and a key mark of leadership in legislatures throughout the country.

SEN. MICHAEL SANCHEZ
Calling the Plays from behind the Scenes

February 8, 1999. The injury was serious. Sen. Michael Sanchez, who each year rallied the older, less toned and more penalty-prone senators in their annual basketball game against the House, was sidelined. He would not be taking to the floor at the School for the Deaf in the next few minutes or playing basketball again that year. But if Sanchez was down he was not out. In spite of a painful torn Achilles tendon, Sanchez resumed his duties on crutches, convening his committee and not missing a beat during the remainder of the long session. Sanchez's grit and competitiveness have been hallmarks of his sometimes gentle, sometimes scrappy leadership style in the New Mexico Senate.

Sen. Michael Sanchez thinks of himself as a coach, uniting his team, protecting his players, and advancing the ball down the field—despite unforeseen injury or loss. Surrounded by baseball memorabilia in his law office in Los Lunas, the former Belen Eagles quarterback reflected on his role as the Senate majority leader, a post he has held since 2005.

"Leadership is something that you earn from the group," Sanchez told me. "It's derived from the group—the group itself is really the leader but you can direct it once you listen to people and figure out a way to solve problems and reach compromise within your caucus."

"Good followers make for good leaders," former Senate pro tem Les Houston had told me—but sometimes the caucus that a leader inherits is dysfunctional, with committee chairs too independent or (conversely) too deferential, and members noncommittal or indifferent to policy issues. It's a problem that plagues leaders in every state capital.

With so many controversial issues, and a Senate filled with mavericks, leading the diverse Democratic caucus in New Mexico is not an easy task. Sanchez says it boils down to listening to the dissidents and minority members and understanding their desires. "You have to be able to take the pulse of the body," he says. "I don't believe in making all the decisions" (see fig. 17).

Sometimes a compromise can't be found, but if you are civil and do not shut anyone down, nine times out of ten you can come to an understanding—and solve a problem. For Sanchez, this work is often done one-on-one, out of the public eye, not in caucus or on the floor.

Most often, Sanchez has to corral the minority of conservative Democrats, like Tim Jennings, who is also a good friend, or make sure he has enough other votes so that some of his caucus can vote against a bill or "walk" without voting on it at all.

When he chaired the Senate Judiciary Committee, Sanchez would often assign his staff to work with sponsors and opponents of a certain bill to come up with something they could all live with. In 2005, he helped me with my bill to require young all-terrain vehicle (ATV) users to wear safety helmets and riders to abide by environmental protections. It was a bill that was opposed by the industry and some gung-ho riders, but we came up with a compromise, which passed the Senate and, later, the legislature. In 2011, Sanchez used the same method to help me pass a bill to make health insurance hikes more transparent and fair. It was a bill that could easily have been killed by the powerful insurance lobby, but Sanchez provided an opening by bringing Republican Sen. Carol Leavell (an insurance agent) and Sen. Mary Kay Papen to the table. Without his guidance they would have opposed the bill, and this important insurance reform would have fallen through the cracks. He also deserves credit for getting Sen. Phil Griego to turn a tobacco tax bill loose from his Corporations Committee in 2010 (see chapter 7), thus enabling its passage.

Sanchez says he is trying to earn the respect of members based on his actions and not on fear of punishment and retribution, a style characteristic of past Senate leaders like Aragon and Smalley. He is gratified that the budget and capital outlay process are no longer used to reward friends and punish enemies and proud that the Senate is now a more civil and orderly place.

But to protect the integrity of the institution, some say Sanchez has gone too far behind the scenes, injecting himself into members' affairs, cautioning them about personal indiscretions or drinking habits, or coaching them on how to speak or not speak on the floor. "I take responsibility for them because it reflects on all of us," he says. Yet many legislators are grateful to him for his guidance in presenting a bill or delaying a hearing until the time is ripe. He has counseled committee chairs on fair procedures and defused tensions, but others wonder whether he tries to orchestrate too much, too secretly. Some doubt that he always has their best interests in mind, particularly if he disagrees or feels that somehow a proposal is an insult to the institution.

Sanchez's well-known opposition to open government measures, including webcasting and public conference committees, was grounded in a defense of the traditions of the Senate. He takes umbrage easily when ethics, governmental conduct, or campaign finance reforms are suggested. He often lashed out against me and other advocates who dared to suggest that the public didn't fully trust legislators.

A trial lawyer, Sanchez does not hesitate to unexpectedly single out opponents in the audience or his critics in the press gallery, accusing them of hypocrisy or even lies. Sanchez has publicly gone after the head of the Drug Enforcement Administration, Governor Richardson's domestic violence czar, tobacco lobbyists, and the directors of Think New Mexico, Common Cause, and the Albuquerque Chamber of Commerce. The outbursts may sometimes be justified, but, for those on the receiving end, they don't feel like the civility Sanchez says he is trying to cultivate in the Senate.

Being the bad guy, however, is something that Sanchez feels is part of the job description, especially on the last few days of the session when he must decide which bills to call up for a vote and which ones to leave on the table. How does he decide? He consults with the sponsor, tries to balance Republican and Democratic bills, and tries to figure out how much debate the bill will create.

Sometimes, he says it just doesn't pass his smell test. A sponsor will tell him confidentially that it's not that important or his experience tells him to wait another year. "Emotions don't play a role in deciding which bills I place on the calendar," Sanchez told blogger Heath Haussaman.[12]

Hmm. In the New Mexico Senate, it's hard to believe that emotions don't play a role in everything. As we will see, compassion, loyalty, and personal connections have made the difference between defeat and victory when it came to medical marijuana, mental health parity, and an end to the death penalty. And emotions define leadership as well. Aragon's charisma engaged the emotions and defined a confrontational partisan leader. Jennings's conflicts with the governor were personal conflicts, and emotions ran high. Although Sanchez, like Romero, has professionalized the process, his search for what is "best for the whole body," including the minority, is not scientific. It is intuitive—for better and worse.

Sometimes the leader gets it right, and his intuition is in sync with the members. Richard Romero recognized when the public mood was right to overthrow a leader who had overreached. Jennings and Smith may have been in sync with the state's more conservative, antigovernment constituents who want few new laws. Whether Sanchez can create a consensus for a more Democratic agenda is still unknown, and his behind-the-scenes methods make him hard to judge.

It's hard to assess which of these Senate leaders was most successful. Each had a different goal and worked toward it at a different speed. Aragon saw himself as the champion of the state's underrepresented, the poor and ethnic minorities, and he worked day and night, pushing the envelope in whatever direction he could. Jennings saw his role as simply limiting the damage the legislature can do with too many unnecessary laws. All of them tried to increase the power of the Senate vis-à-vis the executive and the House. I liked and admired each one of them greatly, and I was especially grateful to Richard Romero for changing the direction of the New Mexico Senate. But, with what I saw going on around me, I tried not to be blindly loyal to any of them, a stance that often placed me outside the system, a stranger in a strange land.

CHAPTER 4

Special Interests, Lobbyists, and Citizen Legislators

"You've Got to Dance with Them What Brung Ya"

Politicians and governors come and go. Lobbyists are always there.

—CONCI BOKUM, WATER LOBBYIST

D URING MY FIRST TERM IN THE SENATE, BACK IN THE 1990S, IT suddenly dawned on me that, regardless of how many speeches I gave extolling the virtues of public service or how sincerely I expressed my positions on the issues to the media, a certain slice of the community didn't believe me—no matter what I said or did. These weren't just partisan opponents. They were ordinary citizens, many of them young people, who believed that in New Mexico and in the rest of the country all politicians are the same. Politicians will say anything to get reelected, or get a "wet kiss" from the news media, right? Most of all, a growing number of cynics believe politicians tailor their actions to fit the wishes of their campaign contributors who are, for the most part, special interests. I knew that this was the conventional wisdom, but I never imagined it would be applied to *me*. Then I began to see the polling results. A 1999 poll taken by Research and Polling indicated that 82 percent of voters believed that special interest contributions to legislators' campaigns affected their votes either "a lot" (47 percent) or "some" (35 percent).[1]

No wonder I was feeling the effects of this credibility gap. But was this merely a perception problem or was it true? I was determined to find out whether special interests controlled the Roundhouse. And I wanted to know if, as my friends and neighbors seemed to believe, a tight group of insiders composed of lobbyists, campaign contributors, and key legislators controlled what bills passed and failed in the New Mexico legislature. If this was true, I wanted to know who they were.

It's a question that citizens and advocates in every state ponder more and more as the process is unveiled in the media and blogosphere. In New Mexico, just asking the question didn't endear me to many of my fellow members who bristled at the thought that lobbyists might influence their vote or that special interests had inordinate influence. Testing the proposition with reform bills that challenged the fireworks industry, tobacco manufacturers, pharmaceutical giants, and health insurance companies didn't garner me as many campaign contributions as I might have gotten if I had kept my mouth shut.

The answer is far more complex than I initially thought, and to "get it" you have to understand the unique political culture of the New Mexico legislature.

I have a collection of trinkets and baubles from my sixteen years in the legislature. Most were placed on my desk in the Senate chambers by attendants. Others were delivered to my office or my front door by lobbyists or other envoys. Items that could be mailed flooded my mailbox or arrived via Fed Ex. Once, when we were debating a gift act to restrict donations, I tried to inventory the items to see whether there was anything that was really valuable, but I realized I had given most of them away. Still, each year I would bring home box after box containing things like teddy bears; thermos containers; mouse pads; flashlights; blocks of cheese; thermometers; bags of peanuts, potatoes, or pinto beans; cookies; wine glasses; pens of all types; jars of salsa; digital clocks; pins that blinked or flashed; posters; pencil holders; t-shirts; countless canvas bags; portfolios; and CDs. All were inscribed with the logo of the supplicant organization, many of them small towns or schools. And all had a fact sheet or message attached. Most included food.

I still have some of my favorites, based on the kitsch value alone: a urine specimen container (unused, I hope) filled with candy handed out by the district courts; a maroon leather binder with SENATOR DEDE FELDMAN and the state seal of New Mexico on the front donated by "The Friends of the Legislature" (i.e., Qwest, Xcel, the Modrall law firm and the New Mexico Broadcasters Association); an insulated green Del Norte Credit Union lunch sack; a huge black canvas bag imprinted with the name of every casino in New Mexico; and a CD of a group called the

New Mexico Singing Churchmen from the Baptist Association of New Mexico. My all-time favorite is the mug from the New Mexico Institute of Mining and Technology that, when filled with hot water or coffee, turns into a version of Van Gogh's *Starry Night* that somehow incorporates an image of a giant telescope near Magdalena.

Most of the gifts are of insignificant value, all falling well beneath the $250 cap for individual gifts set by the 2007 Gift Act. Still, some push the limit, like the free ski passes handed out by the New Mexico Ski Association (good for two at each of the state's ski areas), the electric toothbrushes from the New Mexico Dental Association, or the golf passes handed out by the New Mexico Golf Tourism Alliance. For lobbyists and their clients, who are required to report expenditures made during each legislative session, the cost of the gifts can add up. The ski passes and greens fees for all legislators, for example, were valued at about $28,000 each—a pretty big expenditure for the nonprofit organizations, who use it to buy good will and encourage decision makers to become familiar with their resorts.

Long before the Gift Act was passed in 2007, gifts to individual legislators were more lavish. Tickets to professional football games (even the Super Bowl) and Lobo and Aggie basketball games were commonplace. Old time lobbyists recall how boxes of liquor and soda were delivered to offices in the capitol at the beginning of each session—after ascertaining what thirsty legislators preferred. Crown Royal was a favorite. Some legislative leaders had insatiable appetites for *biscochitos* or certain other types of food. One lobbyist recalls how one senator would request that, since the lobbyist was picking up lunch for their meeting, could he bring a case of beer and a dozen burritos for the group?

The first year I arrived in the Senate, eager to network and meet fellow legislators, lobbyists, and their clients, I gained twenty pounds. I religiously attended the major dinners for all legislators listed on the social calendar and slurped up as much free booze as I could. After all, didn't former California Speaker Jesse Unruh say that you have no business being up here if you couldn't eat their food, drink their booze, screw their women (well, not me), and then vote against them? But, hey, it was hard to keep up. There was the fancy auto dealers dinner at the El Dorado Hotel, the Cities of Gold dinner at La Fonda started by long time lobbyist Bob Gold and his clients, the Presbyterian Health Care event at the posh La Posada, the Lutheran Advocacy Ministry–New Mexico lunch, the president pro tem's dinner at Quail Run sponsored by the utility companies, Echols Enterprises' dinner and show at the Santa Fe Convention Center, "The Party"

sponsored by lobbyist Tom Horan, and Agfest, a smorgasbord of state agricultural foods.

Often lobbyists and organizations go in together to sponsor some of the
biggest events for staff, elected officials, and members of the larger community. The 100th bill party is a legislative tradition that dates back decades
and usually involves a dance band from northern New Mexico, sometimes
with politico musicians like saxophonist Attorney General Gary King (a
former representative) sitting in. The Flor de las Flores award dinner, sponsored by the Hispanic Roundtable, and long dominated by Sen. Manny
Aragon, was held each year at the Santa Fe Convention Center. Free tickets
from various airlines, Navajo rugs, Nambé bowls, jewelry, and other presents were heaped upon awardees, selected personally by Senator Aragon for
their contributions to the Hispanic community.

After a while, like other legislators, I became selective about which events
I went to. Often the dinners conflicted with late committee meetings or I
was just too tired to go out on the town, but the events were always there.
They were, after all, a free source of good food for legislators whose per diem
wears a little thin in expensive Santa Fe. And you've got to eat, right?

During the 2012 session lobbyists spent more than $260,000 for meals,
gifts, and special events for legislators, according to reports filed with the
secretary of state.[2] That's not counting campaign contributions from lobbyists and their clients.

Some of that money goes to group dinners for individual committees and
their staffs, like the one sponsored in 2011 by the University of Phoenix for
the House and Senate Education Committees at the Bull Ring ($6,761) or
another sponsored by the brother and sister lobbying duo, Mark and Stella
Duran, at the Restaurant Martín for the House Energy and Natural Resources Committee and staff ($2,916). In the Senate, the Corporations Com-
mittee is often fed by another lobbyist duo, siblings T. J. and Ty Trujillo,
who run a tab at the downtown watering hole, the Bull Ring, where many
lobbyists and legislators hang out on a regular basis.[3] My own Senate Public
Affairs Committee was often the recipient of pizza, sandwiches, and other
food, which we usually ate during late evening committee meetings. I, too,
was caught up in what political scientist Lawrence Lessig called the "legislative subsidy model" of lobbying, wherein legislators become dependent on
the services of lobbyists to meet some basic expenses for which we are not
reimbursed.[4]

None of these dinners violate any law or legislative rule, and both lobbyists and legislators maintain that they are simply a way to get together.

Usually, the conversation is not about issues being heard by the committee. "It's just an opportunity to facilitate the committee getting together in a social setting so they can talk and mingle," Mark Duran told the *Santa Fe New Mexican*.[5]

What do the lobbyists and their clients get out of it? The answer, almost everyone involved agrees, is not votes or access, but goodwill and the development of personal relationships. And it doesn't hurt if some of those personal relationships are with committee chairmen who have the power to block or facilitate passage of bills, since the bills must pass through their committees before coming to a vote on the floor of the Senate. Here, even more than in other states, friendships and personal relationships are the coin of the realm.

In 2012 there were over 744 lobbyists registered, as required, with the secretary of state's office. Among them were ordinary citizens who do not receive salaries, directors of nonprofit organizations, university presidents, administration officials, and paid lobbyists, some of whom have dozens of clients. That's almost seven lobbyists for every legislator. A few major interest groups dominate the scene, fielding large numbers of lobbyists. In 2012, the groups with the largest number of lobbyists on the ground were: ideological and single issue groups (167); businesses (155); health care and pharmaceuticals (150); local and tribal governments (150); education (142); and oil, gas, mining, and other energy-related companies (105). There are lots of different groups within each category, often working at cross-purposes.[6] With that mob, it would take a lot of schmoozing, a lot of hobnobbing and pressing the flesh, to even know who is who (see figs. 8 and 18).

In reality, however, there are far fewer full-time, year-round lobbyists. Some estimate the core group of "suits," as they are sometimes called, at about forty to fifty. Many are former legislators themselves, or are related to current or former lawmakers. In 2012, when I presented my last bill to prevent legislators from immediately becoming lobbyists after serving in the legislature, I could count at least thirteen former senators and eleven former representatives, many of them former leaders pressing the flesh in the halls of the Roundhouse. The senator/lobbyists included former president pro tem Richard Romero, former majority leaders Tito Chavez and Tom Rutherford, and former committee chairs Roman Maes and Otis Echols. Former senators Bobby McBride, Walter Bradley, Arthur Rodarte, Diane Snyder, Kent Cravens, Christine Donisthorpe, Les Houston, Mickey Barnett, and Maurice Hobson also lobby for various clients. Former representatives now lobbying include Raymond Sanchez, Tom Horan, John Lee Thompson,

Hoyt Pattison, Andrew Barreras, Joe Nestor Chavez, Michael Olguin, Dan Silva, Joe Thompson, Dick Minzner, and John Underwood. And the ranks of former legislators who become lobbyists swell after each election. Sen. Clint Harden, Rep. Andy Nunez, and former House judiciary chairman representative Al Park became lobbyists in 2013.

Often legislators refer to their former colleagues as "Speaker" Sanchez or "Senator" Snyder. One committee chair in the Senate, Sen. Linda Lopez, went even further with former senator Kent Cravens. Cravens stepped down from his seat representing Albuquerque's Northeast Heights in the fall of 2011 in favor of a lobbying job for the New Mexico Oil and Gas Association. Spotting him in the audience of the Rules Committee where he had served for many years, Chairman Lopez joked that his seat was still warm. "If you'd like me to stand in and vote, I'd be glad to," replied Cravens. It was a joke, of course, but it highlights the special advantage former colleagues have in approaching legislators.

This was something I pointed out to members of the same committee a few days later when, for the third time, I presented a bill to require a one-year pause between leaving office and becoming a paid lobbyist. Twenty-six states have similar moratoriums on lobbying by former legislators and restrictions are in place across federal and local governments.

"It's a matter of public trust," I argued. "We've developed a culture here where former colleagues have more access than the general public. Understandably we trust them more than people we don't know, and that gives them an advantage."

But a majority of the committee, as usual, disagreed.

"I don't think volunteer legislators should be restricted in what they can do after leaving here," said committee member Sen. Gay Kernan. They have made sacrifices and may need the money, the senator from Hobbs argued. She did not address the impression that legislators might profit by virtue of their former status.

"I've never known a legislator that was retired who had any influence," said Sen. Stuart Ingle, who, as everyone knew, often mentions lobbyist Tom Horan as his best friend. Decades earlier, Horan, as Ingle tells it, saved his life after he had an aneurysm. "And I have never known a legislator that paid attention to former legislators. I do not think this is a problem we have in this legislature."

Needless to say, the bill died an immediate death, with only me, Sen. Peter Wirth, and Senator Lopez voting in the affirmative. The lobbyists in question, who made up the bulk of the audience that day, felt a sense of relief.

If the fact that some of the top lobbyists in Santa Fe are former legislators seems a little incestuous, it is only part of the family atmosphere that exists in the Roundhouse. A good number of lobbyists are related to legislators. Mark Saavedra, the chief lobbyist for the University of New Mexico, is the son of House Appropriations Chairman Kiki Saavedra, as is Randy Saavedra who lobbies for the New Mexico Institute of Mining and Technology. Allison Smith, lobbyist for the New Mexico Restaurant Association, is the daughter of Sen. Mary Kay Papen, of Las Cruces. Jerry King, who used to lobby for the National Rifle Association, is the cousin of Rep. Rhonda King. Vanessa Alarid, who lobbies for Pfizer, the New Mexico Independent Auto Dealers, and many others, is the wife of Rep. Moe Maestas. The most well-known example is former speaker Raymond Sanchez, the brother of Senate Majority Leader Michael Sanchez. During most sessions the former speaker (who is the older brother) is camped out in the majority leader's office. To think that he had no influence on his brother would be a stretch. To say that he controlled his younger, somewhat unpredictable, brother would also be a stretch. A number of lobbyists, however, told me that a strategic phone call from Raymond to the majority leader, who controls which bills are heard on the floor of the Senate during the last crucial days of any session, could move your bill up—or down—on the agenda.

Lobbying as a family business makes sense, and not only when the target of your activities is your brother, mother, or father. When you have a big roster of clients, you need help. Who better than your son, daughter, or sibling to help you monitor the activities of various committees, write reports back to your clients, or socialize with the people with whom they grew up? Former representative Tom Horan, whose father was a legislator and then a lobbyist for the City of Albuquerque, now works with his son Larry and hopes to bring another son into the business soon. Tom Rutherford, whose father was also both a legislator and then a lobbyist, now works with his son Jeremy. Longtime lobbyist from Silver City Tony Trujillo is semi-retired, but his sons Ty and T. J. are very active. Dan Weaks, a former legislative and gubernatorial staffer, lobbies with his wife Marla Shoats and, more recently, his son Jason. Sam Ray, longtime utility lobbyist, introduced his daughter Matejka to the business. She now has a number of clients. Siblings Randy and Mark Saavedra each have their own clients as do Adela and Mark Duran. But they help each other when needed.

The family atmosphere at the Roundhouse is a friendly one, and not, as you might expect, unwelcoming to newcomers. But it is most comforting to those in the in-crowd, which, during each session, expands to include other family members as attendants, analysts, or staffers. This is, after all, New Mexico, a small state where everyone knows each other and is somehow related.

~~

The first week in December 2011 was a busy one for the leaders of the New Mexico Senate. The session was coming up and, even more important, elections were just around the corner. Redistricting was still unresolved since Governor Martinez had vetoed the legislative plan and everyone was talking about which redistricting map which court would accept. Rumors abounded over who was running for reelection and who was not. With a number of legislative victories in 2010, Republicans felt they were surging, but Democrats in the Senate had picked up another member with the unexpected appointment of Sen. Lisa Curtis, increasing their majority to twenty-eight. Incumbents of all stripes were on guard since New Mexico had not yet escaped from the grips of a severe recession. There was only one sensible thing for the restless senators to do—start raising money now! After all, it would be too late to start in January, when the ban on fundraising during a legislative session kicked in.

The first of the fundraisers was held on Tuesday night at the Amici Restaurant in Albuquerque, owned by former representative Dan Silva. Hosted by a number of prominent lobbyists, the funds raised went to the Democratic majority leader's fund controlled by Sen. Michael Sanchez. With the departure of Gov. Bill Richardson and a House now more evenly divided between Democrats and Republicans, the Senate had become the Democratic backstop, even more important to counter the new, popular Republican Governor Martinez.

Aside from senators, lobbyists were the main attendees at the function. As Sanchez introduced the senators, they spoke to the Roundhouse regulars about their Democratic values, their accomplishments, and their gratitude to the special interests who they said were like family. Sanchez introduced a young man from Del Norte High School who had cancer—an inspiration to him and to those who believe people like him should not be left by the wayside. People like Democrats, that is. Everyone clapped and turned in their checks.

The very next night at the Albuquerque Country Club the same crowd assembled, this time to cheer and contribute to Senate Minority Leader Stuart Ingle. Chuckling at the irony of having the same people give to opposite sides, applaud the partisan remarks, and chat up the senators, I overheard Ingle and Sanchez laughing about it during the December meeting of the

Rules Committee. When I asked about the irony, Ingle said, "I'll get about a third of what the D's get: they [the lobbyists] know the score."

Knowing the score means giving big to both sides, tilting a bit toward the majority with its committee chairs and floor leadership, but basically rewarding your friends and snubbing your opponents. The savvy behavior makes a big difference in who wins and who loses—both on election day and during the legislative session.

Collecting the data on campaign contributions in New Mexico has not been easy, despite the requirement that contributions be publicly disclosed and displayed on the Secretary of State's website. But with the help of several interns, followthemoney.org (the website of the National Institute of Money in State Politics), and an excellent analysis of 2008 campaign finance reports completed by the *Albuquerque Journal*, we can piece together some important trends. Contributions of over $250 accounted for 95 percent of the money raised by legislators to run for office in 2008 according to reporter Thomas Cole, who continues to perform a great public service by getting this data out to the public through his front page *Albuquerque Journal* column.[7] Since most people can't afford that, I am guessing that the bulk of these contributors represent either special interests, lobbyists, or people who are pretty well off.

According to followthemoney.com, the industries that contributed the most to candidates in 2008 were (in descending order) the oil and gas industry ($1,586,597), lawyers and lobbyists ($1,273,458), real estate ($820,675), candidate committees ($747,403), education ($560,762), candidates financing their own campaigns ($519,037), party committees ($487,175), conservative policy organizations ($358,178), health professionals ($352,389), tribal governments ($329,385), home builders ($321,375), hospitals and nursing homes ($292,285), general trade unions ($267,808), and public sector unions ($252,246).[8]

Thomas Cole's account of the twenty biggest contributors for that year, published in the *Albuquerque Journal*, jives with followthemoney.org's summary. According to the newspaper's analysis, the twenty top givers in 2008 were

1. Mark Murphy (representing various oil and gas companies and a PAC) $435,318
2. The Yates family's oil and gas companies $132,040
3. The Committee for Individual Responsibility (trial lawyers) $120,400

4. Realtors Association of New Mexico $116,230
5. Conservation Voters New Mexico PAC $111,886
6. The officers of Marbob Energy Corp. $94,350
7. New Mexico Medical PAC (physicians) $78,050
8. New Mexico Hospital Health Systems Association $72,450
9. ConocoPhillips $68,550
10. Plumbers and Steamfitters Local 412 $63,400
11. Isleta Pueblo $53,950
12. New Mexico Homebuilders Association $47,350
13. Altria Group (previously Phillip Morris USA) $46,950
14. Car of New Mexico (the automobile dealers' PAC) $45,800
15. American Federation of State, County, and Municipal Employees $44,673
16. Santo Domingo Pueblo/Kewa Gas Limited and Pueblo Gas $40,400
17. Chevron Corp. $40,350
18. PNM Responsible Citizens Group (PNM Resources' PAC) $39,000
19. Health Care Service Corporation (Blue Cross, Blue Shield of New Mexico) $38,850
20. American Federation of Teachers/Albuquerque Teachers Federation $38,100 [9]

Often, lobbyists were the purveyors of these contributions as well as contributors themselves. In 2009, the *Albuquerque Journal* profiled the top lobbyist contributors for 2008. At the top of the list were veteran lobbyists Nancy King and Gary Kilpatric, lawyers at the Montgomery and Andrews firm in Santa Fe. Together they represent eighteen clients and gave more than $330,000 to legislative candidates. Number two was Joel Carson, a lobbyist for Yates Petroleum and Navajo Refining, who gave $166,990. Other top lobbyist contributors included

Dan Weaks (lobbyist for the New Mexico Hospital Association and fourteen others) $147,974
Dan Najjar (lobbyist for Lovelace Health Systems, Intel, Santa Ana Pueblo, and nine others) $137,250
Randy Traynor (lobbyist for the New Mexico Homebuilders and seven others) $132,040
Jerry Fanning Jr. (lobbyist for Yates Petroleum) $132,040

Peter Mallery (lobbyist for the New Mexico Trial Lawyers and
   eight others) $121,650
Sandy Buffett (executive director of Conservation Voters of New
   Mexico) $112,636
Drew Setter (lobbyist for Isleta Pueblo and twenty-one others)
   $112,1000 [10]

Many of the top lobbyists downplay—and even ridicule—the idea that
their contributions influence the way legislators vote. In the aftermath of
one story about the contributions Nancy King told the *Albuquerque Journal* that the public and the press put more emphasis on the contributions
than the legislators themselves. And Dan Weaks said he didn't think that
legislators sold their votes for $250 or even $1000 contributions. [11]

He's probably right, but the contributions are only one tool in the lobbyists' tool kit and they should be taken in context. The lobbyist tool kit also
includes personal relationships that may have been developed over years,
technical knowledge of a certain field, the fact that the lobbyist represents a
key industry or group back home, or even their ability to solve constituent
problems for the legislators.

The New Mexico legislature—just like any institution—is built on personal relationships, but relationships come in all flavors. Some are good,
some are bad, and some are ugly. Some legislators and lobbyists from the
same part of the city or the state are old buddies. Some bonded at an early
age in St. Michael's High School in Santa Fe or the New Mexico Military
Institute. Some, including Sen. Manny Aragon's inner circle of friends, lobbyists Ricardo Barros and Dan Lopez and Senate staffers Frank Martinez
and Bobby Gianinni, even wore the same ring, which I thought was mighty
strange. But then there were all kinds of alliances of convenience based on
reciprocal favors, loyalty to the same team, mentorships, and even lasting
enmities.

No matter what the exact relationship, even if it is not actually friendship, credibility is key for an effective lobbyist. "If they are truthful you will
listen to them again. . . . Although they are paid, they know more than
anyone else," says Senate Minority Leader Stuart Ingle.

"A good lobbyist will tell you what they want, lay it on the table, the risks,
the downside, the upside," says former House Appropriations and Finance
chairman Max Coll. "But sometimes they get you out on a limb and saw it
off." That's when the relationship changes.

Lobbyists caught in a lie are sometimes subject to the wrath of irate legislators who have to make hundreds of decisions with inadequate information and conflicting loyalties. Municipal League lobbyist Bill Fulginetti recalls a time when an opposing lobbyist told a committee chair that the sponsor had withdrawn Fulginetti's bill. He hadn't. Fulginetti pointed it out to the chair, and the bill was immediately passed—unanimously, without debate.

I came to trust many lobbyists, some like Jim O'Neill or Dick Minzner for their technical knowledge of tax issues, others because they were advocates for health care or open government who were on the same side of the issues as I was. I worked with many of them to draft legislation, negotiate with the administration or lobbyists from the other side. They could bring in unlikely allies and expand the coalition supporting the bill. Especially as a new legislator, I respected the knowledge that lobbyist lawyers and old hands like Tom Horan had of the system itself. They could often summon up the legislative history of an issue at a moment's notice.

I was particularly grateful to lobbyists from the Trial Lawyers Association and the pharmaceutical corporations in 2011, who worked out a compromise on an important bill I had sponsored two years earlier. The bill, to allow patients to donate their unused prescription drugs back to the doctor or clinic that had prescribed them, had been blocked by an impasse between the two special interests. But, with the help of Rep. Ken Martinez, then House majority leader, the two sides negotiated a compromise. And it passed with little ado. The law is now in effect and doctors are re-prescribing drugs some of their patients can no longer use to others who cannot afford them. The law enables cancer and MS patients in particular to focus on getting well and not on how to pay for the life-saving drugs.

There are basically three types of lobbyists, says former representative and lobbyist John Lee Thompson: the citizen lobbyist, the technical lobbyist, and the political lobbyist. "I'm a political lobbyist, he said. I don't really know about the details of ophthalmology, railroads, horseracing, or the Middle Rio Grande Conservancy District (his clients), but I know how to get a bill passed or how to kill one."

I've had a special liking for John Lee ever since he got up in the Public Affairs Committee one day and, with tongue in cheek, testified against a bill cracking down on voter fraud if it was discovered that some of those who voted were actually dead. The former representative, who was then lobbying for the funeral directors, said, "Now wait a minute; those are our guys you're talking about (the dead ones) and we need to protect their rights. Some of them even live in Española, he continued, referring to the popular joke about voter fraud in Rio Arriba County. (Here's the joke: Calling about the allegations of fraud and the perennially late returns from the county, the secretary of state finally got local officials on the phone and asked how many votes were still outstanding. The reply: How many do you need?)

Citizen lobbyists, like those representing the League of Women Voters, the Sierra Club, the National Association of the Mentally Ill (NAMI), the American Association of Retired Persons (AARP), the New Mexico Conference of Churches, the Gallup Chamber of Commerce, the Nurses Association, and other nonprofit groups are typically unpaid and thus not considered "professional" lobbyists. Still, they can be very effective, especially when they represent members throughout the state or, conversely, are concentrated in one or two districts (which just might be yours, if you're the lucky target). One such citizen legislator, Corrine Wolfe, a social worker, was responsible for many of the laws we now have about foster care and children. Her tireless work is memorialized by a photo on the wall just outside of my office on the third floor, where many of the lobbyists congregate while awaiting hearings (see fig. 18). Often there is a bouquet of fresh flowers beneath her picture. Corrine died in 1997.

Technical lobbyists are hired because they know one area of the law. Perhaps they were former legislative council service staffers like John Anderson, who lobbies for the New Mexico Medical Society and the New Mexico Bankers Association. Or perhaps they know health care or local government financing like Dan Weaks, another former legislative staffer, does. Sometimes the heads of hospitals, universities, federal agencies, major industries, clinics, or other organizations will testify themselves, and they are generally considered more credible than paid lobbyists. They are particularly effective with individual legislators who live in the area served by the hospital, clinic, or university, or if the institution is a major source of jobs in their district.

"Political" lobbyists know their way around the Roundhouse. They know how the system works, down to the details of how the actual paper the bills are written on flows from one office to another. They know it is easier to kill bills than pass them, particularly in a short session, and most importantly, they know how the committee process works. They know which committee chairmen are friends and which are foes. They know that the Senate Corporations Committee and the House Business and Industry Committee are the best places to kill tax increases, new programs, or regulations. They know that the Senate Finance Committee members don't like revenue from fees or taxes earmarked to a specific agency, but want it to go to the general fund.

They know which legislators arrive at committee meetings late—or not at all—and exactly who will be in the room at the right or wrong time for either passage or defeat of their bill. They know some committee chairs will delay or just not hear certain bills and others will hear all bills referred to that committee in the order received.

Armed with this knowledge, a political lobbyist's job is to navigate the bill through the maze, garnering enough votes at each stop to either kill or pass the legislation. Since all bills must be introduced, assigned to committees, pass through those committees, come to the floor for a vote, and then repeat the drill in the other chamber, the process can be a long, drawn-out one. Or it can be extraordinarily fast, with the right grease applied by the right leaders at the right times. Either way, time is of the essence.

"Anybody can lobby the legislature during the first fifty-seven days in a long session or the first twenty-seven days in a short session," says Tom Horan, who lobbies for Presbyterian Health System, the City of Albuquerque, and a host of others clients. "But not the last three days. That's when a good lobbyist can make a difference."

That's where a friendship with a committee chair can get your bill passed under the wire, or get an amendment attached that renders the whole thing useless, or, alternatively, it can actually enable the bill to pass. That's where a personal relationship, or a trade-off with the Senate majority leader, can get your bill delayed or put it on the fast-moving consent calendar reserved for noncontroversial bills.

Some lobbyists are hired specifically to work on one legislator. These "specialists" stick like glue to their friendly target up until the crucial vote, sometimes taking his clothes to the cleaners, or giving her a ride back to her hotel after a long committee meeting. Often these lobbyists act more like personal staff rather than lobbyists. For several years, I did not realize that Vince Montoya was a lobbyist for the liquor industry and not the analyst for the House Business and Industry Committee. He was always in Chairman Fred Luna's office and appeared to be in charge of what bills were heard by the committee. Luckily, Vince seemed to like me and would get my item on the agenda from time to time.

In the same special way, insurance lobbyist Charlie Young was a fast friend of Senate Finance Committee Co-Chair Joe Fidel. Liquor lobbyist Maurice Bonnell, and later T. J. Trujillo, was never far from Senate Corporations Committee Chair Phil Griego. With enough of these specialists, and a bunch of temporaries hired on a short-term basis, an industry can actually field a team of lobbyists to play man-on-man defense—or offense—with all forty-two senators. This tactic is usually reserved for really big bills, like the legalization of Indian gambling or the increase in a tobacco tax. Then almost every legislator is "covered." And watch out if you have to go to the bathroom or, God forbid, out of the building. You will have a friendly lobbyist following you.

Usually lobbyists do not operate in these kinds of teams since special interest are so diverse they can rarely agree on any one issue. But sometimes, at hearings on consumer protection issues or health care issues, it sure looked that way. All the advocates for seniors, Medicaid recipients, church groups, or the League of Women Voters would be lined up to testify in favor of a measure to, say, prevent discrimination by insurance companies against people with preexisting conditions. Then, a much larger, more well-heeled group of insurance lobbyists, in suits mainly, would show up to testify against the same bill. It was hard not to think it was one team vs. the other. And I had to choose sides. So do all legislators.

What goes into that decision goes to the core of what democracy is supposed to be and what it has become. The answer to the question, "How do I vote," varies from issue to issue and legislator to legislator. But here are the considerations flashing through every legislator's brain: what do my constituents think, what do the facts say, what does my conscience dictate, what does my leadership want, how do my contributors feel, will the governor veto this, and what do the friends I trust the most say?

In these parts, Texas columnist Molly Ivins stated the conventional wisdom: "You Got to Dance with Them What Brung Ya."

But who actually brung ya? The usual suspects fall into two categories: your constituents who voted you into office and your contributors, many of them lobbyists, who enabled you to run a campaign and have eased your way once in office with dinners, constituent services, and other amenities.

Keeping up with your constituents' needs and opinions—from Santa Fe— is not easy, and of course they do not all speak with one voice. With no staff or stipend, few legislators do regular polls and/or hold town halls to find out their specific opinions on the issues as they arise. (I was the exception, I think, doing one survey every year.) On the other hand, the money from special interests comes to incumbents fairly regularly and the friendly lobbyists are all around you.

"The unfortunate thing is that the process of policy making has become infiltrated, if you will, with money," Bob Gallagher, a lobbyist for the biggest spending and arguably the most powerful industry, oil and gas, told the *Albuquerque Journal*.[12] Gallagher said the industry had to spend big because it just couldn't afford to have what it perceived as antibusiness legislators making laws that would hurt the industry.

Tom Horan bemoans the change from the more traditional kind of lobbying to something different. "Lately it has more to do with campaign contributions and entertainment than the competence of the lobbyist or their credibility," he says.

But do these ever-expanding contributions directly influence votes? To answer this question, the good government group Common Cause tracked both contributions and votes in a number of *Connect the Dots* reports on various industries, including health care and oil and gas. Although they are careful to say that you can't say that the money causes a legislator to vote a certain way, there's a strong association. In all their reports, on average, those who received more money from an industry voted for that industry's position.[13]

Senate President Pro Tempore Tim Jennings bristles at this thought. "I don't check my list of donors before I vote, Jennings told the *Journal*.[14] Although, like all legislators, Jennings is aware of who gave him what, these are not the determining factors, he says. "You always know who butters your bread. It doesn't mean it's the only meal you're going to eat."

Jennings says that friendship in New Mexico means more than contributions. All politicians, all people, want to be loved or at least liked by those closest to them. At the crucial moment these friendships, the contributions, the facts as offered by either staff or lobbyists—they are all spinning around furiously in the giant washing machine that is the legislative session.

"I don't know who to trust," Senator Mary Jane Garcia said during one confusing debate about education policy in 2012. The interest groups were arrayed on both sides of the issue; the governor wanted one thing and the Democratic leadership another. Garcia's solution, in this case, was to vote for both of two competing bills.

"Once you're here a little while you know who you can trust," says Stuart Ingle. "I ask both sides and get the legislative council service to do the research."

The problem with the system, as I see it, is that often the people that the legislators trust, those with whom they have become friendly over the years, are the same people whom they depend on for campaign contributions, food, fun, and fellowship. Sometimes these are constituents or citizen lobbyists, but most often they are the professionals—and the public feels left out.

As distrust of the legislature grows, legislators reluctantly address what they call "the perception" problem. The Gift Act, passed in 2007, was the only one of a packet of reform measures suggested by the governor's campaign finance and ethics reform task force to survive that session and that happened only after it was repeatedly questioned on the Senate floor. Opponent Sen. Shannon Robinson, for example, said, "All we are saying is if you run for office in New Mexico, you take a vow of poverty."[15] To meet these concerns, the bill was watered down to make the gift limit high enough to allow almost everything the legislators were then receiving from lobbyists.

Other measures to ban campaign contributions from lobbyists or provide at least a one-year hiatus before a legislator could begin lobbying his former colleagues have never emerged from committee. Yet another, which I thought was just common courtesy, was ridiculed by lobbyists. In 2007, Rep. Jeff Steinborn carried a bill that would have required lobbyists to wear name badges, listing their clients. That way, he reasoned, the public, the legislators, even the sergeants at arms assigned to clearing the floor of each chamber and restricting access to legislators during the last crucial last days of the session would know who was who. Although the practice is common in other state legislatures, it was portrayed as "Mickey Mouse," even absurd, and it, too, never emerged from committee. Still, the transparency measure would have gone a long way to reveal who those guys (and gals) in suits are and even shine a little light on the conflicts between special interests. The public currently can get this information (along with special interest and lobbyist contributions and expenditures) from the secretary of state's office, but it is a long and cumbersome process and it is usually completed only long after the issue has passed, too late to affect its outcome.

Another piece of information, guarded even more closely, is how much lobbyists make. Legislators and lobbyists take umbrage at even the suggestion that this information should be made public, asking why this occupation would be singled out above all others. I've made informal inquiries of various lobbyists and found out that payment depends on whether the lobbyist works for a client year round or only during the legislative session. A lobbying contract can be for simply monitoring issues or for the passage or the defeat of a certain bill. Sometimes lobbyists can be hired midsession to kill a certain bill; sometimes they are hired preemptively so the other side will not hire them for their relationship to a key legislator or technical knowledge. Some lobbyists have ten to twenty clients; others have only one small nonprofit organization. Contracts can run from $3,000 to $40,000 per month for one piece of legislation or to lobby for capital appropriations made for specific projects like buildings or roads. One lobbyist told me he

made between $15,000–$45,000 per client, per year. Another told me he had
a mixture of retainers from a variety of clients ranging from $36,000 to
$84,000 each. Both said that expenses—including campaign contributions
and entertainment—ate up a good portion of their fees. Even so, considering that some lobbyists have as many as fifteen clients, that means quite a
few of them can be earning as much as a half a million dollars a year. Quite
a difference from the legislators themselves, who are unpaid, except for the
per diem and reimbursements they get for a dozen or so trips to Santa Fe.

Since lobbyists are not required to report how much they are compen-
sated, except for those who are employed by public agencies, which are required to report how much they spend on lobbying, I am just making
informed guesses here. But aren't we entitled to this information—in the
name of both transparency and accountability? Given their huge role in
policymaking in New Mexico, lobbyists should be required to report how
much they are earning.

As long as New Mexico is a sparsely populated state, where politics are
dominated by relationships (which I hope is forever), and as long as legislators are staffless and unsalaried, lobbyists will have an unusual amount of
influence here. That's not to say that lobbyists are bad or unethical, it's just
that combined with the amount of money that it now takes to win a legislative seat you have a toxic mix, which, when swallowed by the public, leaves
an aftertaste of distrust that is damaging to our faith in democracy.

It will be left to new generations of legislative reformers to continue the
fight to control lobbyists and special interests—perhaps, by expanding the
restrictions on gifts and limits on contributions that were won in 2007 and
2009. One thing is sure; the battles will be hard fought. Money will pop
up in a new area once it is restricted in an old one, but it is worth the fight.
For those who love New Mexico, there is nothing more important.

FIGURE I
A filibuster by Sen. Bill Davis, a Republican from Albuquerque, drove the Democrats into disarray on the final day of the 1997 session. The nonstop talkathon prevented the passage of a huge capital-outlay bill for bricks-and-mortar projects around the state. President Pro Tem Manny Aragon could have stopped it. Photo by Jaime Dispenza, © *Albuquerque Journal.* Reprinted with permission.

FIGURE 2
Democratic members of the New Mexico Senate gather around Pro Tem Manny Aragon (center, bottom) during the final moments of the 1997 session. A filibuster by Sen. Bill Davis ended the session before passage of the all-important capital-outlay bill. Many senators felt that Aragon could have stopped it. AP photo by Eric Draper, © Associated Press. Reprinted with permission.

FIGURE 3
Buffalo and other Pueblo dances in the capitol rotunda are fairly common during the legislative session. The drumbeat can be heard by the senators in the chamber below. Photo by Cliff Rees.

FIGURE 4
Rodeo queens, basketball stars, musicians, and dignitaries of all types are recognized from the rostrum of the New Mexico Senate. Here the New Mexico State Fair queen chats with lobbyists in the president pro tem's office in 2013. Photo by the author.

FIGURE 5
Gov. Bill Richardson addresses the legislature on opening day 2009 in the House chambers. Senators, representatives, guests, and staff crowd around as the governor announces his priorities for the session. Photo by Cliff Rees.

FIGURE 6
Debate can be intense, particularly if it's 3:00 a.m. Here Sen. Bill Sharer, a Republican from Farmington, yells during a 2004 debate. Sharer was protesting a measure pushed by Gov. Bill Richardson and legislative Democrats that would cut taxes on some grocery items and medical services and make up for lost revenue with tax increases on other items. Photo by Jeff Geissler, © *Albuquerque Journal*. Reprinted with permission.

FIGURE 7
Members of the dance troupe Baile Folklorico de Santa Fe perform on the floor of the Senate during the 2013 session. Photo by Dean Hanson, © *Albuquerque Journal*. Reprinted with permission.

FIGURE 8
Citizen lobbyists for the New Mexico Cattle Growers Association confer in the west entrance area of the capitol in February 2013. Photo by the author.

FIGURE 9
Republican senators huddling with staff on the floor during the 2004 debate over the removal of the gross receipts tax on food. The Republicans were desperate to stop the cut but were unable to counter the unified Democratic initiative. Photo by Pat Velasquez, © *Albuquerque Journal*. Reprinted with permission.

84

FIGURE 10
Beans and chile are matanza staples.
Here they're dishing them out at
the annual Valencia County event.
© *Valencia County News Bulletin*.
Reprinted with permission.

FIGURE 11
Talk about pork barrel politics! In
New Mexico campaigns, candidates
often stage huge traditional Hispanic
barbeques called matanzas. The main-
stay of a matanza is a pig roasted
underground overnight. But first you
have to save some of the fat for the
chicharones. © *Valencia County News
Bulletin*. Reprinted with permission.

FIGURE 12
There's no substitute for retail politics. The basis of grassroots campaigning is talking to people where they live about the issues they care about—whether they are the neighbor's barking dog or the lack of affordable health insurance. Photo by Cary Herz.

FIGURE 13
Two weary state senators, Joseph Fidel of Grants and Majority Leader Manny Aragon of Bernalillo County's South Valley, embrace on the floor of the Senate in February 2004 at the end of what many lawmakers called one of the most demanding legislative sessions ever. Photo by Pat Vasquez-Cunningham, © *Albuquerque Journal.* Reprinted with permission.

FIGURE 14

Sen. Linda Lopez holds her newborn son, Lorenzo, as she is sworn in on February 6, 2001, on the Senate floor. The Democrat from Albuquerque was hospitalized after the birth and was unable to begin serving her second term immediately. Her absence swung the vote for president pro tem to Sen. Richard Romero, upsetting previous pro tem Manny Aragon. Photo by Dean Hanson, © *Albuquerque Journal.* Reprinted with permission.

FIGURE 15

President Pro Tem Richard Romero (on the right) makes a point at a 2003 capitol news conference with Sen. Dede Feldman (on the left) and U.S. Sen. Jeff Bingaman (center) in the rotunda. © 2003 *The New Mexican, Inc.* Reprinted with permission. All rights reserved.

FIGURE 16
Roswell Senator Tim Jennings (center) is sworn in as president pro tem in 2009. Supporters Sen. Howie Morales (on the left), who was appointed to replace Sen. Ben Altamirano upon his unexpected death, and Sen. Mary Kay Papen (on the right), who became pro tem in 2013, look on. AP photo by Jeff Geissler, © Associated Press. Reprinted with permission.

FIGURE 17
Majority Leader Michael Sanchez (on the right) makes a point as then president pro tem Ben Altamirano (on the left) thinks it over. AP Photo by Jeff Geissler, © Associated Press. Reprinted with permission.

FIGURE 18

Lobbyists checking on the status of their bills in—where else—a third-floor lobby.
The popular lobby features a weaving by New Mexico artist Nancy Kozikowski and a
secular "shrine" to Corrine Wolfe, a children's advocate and lobbyist who frequented
the Roundhouse. Advocates and lobbyists often place flowers beneath Corrine Wolfe's
photo. Photo by Cliff Rees.

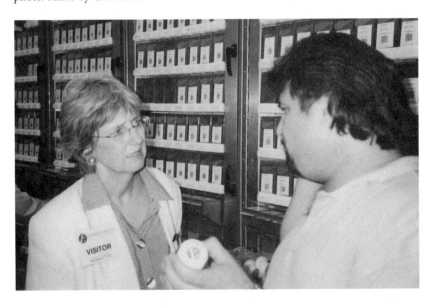

FIGURE 19

Senator Feldman examines a bottle of medication at the Express Scripts facility in
Albuquerque. "Now, tell me again why these prescription drugs cost so much? I just
went down to Las Palomas and purchased some for one-quarter of the price." Actually
Express Scripts isn't a drug manufacturer, but a drug benefit manager—a middle man
in the bizarre labyrinth of prescription pricing. Photo courtesy of the author.

FIGURE 20

Albuquerque Journal cartoonist John Trever nails it again, catching Manny Aragon's movida to attach an amendment taxing cigarettes to a bill to ban smoking in the Roundhouse. First Lady Dee Johnson long sought the ban, but her husband, Gov. Gary Johnson, vetoed it when the tax was attached. © 1998 by John Trever, *Albuquerque Journal*. Reprinted with permission.

FIGURE 21

Senator Feldman persuading reluctant legislators to vote for a cigarette tax increase during the special session in 2010. After two hours of intense debate and attempted amendments, the tax increase passed. Photo by Roberto Rosales, © *Albuquerque Journal*. Reprinted with permission.

FIGURE 22

Sen. Shannon Robinson gives the Bull Moose salute, a signal that this is a bill rural ranching interests could unite around. Robinson, at the time, was a Democrat who represented the Southeast Heights in Albuquerque. After his defeat for reelection in 2008, he became a Republican. Photo by Katharine Kimball, © *Albuquerque Journal*. Reprinted with permission.

PART III   Dances with Wolves

New Mexico Advocates Take On the Big Boys

SOME OF THE BIGGEST SPECIAL INTERESTS IN THE NATION ARE FIERCELY engaged in state legislatures where they compete head-to-head with health and consumer advocates. Often these "Big Boys" fare better in the states when the way is blocked in Washington, D.C. The New Mexico Senate is one of their battlegrounds, and chapters 5–8 tell the tale of how these battles were fought. With campaign contributions, captive committees, and well-connected lobbyists, Big Pharma, Big Tobacco, and the NRA are striving to protect their bottom lines in the state, whether they involve a favorable price or an expanded market for their products. In addition, the state fireworks industry (also covered in this section) does an elaborate dance with the guardians of public safety. Sometimes special interests win; sometimes they lose, depending on the stance of Senate leadership and the skill of grassroots organizations. The legislature has a different history with each issue. With supportive leadership and effective advocacy, the legislature has held its own in the face of Big Tobacco and struggled to dance a delicate two-step with the wolves from Pharma. But since 2001 it has almost completely capitulated to the NRA—in spite of the high rate of gun violence and suicide in New Mexico. And even with drought and devastating fires hitting the state almost every year, it has not done much better when it comes to the fireworks industry.

CHAPTER 5

Burn Marks from the Fireworks Industry

> Here's an example of special interests and
> private gain trumping public health and safety.

—SEN. DEDE FELDMAN, SANTA FE NEW MEXICAN, MARCH 6, 2011

*J*UNE 24, 2003. THE FIRE CAME UP QUICKLY ON A DRY TUESDAY afternoon in the southern part of my district, on the west side of the river near Interstate 40. It was caused by a couple of kids playing with fireworks in the bosque, as we call the cottonwood forest lining the banks of the Rio Grande. Fanned by the summer winds, it spread quickly. Within a few hours a house under construction on the west side of the river was on fire, and my friends the Kirschners were battling to save their home overlooking the river. Flying embers had ignited their roof and had spread to the east side of the river as well, where the thick groves of cottonwoods were beginning to catch fire. By now every fire unit in the city and county was responding, cordoning off the residential areas on both sides of the river.

Orders to evacuate came rapidly. Residents of Thomas Village and then Dietz Farms, two lovely, longstanding North Valley neighborhoods, were given a half hour to gather their important possessions and get out. Since it was midafternoon, most people were at work. They were now rushing to get into the area to save pets and gather photos and insurance policies.

Three years earlier, the residents of Los Alamos had been evacuated during the devastating Cerro Grande fire, which reached into the mountain community inhabited by scientists and workers from Los Alamos National

Labs and their families. Over four hundred homes were burned to the ground. Families were not resettled until years later.

But it couldn't happen here in the heart of Albuquerque, most people thought. We're not a forest community. We don't expect the panicked calls from our kids, anxiety attacks about the neighbor's horses, or the hard choices about what to save and what to sacrifice. As my neighbors and constituents gathered in the parking lot of the Sheraton Old Town (now the Hotel Albuquerque), I began to worry about my own house, just across the boulevard from Thomas Village. Surely the fire couldn't spread that far, could it?

Some of the appealing features of Thomas Village (population 2,000) and Dietz Farms (population 1,200) are the mature landscaping provided by the huge cottonwoods that wind into the neighborhoods and the proximity to the trails lining the acequias, or ditches, which, in some parts of the North Valley, are still used for irrigation. These defining characteristics of these neighborhoods had now put them at risk for devastation.

By the next morning, as the fire raged on, the Sheraton Old Town was filling up with families and their pets. My friend Helen Whitesides and her sister Liz Gordon were among the refugees, hanging out in the parking lot listening for news from the car radio, hoping the evacuation orders would be lifted.

Just like everyone else, I felt helpless. My desire to protect the bosque was one of the things that propelled me into politics. And now 150 acres of it was going up in flames. The much loved Rio Grande Nature Center, with its beautiful headquarters designed by Antoine Predock, was directly in the path of the fire, now moving north. But with the use of helicopters provided by the state the fire was held at bay, and the nature center was spared. The coordinated response from fire crews coming from outside of Albuquerque was crucial, along with the use of special equipment designed for wildfires.

The news the next few days was not good. Another fire had started near the Montaño Bridge and it was spreading south, about to join the fire traveling north. Even worse, it was threatening the Bosque School, a new private middle and high school whose curriculum was based on the riverside forest now engulfed in flames.

The firefighters rose to the occasion, saving the school with a last ditch technique they improvised on the spot. For an entire night they held up a wet curtain created by their fire hoses which deflected the fast flying sparks and embers headed toward the school. The fire was gradually put out, and miraculously no lives or homes were lost. But 263 acres of bosque were destroyed and $1 million spent by the city, the state, and the Federal Emergency Management Administration (FEMA) to deal with the fire.

The events of 9/11 had made all of us revere firefighters, but seeing our own men and women put life and limb at risk here in the North Valley left me in awe. Like legislators everywhere, I wanted to solve the underlying problem.

The crisis began with a group of kids fooling around with fireworks in the tinderbox conditions that precede the Fourth of July almost every year now that New Mexico is in a period of extended drought. The fireworks are readily available at roadside tents that spring up close to the holiday or at permanent outlets. As firefighters began to point out to me, there were gaping holes in what cities, counties, and even the state could do to restrict their use or sale, even when fire danger was high or multiple fires had already broken out in the area.

Under current law, passed by the legislature in 1996 with the support of the fireworks industry, municipalities have their hands tied by first having to hold a hearing to determine if conditions warrant restrictions no less than twenty days before a holiday for which fireworks may be sold. Of course, conditions can change in an even shorter period, and even if a huge fire started the week before Independence Day, cities could not act in time. Moreover, cities can only ban the sale or use of some fireworks (missile and stick type rockets, helicopters, aerial spinners, and ground audible devices), and they can only restrict the use of everything else that sets off showers of sparks to areas that are paved, barren, or have an accessible source of water. For firefighters, that makes enforcement almost impossible.

To address their concerns, I met with the New Mexico Municipal League, which represents cities and towns throughout New Mexico, and drew up a bill for introduction in the 2004 legislative session. The bill had the support of Albuquerque and Bernalillo counties. Firefighters throughout the state came to Santa Fe to testify in support of giving the cities the authority they needed and to allow the governor to temporarily ban fireworks when fire danger reached a certain level defined narrowly by the "energy release component of the national fire danger rating system." The level was set at 97, which we later found out would rarely be reached in New Mexico even if the forests were on fire.

Naïvely, I assumed that the public safety features of this bill would be obvious, especially with the recent fire, and that the provision for temporary restrictions would rarely be used. With uniformed firefighters from all over the state in the audience, I was confident as I brought the bill before its first committee—the one that I chaired, Senate Public Affairs.

But enter stage right the lobbyist for the fireworks industry, who was then Scott Scanland. Scanland is well known to legislators. A few summers earlier, when an interim committee met in Roswell, where his fireworks client had an outlet, he sent legislators home with huge shopping bags filled with fireworks. The fireworks industry was only one of his clients, which took up a whole page in the secretary of state's lobbyist registration. The others include payday lenders, pharmaceutical and chemical companies, race tracks, airlines, cities, and colleges around the state. After apologizing for the absence of his fireworks clients that night (the committee was meeting late), Scanland gave a dramatic speech lamenting the bill's restrictions and defending the mom-and-pop businesses that depended upon the sale of fireworks for their livelihood. These are true Americans, he said, wiping tears from his eyes, and now we want to put them out of business.

The committee bought the Academy Award–winning plea lock, stock, and barrel, and, with little courtesy to either the chairman or the firefighters, the bill was tabled without further debate. In other words, it was dead. The bill seemed like such common sense that I had not worked it very hard, leaving the heavy lifting to the firemen. But some of the committee members had heard from distributors in their areas, and others just didn't see the need to restrict business in any way. Although Governor Richardson had allowed the item to be placed on the agenda for the short 2004 session and had been all over the media during the Albuquerque fire, he didn't push the bill hard.

I tried to toss off the defeat and not hold it against my fellow senators. Instead, I went on to the next issue, knowing that in the legislature there are no permanent allies or permanent opponents.

Six years later the issue came back with a vengeance. The year 2011 was the worst fire season New Mexico had ever experienced, starting early with fires near Silver City and continuing with fires in Ruidoso, Eddy, and Roosevelt counties in the east; Catron in the west; and then the Track fire near Raton in the north. As the summer began the fires were closing down tourist attractions like the Carlsbad Caverns and the Gila Cliff Dwellings, and they were forcing evacuations throughout the state. The season reached a crescendo on June 26, 2011, when the Las Conchas fire, the hottest fire the state had ever seen, ignited 43,000 acres in its first day, scaring the hell out of Los Alamos, Española, Cochiti, and Santa Clara residents. The Las Conchas fire grew to engulf 244 square miles or 156,000 acres, engaging over 2,500 firefighters from around the West and destroying sixty-three residences. Firefighters fought the fire from base camps near Jemez Springs, shifting to the north when the fire hit the Santa Clara reservation. It was the largest fire in state history until the next year, when a fire in the Gila National Forest destroyed even more acreage. Altogether in New Mexico, the fires burned almost a million acres, costing the state and federal governments over $22 million.

Even with help from "hot shot" crews from around the nation sent by the U.S. Forest Service, the state's resources were stretched in every direction. Equipment and fire teams were moved around the state from fire to fire. Gov. Susana Martinez gave daily briefings; the state forestry division and local fire chiefs were looking for every tool they could muster to meet the crisis.

Meanwhile, as the Fourth of July approached, the fireworks merchants were plying their wares along the highways and in big-box stores like Walmart. Although fireworks caused only one of the blazes, Governor Martinez clearly saw the danger. She used the bully pulpit to ask citizens to not use fireworks themselves and instead go to public displays. Realizing that she had no power to ban the sale of the incendiary devices, she asked stores to voluntarily stop selling fireworks. Some, including Walmart, pulled the products off the shelf; others continued, prompting the governor to call for a bill in the upcoming special session to give her the power to temporarily ban and restrict the sale of fireworks in time of extreme drought and fire danger.

As Las Conchas wound down, the governor gathered a bipartisan group of legislators together for a news conference in Albuquerque to press for a bill to ban fireworks. The event, at which the mayors of Santa Fe and Albuquerque spoke, was held at the scene of the 2003 bosque fire. Given my experience, the governor asked me to sponsor the bill along with Republican Sen. Sander Rue and Republican Rep. Nate Gentry. I jumped at the opportunity, thinking that this time, with the help of the governor, a bipartisan coalition, the news media (which was already beating the drum for a ban), and a huge crisis, we could make it happen.

My constituents, who could not believe the fate of the bill in 2004, had already been contacting me to do it again, and now I was game. And I knew we had to strike while the iron was hot.

Gentry, Rue, and I got together with the governor's office, state forestry officials (who had not been involved in the 2004 effort), and local fire chiefs to write the bill. We were careful to not give the governor too much power and to set a reasonable standard to trigger restrictions. It had to be more specific than "drought," since New Mexico now seemed to be in that state permanently.

Our best shot was to get it before the legislature immediately during the upcoming special session on redistricting while the public was still engaged and the lobbyists did not have time to organize. But we ran squarely into a partisan problem. Regardless of the merits, the Democratic leadership didn't want the governor to get credit for the popular measure. They were determined to focus on redistricting and redistricting only, they said, and to throw other issues (Martinez had a whole list) into the mix would invite horse trading for precincts and open up a "box of Pandoras," as former governor Bruce King used to say. I bought the argument, to some degree, but suspected that Majority Leader Michael Sanchez, and President Pro Tem Jennings, didn't want the bill anyway.

The delay was frustrating, but nothing compared to what was to come. As early as December, when Rep. Gentry and I eagerly pre-filed the bill so that it would be heard early during the short thirty-day session, we began trying to contact the industry's lobbyists to see if we could come up with a compromise. The industry had floated a weak, alternative bill that Sen. Phil Griego, a Democrat from San Jose, was said to be introducing and we were trying to meld the two bills. But T. J. Trujillo, the lobbyist for American Promotional Events (formerly TNT Fireworks) was evasive, and although he was always in Senator Griego's office, the two of them could never make time to meet with me.

Meanwhile, calls, e-mails, and letters from the public were pouring in from supporters of the ban to the governor, the Senate, and House members.

Shirley McNall from Aztec wrote that she and her family were held hostage in their home every Fourth of July because they were afraid of another fireworks-caused fire. "We have endured at least three fires on our property that were ignited by the careless use of fireworks off our property. . . . We feel fortunate we were able to put out the fires ourselves each time," she said. Other comments came from the signatories to an online petition circulated by SignOn.org, which gathered seven thousand signatures and notes for the measure. There was also a growing list of mayors, fire departments, village councils, and counties who supported the measure.

By the time the bill hit its first major committee, Senate Public Affairs, the list of local government supporters was up to thirty-five, including the New Mexico Association of Counties and the New Mexico Municipal League. There were so many people who wanted to testify for it that it was difficult to determine who would be most effective. The Los Alamos fire chief? The state forester? The mayors of Ruidoso, Red River, Silver City, or other towns that had been evacuated? It seemed like there was someone from every town, and when the vice chair asked all those who support the bill to stand up, there must have been more than forty who rose.

But suddenly there was a problem. The fireworks industry had swung into action and its lobbyists had been busy sounding the alarm. It's hard to gauge the size and profitability of the industry, which is composed of a half-dozen large companies that import Chinese fireworks and a proliferation of retail outlets, most of them open only two weeks out of the year. Still, Fire Marshal John Standefer says profit margins in the industry are high, especially for big players. The largely seasonal business is localized in several communities: Roswell, Las Cruces, and Farmington. With over five hundred retail licenses, lobbyists said their sales amounted to between $28 and $30 million each year.

Some of the retailers were at the committee meeting, including Eddie Arnett, a co-owner of a Roswell-based business; Amy's Fireworks; and Jimmy Navarez, the owner of Diablo and Planet Fireworks in Las Cruces. They argued that the measure would affect their livelihoods. They didn't object to giving the local governments additional authority to restrict fireworks, they said, but they didn't want the governor issuing any orders. The substantive arguments were made by their main lobbyist, T. J. Trujillo. He stressed that fireworks are not the major cause of fires in New Mexico and that under the standards in the bill no one would have been selling the items in the past several years. There were already adequate restrictions in place at the local level, he added—even though Bill Fulginiti from the Municipal League had testified that the cities wanted more.

The state forester, who was testifying for the bill with Rep. Nate Gentry and me, had already acknowledged that fireworks did not cause the Las Conchas fire but that they did play a role in the Track Fire near Raton. Also, the Bernalillo County fire chief said that over the past five years his area had experienced an average of four major fires caused by fireworks.

"The wind and the heat are beyond our control," Gentry and I countered as we sat at the witness table, sensing that support was ebbing away. "But fireworks are one of the few causes of fire that we can control."

"My village loves fireworks," said Sen. Mary Jane Garcia, from Doña Ana, a small village in southern New Mexico. Garcia and Sen. Cynthia Nava, another southerner, were clearly sympathetic to "Jimmy," as they called him, from Diablo Fireworks.

"Even if there is a ban, people will be able to get fireworks from the reservations," said Sen. Tim Eichenberg, adding the familiar refrain of those who believe that every new regulation has to be ironclad and foolproof before it can be considered. Those are things that need to be worked out between the governor and the tribes on a nation-to-nation basis, we countered, pointing to the provision in the bill that allowed for tribal consultation.

The room was packed with firemen, with opponents in the rear. A motion to table the bill was made, which failed narrowly with all the Republicans voting against their governor's bill. Usually when that happens in a committee, another vote is taken, either a "Do Pass," a "Do Pass with no Recommendation," or a "Do Not Pass."

With the chairman of the committee sponsoring the bill and so much public support, the senators had mercy. "There seems like there's a lot of common ground here," said Senator Nava, "especially since the fireworks people say they don't mind additional local control, but not the governor."

With no other choice, I agreed and expressed willingness to work it out with industry lobbyists, whose ranks had suddenly swelled to include Dominic Silva, who, like Nava and Garcia, is from the Las Cruces area. The committee, now off the hook, voted 6 to 2 to send SB 5 on to the Corporations Committee with no recommendation.

Eddie Arnett, of Amy's Fireworks, couldn't believe it. He was certain the bill would be killed as quickly as it was in 2004.

"What the hell are they doing?" he asked after the hearing. "It's a free country." Arnett said that if the bill had been in effect he would have been able to be open only one year in the past eight.

Representative Gentry and I had already roughed out the framework of a compromise, meeting most industry objections, removing the governor's ability to order a ban, and largely leaving it to local government and the state forester. The criteria of when restrictions would be triggered were still unresolved, and, with the help of the governor's staff, we sought a meeting with the lobbyists. Assembled in the governor's office, the lobbyists—T. J. Trujillo and Luke Otero for TNT and the hastily hired Dominic Silva for Diablo—seemed friendly enough. They assured us that a compromise, based on a combination of Senator Griego's SB 300 and my SB 5, would probably work. They just had to get back to Senator Griego and their clients.

But somehow, T. J. Trujillo, who spent most of his time in Senator Griego's office or before the Corporations Committee representing payday lenders, mining and oil companies, drug manufacturers, and jockey clubs, among others, could never seem to get ahold of his client to endorse a compromise proposal. But in the meantime, he had been busy.

He and fellow TNT lobbyist Luke Otero had been taking members of the Corporations Committee to lunches and dinners throughout the session. Reports to the secretary of state indicated that Trujillo spent $3,808.99 on meals for various legislators.[1] It was a pattern that repeated the previous session's social calendar when Otero spent $1,439 wining and dining various legislators and Trujillo spent $3,881.[2] Some of that money was spent on

Corporations Committee dinners shipped in from Restaurant Martín and other high-end Santa Fe eateries to feed the committee as it heard supplicants at its regular afternoon meetings (using white linen napkins and the good china).

American Promotional Events knew how to target its campaign contributions as well. Although the total amount given by the fireworks company pales in comparison to oil, gas, and pharmaceuticals (the same lobbyists represented many of these clients and had facilitated contributions on their behalf as well), it knew how to pick the proper recipients. Four of the members of the committee—Sharer, Griego, Munoz, and Ulibarri—had received $500 checks just weeks before the 2012 legislative session began.[3] The previous year, in 2010, the company spent $4,400 in campaign contributions to legislators. That was about the annual average for the company's New Mexico contributions in the past ten years, which totaled $42,000. (Gov. Bill Richardson was the biggest recipient, receiving a total of $6,000 for his gubernatorial campaign in 2002.) But in 2011, the year of the fires, TNT upped their contributions to legislators to $7,500.[4] And they knew where to go after the likely votes—the Corporations Committee.

Meanwhile, even though Trujillo had not gotten back to me with the seal of approval from TNT Fireworks, I decided to present the compromise anyway, contained in a "substitute bill" for the original. A substitute is often used in the legislature when there are too many changes to use amendments. The changes in this case were almost everything that the industry's representative had wanted—a lower standard for triggering restrictions, with a ban on the use and sale of fireworks only declared by local governments or the state forester through regulations. The Senate Corporations Committee heard the substitute for SB 5 and SB 300 (Griego's) on February 5.

T. J. Trujillo was nowhere to be found, but the room was stuffed with dozens of firemen, foresters, and mayors who were supporting the now stripped-down bill. Conscious of the time, Chairman Griego was impatient and admonished me to limit my speakers. Although the new bill clearly placed regulation in the hands of the local governments and the state forester, the opponents debated the old bill as if no changes had been made. And they were turning up the heat.

Jim Burnham, a dealer from Farmington, spoke about how he sold fireworks as a boy and got to go to college and become valedictorian all because of his family's fireworks business. Fireworks also put six of his brothers through college. Eddie Arnet from Amy's said that putting the state forester in charge of fires was like giving the fox the key to the hen house. "This is

America. We're talking about a free country and independence. These fire-works are used for Fourth of July. We're talking about sparklers in grand-mother's birthday cake."

There was no chance to say that the sparklers would not have been af-fected. And there was no chance to respond to Public Regulation Commis-sion (PRC) Chairman Pat Lyons, who made a guest appearance to counteract the support of the fire marshal and other PRC commissioners. Responding to my comments about the 2003 Albuquerque fire caused by fireworks, Lyons said simply that the bosque needed to be burned anyway.

After the testimony, committee members got their turn. Sen. John Sapien said that the fireworks debate had become politicized and would be used as a wedge issue since it had so much public support. He was voting for it, but under protest. Sen. George Munoz, from Gallup, said the bill was a one-sided one for cities, and that a ban would not be fair to the Fourth of July itself. Because displays would continue, and people could bring in fire-works from neighboring states or the Navajo reservation, the whole thing was a hypocritical ploy, he implied. The comments made no sense.

Sen. Bill Sharer, as was the custom in the Corporations Committee, moved to table the bill, and it went down in flames, 6 to 4. Only Sens. Tim Keller, Lynda Lovejoy, John Sapien, and David Ulibarri voted for the bill, and Ulibarri did so only after it was apparent that it was going to be tabled.

In the hall outside the committee room, Sen. Phil Griego shook hands with the bill's opponents and told KNME-TV that the people of New Mexico are smart enough to understand that fireworks are not a good idea in times of high fire danger and that a new law was not needed.

My own assessment, which I, too, shared with the news media, was that this was a textbook example of how special interests and private gain trumped public health and safety. The governor agreed. She said that her office had received over seven hundred calls from mayors, fire chiefs, and concerned New Mexicans who were worried about the prospect of fire-works wreaking havoc and destruction in communities that had already faced weeks of wildfire threats. In a press release after the vote, she said she was frustrated that in times of emergency our local governments and the state had their hands tied and were unable to prevent damage or loss of life.

"We all hope and pray that we do not experience another dangerous fire season like we experienced last year, but if it happens again, New Mexicans can rightfully express disappointment that the special interest lobby pre-vailed among a small group of senators in defeating a bill that would have given cities, counties, and the state the tools they need to keep our commu-nities safe during the most extreme wildfire emergencies."

The fireworks industry did not need to compromise. And no wonder it was playing "slow ball" with me in my attempts to do so. It already had the votes.

Asked whether the $500 contributions made to committee members, including himself, had anything to do with it, Griego told Steve Terrell of the *Santa Fe New Mexican*, "Of course not. Give me a break. Five hundred dollars isn't going to change my mind on anything."[5]

I don't know whether Griego wanted to leave the impression that it would take more than that, but when I read the statement that's what I wondered. Then I put the contribution in the context of the thousands of other dollars he and his committee had gotten thanks to T. J. Trujillo and Luke Otero. Griego got $2,000 from T. J. Trujillo on behalf of Occidental Petroleum in 2011,[6] $500 on behalf of Advantage Capital Partners, and $300 on behalf of Gallagher and Kennedy (where Trujillo works) shortly after the 2012 session ended.[7] And I concluded the sum is greater than the parts.

For special interests, the Corporations Committee in the Senate and the Business and Industry Committee in the House are wise investments. And the chairmen often rake in more campaign contributions than the leadership. But if it were just a question of money and personal relationships between the lobbyists and the strategic committee members, nothing would emerge from the black hole. Yet occasionally, as you will see, an insurance reform, a tax hike, or a halfway progressive measure will survive. That happens when the Democratic leadership and the caucus together curb their committee chairs or when the governor strong-arms key legislators. When it came to fireworks, though, the Democratic leadership did nothing. Majority Leader Michael Sanchez had opposed even putting the measure on the agenda in the special session that fall and, right before the 2012 session, he told me he was opposed to the whole idea, especially if it meant allowing the governor to have more power. The best he could do, he said, was to promise that he would not go behind my back and get it killed. The governor sincerely tried to put some muscle behind the measure, but she was not convincing enough to outweigh the special interests, even with her own party members. Finally, although the media and the public kept the crisis alive in letters, e-mails, and news reports, the fire season was over and the Las Conchas disaster receding from memory.

Delay, a favorite tactic of special interests, had worked again.

CHAPTER 6

A New Mexico Two-Step with the Lobbyists from Big Pharma

G ASPAR LACA IS ONE OF THE BEST-DRESSED MEN AT THE ROUND-house. A lobbyist for the pharmaceutical giant GlaxoSmithKline, his Armani suits and silk ties stand in contrast to the casual attire of most legislators on the Health and Human Services (HHS) Committee, which he attends on a regular basis. Laca has represented Glaxo in southwestern states for over a decade, and he is well liked by a host of legislators, whom he often meets at national conferences put on by the National Conference of State Legislators, the National Association of Latino Elected and Appointed Officials, and the Council of State Governments. Laca's trade group, the Pharmaceutical Research and Manufacturers of America (PhRMA), is always a generous sponsor of these conferences, as is his employer, Glaxo. Whatever the occasion, the attractive, affable, silver-haired Laca is ready with free baseball tickets, dinners, hotel rooms, and, of course, campaign contributions. After all, that's his job.

But Gaspar was not happy with the Health and Human Services Committee as we dug into the complex world of prescription drug prices in 2000, years before Congress enacted a prescription drug benefit for Medicare. And I don't think he was very pleased with me.

Handing me a white envelope as I took a break from chairing the committee to chat with some members of the audience, he said, "This is for your campaign." I looked inside and saw that it was a check. How did he dare to do this in the middle of a hearing where seniors, some of them in wheelchairs, were testifying about their difficulties in paying for their medications? Sure, it's legal, I thought, but talk about shameless! As soon as I realized it was a check, I handed it back and rejoined the other legislators.

In the first part of the 2000s, consumers across the United States were hit with the first barrage of TV advertisements for brand name drugs and huge increases in the prices of Prilosec, Lipitor, Vioxx, and other popular drugs that consumers, encouraged by the ads, were now asking their doctors to prescribe. From 1995 until 2003, the cost of prescription drugs increased 10–15 percent each year, three times faster than other health costs. On average, retail prices of drugs shot up from $38.43 in 1998 to $71.69 in 2008.[1]

Caught in the crunch were approximately 77,000 seniors without prescription drug coverage and folks without insurance at all, estimated to total about 550,000 New Mexicans. Without access to discounts or the rebates available to veterans and Medicaid patients, or to the clients of other insurance plans, these seniors were watching a bigger and bigger portion of their fixed incomes disappear at the drugstore. And legislators were hearing about it from our constituents at the local Walgreens and in testimony from seniors like the ones who were now jammed into room 307 at the State Capitol Building.

"It's only with the kindness of friends that I survive," Gertrude Willard, 74, told the committee at one interim hearing, explaining that she took seven prescriptions daily at a cost of $303 per month. Another woman told of selling off her furniture to pay for her medication, and others talked about the choices they made among food, fuel, and medicine. A Santa Fe man said that he travelled to Juárez monthly to buy medicines for neighbors who pooled funds to pay for his trip. The New Mexico Agency on Aging, led by then U.S. Congresswoman Michelle Lujan Grisham, weighed in with statistics about the alarming number of seniors who were restricting their use of meds due to the high cost.

The price hikes were also taking a bigger and bigger bite out of public programs, which purchase huge volumes of medications for retirees, state employees, prisoners, and Medicaid recipients. In these fiscal hard times, were our public programs getting the best price? That's what legislators from Maine to California wanted to know, but it was a question even college professors (and we had several testify) couldn't answer given the tiered price structure and the dizzying array of discounts available to almost everyone, except those who needed it most—seniors and people without insurance.

Here's the way it works: Under federal law, drug manufacturers sell the exact same pharmaceuticals to different purchasers at different prices. For example, if the retail cost for a particular dosage and quantity of a brand name drug is $100, Medicaid and large health maintenance organizations (HMOs) pay on average $65; federally qualified health centers and hospitals pay $54 (under the 340B program); the Department of Defense and Veteran's Administration pay $46 or less. And you can buy the same drug in Canada for $10! To make matters worse—in a move that would make even the slickest car salesman blush—the drug companies have done their utmost to shield the true price of these drugs from view (see fig. 19).

Here's an example of just how weird it got. Medicaid directors around the country know that their programs are entitled to a "Medicaid Best Price" for their recipients, and many get a supplemental discount. But in the byzantine world of prescription drugs, we soon found out that the "best" price is not the lowest price, and the discount is based upon something called the "average wholesale price" (AWP). The problem is that no one knows what the AWP is. To make matters worse, it's against federal law to make it public; a convenient fact that the growing legions of pharmaceutical lobbyists were eager to point out as they began massing in hearing rooms in state capitols across the country.

By 2001, the committee had heard enough. We knew that we couldn't wait for Washington to solve this problem. In a rare show of bipartisan resolve, members of the Health and Human Services Committee held a news conference in the rotunda at the opening of the session with all of its members in attendance. Together we unveiled a package of eight bills to lower the price of drugs for low income and uninsured New Mexicans, provide a level playing field for all purchasers, create an interstate bulk purchasing project, and use the North American Free Trade Agreement to establish a re-importation program for drugs from Mexico. The centerpiece of the bills was the creation of a prescription drug program for uninsured seniors over the age of sixty-five whose income was below the poverty line. Twenty-three other states had such a program, but not New Mexico. Now was the time to do it, we thought, even if it meant starting a long dance with the wolves from the drug companies.

One by one, committee members, flanked by senior citizens, pharmacists, advocates from AARP, the Senior Citizens' Law Office, the Primary Care Association, and the New Mexico Agency on Aging, stepped to the microphone. It was an impressive show of force, which included Rep. John Heaton, a pharmacist from Carlsbad, Republican Sen. Sue Wilson, and our hero and past chairman Rep. J. Paul Taylor of Las Cruces, himself a senior.

"This is the number one issue for our agenda," said Rep. Danice Picraux of Albuquerque, who had ascended to the position of House majority leader that year due to the defeat of longtime House Speaker Raymond Sanchez the previous November. "And you will see it carried through."[2]

States around the country were tackling the same problem, trying to negotiate prices collectively as a block and proposing the use of "preferred drug lists" that featured generic drugs. None were more aggressive than Maine, which tried to obtain a discount for 350,000 uninsured residents and impose penalties on firms that refused. Big Pharma fought back against every state measure, taking the Maine Rx program all the way to the U.S. Supreme Court, crying "price control" and delaying relief for the state's ailing residents. The Court upheld Maine's action.

As we fought for our package of bills that year, we faced a growing army of out-of-state drug-company lobbyists. The ever-dapper Gaspar Laca was there, of course, as I struggled to explain the complex issue to members of the Senate Public Affairs Committee. So were representatives of Pfizer, AstraZeneca, Eli Lilly, Johnson & Johnson, and Bayer. There were so many lobbyists that the industry-friendly chairman of the Senate Public Affairs Committee moved hearings to the floor of the Senate where the lobbyists could roam freely among members, answering individual questions and running out for coffee or Cokes to satisfy thirsty legislators.

The lobbyists were the ground troops of a growing national campaign mounted in response to the hundreds of bills introduced by state legislators at that time to control the practices and prices of the companies. The campaign was coordinated by the trade group PhRMA, which would escalate its spending to $150 million in 2003 to protect what were then the highest profits in the country.[3] It is equally powerful today.

In 2003 PhRMA spent $48.7 million for advocacy at the state level, deploying sixty lobbyists in fifty states, who joined with their allies from the individual companies, sometimes playing one-on-one defense with individual legislators like Rep. John Heaton, who, as a pharmacist, was just a little too knowledgeable for PhRMA's comfort. In New Mexico, PhRMA's chief national lobbyist, a sweet, grandmotherly figure who was as sharp a lawyer as I've ever seen, testified several times. Marjorie Powell, like other industry lobbyists, supplied fact sheets that highlighted victories against life-threatening diseases won by the high tech industry. That year, the industry would spend $12.3 million to develop strategic alliances with universities, doctors, minority groups, and parents of chronically ill children. An intellectual echo chamber developed to sing the industry's praises and strike fear into the hearts of any who would risk the supply of lifesaving medications by questioning why the same drug in Europe or India, made by the same manufacturer, cost one-tenth the price.[4]

Compared to the huge industry push, the seniors and health care advocates behind the bills brought forward by the committee were a rag-tag bunch, but they kept showing up. As a result of their phone calls and office visits, organized by the New Mexico Agency on Aging Chief Michelle Lujan Grisham and the AARP, Representative Picraux's prediction came true. Three of the bills were "carried through," clearing both chambers of the legislature.

Passing bills in the New Mexico legislature is no easy task, since each bill must run a gauntlet of multiple committees in each house where it takes only a few members to table, delay, or kill bills dead in their tracks. But shepherding a package of prescription drug reforms through the Senate was like herding thirsty deer across the desert, protecting them from yipping coyotes, rattlesnakes, and wolves until they could reach water. We were overjoyed that three of our bills (creating a program for low-income seniors, discounting drugs to low-income and uninsured patients through Medicaid, and allowing seniors to buy into public employee programs) survived to reach the desk of Gov. Gary Johnson. Johnson, however, promptly vetoed the bills, saying they would cost the state too much.

By the time the next session rolled around, things had changed. Facing a $50 million hole in the Medicaid budget, driven in part by escalating drug costs (13 percent over the previous year for parts of the program), the administration was looking to save money without drastically cutting benefits or eligibility. The members of the HHS Committee were only too happy to suggest that the governor put a bill on "call" during the short 2002 session to provide some relief by starting a preferred drug list, or formulary, for that portion of Medicaid not already in a managed care program. An expert committee would determine which drugs should go on the formulary based on their effectiveness and whether a supplemental discount higher than the Medicaid "best" price could be negotiated by the human services department. If a manufacturer did not voluntarily negotiate, its drug would not be placed on the preferred list, and patients would have to obtain prior authorization from their doctor to receive it. The prior authorization process is routinely used by HMOs, which negotiate better prices for both their commercial and Medicaid patients, but it is cumbersome and lengthy. And the companies hate it.

Much to the dismay of the pharmaceutical lobbyists, now on high alert, the human services department recommended the governor put the bill on the agenda, and the games began anew. This time, the human services department weighed in with an estimate that my SB 253 would save $1.5 million per year. Also, by then I had been named to replace the notoriously lobbyist-friendly chairman of the Public Affairs Committee where many anti-industry bills had previously gone to die. After some arm twisting with Democratic members of the committee (whom I later found to have been recipients of handsome contributions from the pharmaceutical industry), the bill passed the Public Affairs and Senate Finance committees, then, much to my surprise, breezed through the floor unanimously. The lobbyists, it turned out, had been holding their fire for the House, where a battle ensued to get the measure out of the Business and Industry Committee and onto the floor. Once again, Michelle Lujan Grisham and the AARP marshaled busloads of seniors to pressure their representatives. Their presence reminded the representatives that 2002 was an election year—and the last year for Republican Gary Johnson, who, after eight years, would soon relinquish the governor's mansion to Democrat Bill Richardson. With only two minutes to go before the session adjourned, SB 253 passed the House on a 35 to 26 vote. It was one of the biggest victories ever against the pharmaceutical industry in New Mexico. But as legislators headed home, the lobbyists were just beginning their campaign to get the outgoing governor to veto the bill.

The period after the session adjourns on the thirtieth day at noon is usually a time to rest up for senators and representatives who have endured a marathon final week composed of all-night sessions, last minute cramming, and high anxiety. But savvy legislators know that this is when they must swing into a new campaign and mobilize their allies to persuade the governor and his (or her) administration to sign their bills.

To get Governor Johnson, who prided himself on a record number of vetoes, to sign the controversial bill, the advocates decided to draw on the success that other Republican governors had found with similar bills. Florida's recently enacted program had saved Medicaid $27 million the previous year, and Gov. Jeb Bush predicted the program would save taxpayers $214 million the following year while preserving access to needed medication. To deliver this message, we put George Kitchens, bureau chief of the Florida Medicaid Pharmacy Services, in touch with his counterparts in New Mexico. In Michigan, a similar program that covered Medicaid recipients as well as other state programs was expected to save $42 million.[5] It was signed by Republican Governor John Engler and, like Florida's program, had withstood legal challenges from the pharmaceutical companies. The message was simple: Governor Johnson should do the same.

But as we were delivering this rational message, the phone in the governor's office began to ring off the hook. Seniors began calling him in opposition to the bill, saying that they would be cut off from life-saving medications. The governor's staff noticed something funny. The callers could give no reason for supporting the veto except that they've been told to call by a group called "Seniors Over 60." Some said they had been told the bill would take away their benefits.

Seniors began calling the AARP, which allayed these trumped-up fears and quickly alerted the media to the phony campaign. The AARP had been very supportive of the bill, making the phone calls a big story in the *Albuquerque Journal*. Winn Quigley, the paper's health reporter, fished out the connection to the pharmaceutical industry. The calls had actually come from 60 Plus, the first of many front groups formed by PhRMA to simulate genuine grass-roots campaigns like ours that were working with legislatures around the country to control drug prices. The "group" operated a website and automatic dialer out of Virginia using industry money. Later in the year, another phony group, United Seniors Association, began a $3 million radio and TV ad campaign touting a Republican-sponsored drug plan then in the U.S. House of Representatives. It would step up to a more political pace during the 2002 election with New Mexico airwaves echoing ads from both 60 Plus and United Seniors Association.

The independent ads came atop nearly $16 million donated by the industry to political parties and candidates throughout the country (74 percent of this to Republicans) for the 2002 election cycle, according to the Center for Responsive Politics. In the previous election cycle (2000) the industry contributed $26.5 million to candidates and parties. PhRMA itself spent more than $50 million on television ads. At that time, these expenditures made the drug industry the biggest industry-group spender in U.S. elections.[6] By today's standards the millions do not seem like much, but they are significant because they were the first in a wave of special interest dollars that have come to dominate health policy debates at the state and national levels.

The phony scare campaign backfired in New Mexico in 2002. The *Albuquerque Journal* editorialized against the deceptive campaign, and Gov. Gary Johnson, who was not up for reelection, signed the bill on March 6, 2002. Ten years later, I still have the message from his office about the bill's signing tacked to my office door.

Within a few months, the human services department began to implement the program by forming a Pharmacy and Therapeutics Committee made up of experts to evaluate both generic and brand name drugs on the basis of efficacy. Approved drugs would be included on a preferred drug list. The efforts came as a thirty-member Medicaid task force prepared a sweeping reform bill that began to examine the huge program in search of ways to save money and increase effectiveness. The uniform preferred drug list, as well as a broader purchasing cooperative to combine the buying power of

Medicaid with other programs for retirees, teachers, and health and corrections department programs, was included in the reform bill. It passed the House unanimously and the Senate with only eight opposing votes. The governor signed the bill immediately, along with several other measures to save money in the Medicaid program. The state was on track to save $20 million in its Medicaid program. For the purchase of pharmaceutical products, it was a new day. Or not.

In the ensuing years, the Richardson administration never implemented the cost-cutting program. It never negotiated for the supplemental rebate it could get over and above the Medicaid best price. It never "carved out" the Rx program from the rest of the Medicaid program, as the Reform Committee had suggested. The administration was pursuing other monumental changes to its health programs, including a behavioral health collaborative to coordinate services in that area. According to Human Services Secretary Pam Hyde, the department could get a better deal through its Medicaid HMOs, which could combine their commercial lines with Medicaid and bargain with more "covered lives." But the department was unable to assure us that any savings were going to the Medicaid program and not to the HMOs or their intermediaries, the pharmacy benefit managers who negotiate with the drug companies. In the following session, the HHS Committee successfully spearheaded a bill (HB 666) that required disclosure of these deals. Sponsored by Representative Picraux, it was signed by the governor, but never implemented. Secretary Pam Hyde refused to release the information, initiating a pattern of secrecy that began to disturb the Legislative Finance Committee and Senate leaders.

The HMOs now managing the state's Medicaid formulary were pleased with the arrangement. But it was an especially sweet victory for the pharmaceutical and health products industry, which had been busy making campaign contributions during the 2002 election year. Governor Richardson, in particular, was a beneficiary of their largess, reporting a combined total of $55,711 in contributions for his governor's campaign in 2002, and $73,500 for the 2006 race.[7] Richardson got even more for his presidential campaign. The Center for Responsive Politics reports that he received $806,564 from the health sector, including the pharmaceutical industry.[8] Meanwhile, pharmaceutical companies donated a combined total of $720,000 to state candidates from 2000–2010, according to a draft of the report *Connecting the Dots: The Role of Campaign Contributions in New Mexico Health Policy.*[9]

At the end of the long two-step with New Mexico policymakers, the pharmaceutical companies had prevailed. Medicaid was not required to use a preferred drug list and the program was not getting supplemental rebates. And we still don't know whether the state is paying top dollar or getting a good deal on the millions of prescriptions filled for Medicaid recipients.

During the rest of the decade, the legislature set up myriad prescription drug programs, featuring discount cards for seniors and low-income New Mexicans. In 2003, the legislature created the Senior Rx, which built on the Medicaid program to provide a small discount to low-income seniors. In 2005, a discount card from Express Scripts was authorized and later expanded. By this time discount cards were a dime a dozen, with each company offering their own deal or combining with others to compete with generics and prices at big-box stores.

For the most part, these programs were not opposed by the companies. The expansion of eligibility brought new customers and usually came at state expense. As always, the discount was off of a basic price that remained out of bounds for state regulation.

During much of that time, the sights of the industry were set on Washington, where Medicare Part D, the much-sought-after prescription drug benefit for seniors, won approval in 2003. When it passed it was hailed as a milestone for seniors by the AARP and the Republican-controlled Congress. But the real victory went to the pharmaceutical companies. Their prize: millions of new customers at the pharmacy window with federal cash in hand, and no limits on price hikes or allowances for bulk purchasing.

States were left to sort out the problem that seniors confronted in choosing among the private drug programs (or PDPs, prescription drug plans) offering the benefit. Each policy had different co-pays, benefits, deductions, and premiums, something that the New Mexico Agency on Aging, along with the AARP and other groups, spent years untangling for confused seniors at meal sites and conferences throughout the state. The cost for the outreach effort further strained hard-pressed states.

With new customers now subsidized by the federal government, competition among the pharmaceutical giants shifted from TV advertising, campaign contributions, and lobbying to more direct marketing to prescribers. The practice, known as "detailing," had been growing since the early 2000s. By 2006 the industry had dispatched over 100,000 sales reps (one for every eight doctors) nationwide, spending $8.2 billion on drug marketing to physicians.

The marketing came in the form of gifts, free lunches, trips, educational grants, samples, and payments for reviewing clinical data, promoting drugs, or simply listening to sales pitches. The practice corresponded with the explosion of what have been termed "me too" drugs that companies develop with few modifications but a higher price and a new spin. The spin often included branded pens, note pads, and payment for attendance at continuing medical education (CME) events, as well as use of a physician's name for ghostwritten articles in medical journals.

These practices came to light after the arthritis drug Vioxx, manufactured by Merck, was taken off the market in 2004 because it caused a higher rate of heart attacks and strokes in patients taking the drug than in those given a placebo. Vioxx, whose pain-killing benefits were no greater than ibuprofen according to most data, had been a blockbuster drug thanks to $78 million in consumer ads each year along with $500 million spent annually to market it to physicians. Merck had an aggressive strategy to facilitate publications of friendly articles in medical literature and pressure the FDA to ignore clinical trials that showed cardiac risks as early as 2000. The result: FDA estimated 35,000–55,000 deaths caused by the expensive drug, which was taken by twenty million Americans.[10]

Not wishing to have their own reputations tarnished, health sciences centers around the country, many of which cooperate with companies in clinical trials and play host to legions of pharmaceutical representatives, began to get nervous. In 2008 the UNM Health Sciences Center forbade faculty and students from accepting any form of personal gift from drug reps and device companies. The new regulations prohibited display of any item bearing industry logos, cut off meals funded by companies, banned payments for trips and attendance at sales meetings, and reduced research funding. Prescriptions were to be based on clinical efficacy and not payment. Disclosure of any ownership, paid consultancy, or financial interest was required. Doctors were told to recuse themselves if there was any conflict of interest.

The sweeping policy had been spearheaded by UNM medical students and residents who approached me a year later to take action to require drug and medical equipment manufacturers to publicly disclose gifts of substantial value to prescribing physicians throughout the state. California, Maine, Minnesota, Nevada, Vermont, West Virginia, and Washington, D.C. already had similar laws on the books, and at least twenty-seven other state legislatures had proposed a disclosure bill in 2007.

How hard could that be, they asked, given that UNM had actually banned gifts and we could set the level high, say at $100, and exclude free samples that patients had come to depend upon. The attorney general even agreed to be the agency to which the companies reported.

Well, it was harder than you might think.

Senate Bill 99 made it through committees to the Senate floor with little trouble. News coverage highlighted the transparency aspect of the bill. Transparency was a big issue in the 2009 session with bills in both houses requiring disclosures from state contractors and more frequent campaign reporting as well as the perennial bill to open conference committees to the public. But when the bill, which required reporting to the attorney general, hit the floor, all hell broke loose. You would think I had attacked Mom and apple pie.

The measure was an insult to physicians and implied that a doctor can be bought for $100, argued Sen. Clint Harden of Clovis.

No matter that the New Mexico Medical Association supported the bill, or that the evidence I presented clearly showed industry payments were reducing the use of generics and increasing overall prescriptions for the newest, most expensive drugs.

Senator Jennings, who, as president pro tem, received $1,800 in contributions from the industry in 2009–2010,[11] used the opportunity to launch into a diatribe about open conference committees (another bill I was sponsoring that year) and what a bad idea that was since it would open up deliberations on the budget while the executive didn't have to open cabinet meetings. It was unrelated, but that didn't stop Jennings.

During the middle of the ninety-minute debate, Sen. Howie Morales, a Democrat from Silver City, approached my desk to tell me that he and other senators had just received an e-mail with detailed talking points to counter the gift bill. The sender was ALEC–the American Legislative Exchange Council, a group that bills itself as one of the largest bipartisan, individual membership associations of state legislators. In recent years, ALEC has been outed as a front group for corporate interests, including the pharmaceutical industry, which introduces special interest "model" legislation into state legislatures throughout the country. In 2011 five of ALEC's twenty-three board members, and a substantial portion of its funding, came from pharmaceutical companies. Not surprisingly, ALEC uses the same tactics the pharmaceutical companies do, giving lavish gifts and educational junkets to legislators, peppering them with slick literature and e-mail, knowing the other side is outspent and outdone.

But in 2009, ALEC was not receiving the scrutiny it is now, and the drug companies' steady stream of campaign cash had become routine. Pharmaceutical and health product companies contributed a total of $11,550 to senators in 2009–2010—an off year for the senators, who would not run for election again until 2012.[12] On February 23, 2009, the Health Care Gift

Disclosure Act went down to defeat on the Senate floor on a 24–16 vote. Senators who voted against the bill had received more money from the industry than those who voted for it. Those who voted for the industry's position received a total of $6,633 in contributions while those who voted against the industry received at total of $5,448.[13] The wolves' fancy footwork had left the advocates like me dancing in the dust. The flow of industry money to New Mexico doctors for speaking, research, travel, and meals continued throughout 2009, totaling $525,885.[14]

But there is always another day. The federal Patient Protection and Affordable Care Act, passed the next year by Congress and signed by President Obama, included a provision called the "physician transparency act," which required drug and equipment manufacturers to disclose payments of more than $10 (including honoraria, food, speakers fees, and the like) to prescribing physicians. Woo hoo! I guess somebody was listening to all that racket coming from the states.

In the years since my dances with wolves, I've learned to do a slower two-step.

In 2011, with the help of the New Mexico Medical Society, I passed a bill allowing patients to donate unused prescription drugs back to the doctor or clinic where they got them. The bill was supported by a host of disease-specific organizations like the American Cancer Society and the National MS Society, but it had died the first time out in 2009, caught in the crossfire between the pharmaceutical companies' demand for protection from lawsuits and the trial lawyers' insistence that no corporation should be immune from consumer protection suits. The popular bill made it through both houses but died on the floor of the House.

Two years later, however, House Majority Leader Ken Martinez, who had held the bill on the House floor in the last few days of the 2009 session, helped to fashion a compromise between the two interest groups. Pharma was flexible. The bill passed unanimously in both houses and was signed by the governor. The board of pharmacy developed regulations to implement the law, and it is now in effect, giving consumers an alternative to dumping life-saving and costly medications down the toilet.

Gaspar Laca, the lobbyist for GlaxoSmithKline who had tried to give me a campaign contribution in the middle of a hearing on prescription drug prices, was helpful in the negotiations and deserves part of the credit, proving that sometimes wolves can dance beautifully—at least when they are not directly threatened.

CHAPTER 7

Holding Our Own in the Face of Big Tobacco

A T ONE POINT IN MY LEGISLATIVE CAREER MY PRIMARY FOCUS was on protecting children from harm. Years of testimony from the New Mexico Department of Health (DOH) and teenagers themselves had convinced me of what the public health guys already knew: New Mexico kids were at high risk from guns, tobacco, and car crashes. And, in comparison to the rest of the nation, the statistics were bad.

Violence comes in all forms in our rural state, but our high rates of homicide and suicide among young people were (and still are) miles above the national average. Teen smoking was no surprise, but, as I found out from my own teenage daughter, there's a New Mexico twist. In the 1990s, rodeos, softball tournaments, and other sporting events were often sponsored by chewing tobacco companies. In one softball tourney in which my daughter played I noted that the opposing pitcher, a fifteen-year-old Girl Wonder from Jemez Pueblo, had a can of chewing tobacco jammed into her back pocket.

The crash rate for teenage drivers was likewise appalling. Like other rural states, New Mexico allowed drivers' licenses for very young people, required little on-the-road training, and had a culture of drunk driving that was only then, in the late 1990s, winding down when the legislature finally banned drive-up liquor windows.

Preventing teen smoking, joy riding, and gun fighting may be a fool's errand here in the Wild West. But, if you want to save young lives and precious state dollars at the same time, here's where you can strike pay dirt. Dr. Bill Wiese, former director of the state's public health division and founder of the masters in public health program at the University of New Mexico, once told me that simply increasing the tobacco tax would make more of a difference than anything else. I took him seriously. But, as I found out, some of the most powerful interest groups in the nation are stationed at practically every mountain pass in the country to block progress in these important public health wars. Their most important outposts are state legislatures—like New Mexico's. I had an initial triumph in these battles in 1999. With the help of the American Automobile Association of New Mexico (AAA) I passed a graduated drivers' license system to better equip teenage drivers with on-the-road training and restrictions on the number of teen passengers. In the years since then the death and injury rate has come down. In 2005, I was also successful in passing a bill to require helmets for children under eighteen who rode dirt bikes and all-terrain vehicles (ATVs), both popular recreational vehicles, especially in rural areas.

On two different issues, tobacco control and gun safety, I had much more trouble. The stakes are high in both areas, and two of the nation's most powerful interest groups—Big Tobacco and the National Rifle Association—are fully engaged. This chapter tells the tale of how the legislature dealt with tobacco issues; the next with how it dealt with gun control over the first decade of the new century. The outcome of these battles was vastly different—with strong leaders, political deals, and grassroots efforts making all the difference.

Floor of the NM Senate, March 4, 2010. In the dwindling hours of the 2010 special session, Majority Leader Michael Sanchez leaned over my desk in the Senate chambers and said, "Don't talk so much."

The Republicans were running down the clock, wearing out the already weary, repeatedly trying to amend the 75-cent-per-pack cigarette tax that had finally made it to the Senate floor. The bill, sponsored by Rep. Gail Chasey, was the final missing piece of the budget puzzle, providing $33 million in state revenue and somewhere between $20–25 million for the state's Indian tribes.

I looked at my lineup of expert witnesses, who by now had been sitting behind my desk on the Senate floor for over two hours. Jim Nunns, Wayne Bladh, and other guys in suits were here to help me field technical questions about the way cigarette taxes are collected, how the funds would be allocated, and whether smokers wouldn't just buy cigarettes in nearby states where they might be cheaper. There were no questions about how many people smoked in New Mexico, how many died, or the rate of tobacco-related illnesses here.

Yet for me, the tax bill was primarily a public health measure that—more than anything else we could do—would save lives by discouraging teens from taking up smoking. Plus, the revenue would help offset the $2.78 per pack that we already pay in New Mexico out of the Medicaid program to treat expensive tobacco-related illnesses like cancer, heart disease, and emphysema.

In 2010, the drive to hike cigarette taxes was the latest chapter in the state's attempt to address the ravages of tobacco, which is responsible for about 2,100 deaths per year in New Mexico.[1] Youth tobacco use, reaching a crescendo of about 33 percent in the late 1990s, and hovering around 25 percent in the following years, has been particularly worrisome. Nationwide, the U.S. Surgeon General even called it a "pediatric epidemic," with 3.6 million middle- and high-school smokers, and the tobacco industry spending $10 billion a year (that's $1 million every hour) on marketing that targets kids.[2]

It wasn't just the surgeon general and public health advocates who saw cigarette taxes and the price hikes they bring as the best way to curtail youth smoking. The industry has long known that price—as well as addiction—is a huge factor in determining sales, particularly to teens. Back in 1982 when Congress was contemplating raising federal excise taxes, R. J. Reynolds' executive D. S. Burrows said, "If prices were 10 percent higher, 12–17 incidence (youth smoking) would be 11.9 percent lower."[3] Internal documents that Phillip Morris was forced to reveal by the 1998 Master Settlement Agreement (MSA) between forty-six states' attorneys general (AGs) and the companies also revealed the dramatic impact of prices on the quitting population. Comprehensive reviews of the literature now estimate a 3–5 percent reduction of overall cigarettes consumed as a result of a 10 percent price increase, with young people three to four times more price sensitive.[4] Kids just don't have the money.

Taxes, however, are rarely imposed because of their health effects. Instead, they are driven by the need for revenue to support programs or to fill in budget holes left by recession or a drop in oil and gas prices. Until 2010, when I took to the floor to usher in the latest increase, New Mexico had a relatively low cigarette tax compared to other states. From the mid-1980s until 1993, the tax was 15 cents per pack of twenty. In 1993, a coalition to raise the tax was led by Senate President Pro Tem Manny Aragon and the UNM Cancer Center, which gained about 15 percent of the proceeds for a new cancer center and its school of medicine.

Aragon, a diehard smoker, had longstanding ties to the tobacco industry. One of his best friends was former senator Bobby McBride, a gravel-voiced lobbyist for Altria (the new name for Phillip Morris) since 1986. The two could often be found smoking (and coughing) in the Senate lounge, or in Aragon's paneled office just off the Senate chambers. Aragon's frequent trips, financed by the tobacco and pharmaceutical industries, were covered extensively by the local media, as were the handsome campaign contributions he received—and recycled to other senators. Aragon's June 1997 trip to Costa Rica, paid for by an organization called the New York Society for International Affairs, received front-page coverage in the *Albuquerque Journal.* The *Journal* discovered that, behind the scenes, Phillip Morris financed the group. Senator Aragon said he didn't know about the company's sponsorship and that tobacco was not discussed. Tobacco company documents released through the MSA also revealed that years earlier he had gone to the Super Bowl in 1991 courtesy of Philip Morris, a fact the company tried to cover up but which was discovered by Larry Barker, then the investigative reporter for KOAT TV.[5] But campaign contributions—and junkets—don't always hold sway. Aragon stood firmly behind raising the tax to 12 cents per pack in 1993, and he used his clout to pass it. Several years later, in 1998, he joined with me and Sen. Billy McKibben to raise it again by another 12 cents per pack. It was an unlikely coalition that year—composed of archconservative McKibben, a Hobbs Republican who had recently been treated for cancer, chain-smoking Aragon, and me, a new and largely unknown senator from one of New Mexico's hotbeds of Democratic activism. We each had our own bill but they were ultimately combined into a "substitute bill," Senate Bill 59, which passed both houses just in time, before the adjournment of the short 1998 session.

In the New Mexico legislature, it's often these kinds of unlikely alliances that are the most successful. None of us got as large an increase as we asked for (we started with a request for a 21-cent increase), but we were all gratified that the resulting $11 million would go to a new program for children's health insurance and, once again, UNM Cancer Center. I was particularly impressed with how quickly Senator Aragon was able to navigate the bill through the House the night before the session ended, but my enthusiasm was nothing compared to McKibben's.

Long known as one of the most colorful members of the New Mexico Senate, McKibben had been hyping his bill, focusing on the tobacco companies as the quintessential bad guys. Later in the year, in November, the Master Settlement Agreement would be approved, requiring the companies to pay more than $200 billion over twenty-five years to forty-six states (including New Mexico) for damages caused by tobacco. The TV was full of stories about how company executives, who had known about the connection to lung cancer for years, had lied to Congress. Day after day, McKibben would go on about the Marlboro Man and Joe Camel (a cartoon character then used by the industry in TV, print, and outdoor advertising to appeal to young children) and the millions spent on an insidious attempt to hook new victims. The flesh and blood of New Mexicans was being sacrificed, McKibben howled, to satisfy big tobacco's insatiable appetite for profit, and there was no end in sight.

Hell had no fury like a reformed smoker—with cancer.

In spite of the rhetoric, and polling data indicating that 63 percent of registered voters statewide favored a 20 cent per pack increase, Gov. Gary Johnson vetoed the measure. The anti-tax Johnson had not been convinced by a bipartisan coalition led by the American Cancer Society, which included his own department of health.

McKibben was furious. He led an attempt to override the veto in a subsequent special session—a politically incorrect move for a senator from the same party as the governor. He called a news conference after the veto, and his quote was picked up by a media he had trained to appreciate his folksy aphorisms.

"Every hearse carrying the body of a victim of big tobacco should have a Johnson for Governor bumper sticker on it," McKibben proclaimed to reporters in March, as the 1998 election season was getting under way.

But cigarette taxes are only one front in the tobacco wars. In the following years, other battles began over how to clear the air and use a windfall coming from beyond our borders.

Tom Udall has always been very health conscious. In 1988, when he was running for a congressional seat in the first congressional district in Albuquerque, I served as his press secretary and actually saw what he put in his mouth—which was all good food. His Mormon stock didn't countenance smoking or even drinking coffee. And outdoor activity was a key value. So it was no surprise, ten years later, that Udall, now attorney general, did battle with the tobacco companies with some relish. In 1998 Udall, along with forty-five other AGs from around the company, was victorious, obtaining the biggest settlement for the state ever. New Mexico's share of the master settlement was $1.12 billion over twenty-five years. In addition, tobacco advertising to youth was restricted, and the companies had to make public years of documents about their lobbying and marketing activities.

Around the country legislatures were deciding what to do with the windfall. It was like winning the lottery. Do you want all the cash up front? Well, you can "securitize" the funds, and sell your rights to future payments for a lump sum now. Do you want to use it for teacher salaries or schools that sorely need a boost? That can be arranged. Or do you want to use the funds for cancer research and health care? Expert opinion began pouring in, from financial consultants I didn't even know existed.

In the end, under the leadership of House Speaker Raymond Sanchez, the legislature decided not to put the money into the general budget fund, but to create a new "permanent fund." Like the land grant permanent fund that was created at statehood, the tobacco settlement permanent fund would become a part of the reserves, invested each year, growing as the market dictated. Half of these funds each year would be withdrawn into a program fund, to be used only for health and after-school activities. Permissible uses included health programs to deter smoking or treat resulting diseases and research into tobacco-related illness.

The enabling legislation (HB 501) created a special joint committee, the Tobacco Settlement Revenue Oversight Committee, which decides what to spend the money on, and handles other tobacco-related bills. In the ensuing years, a special unit of the health department, the Tobacco Use Prevention And Control (TUPAC) program, was formed, beginning immediately to implement a strategic plan to leverage the money, create coalitions, and empower young people and various ethnic groups (especially Native Americans) to become tobacco-control advocates.

It was one of the legislature's finest hours, and the credit should go to Speaker Raymond Sanchez. As other states spent their funds on property tax rebates (Illinois), harbor improvements (Alaska), flood control (North Dakota), and even upgrading tobacco furnaces (North Carolina), New Mexico did the right thing. Our proceeds would not go up in smoke.

Serving on the committee every year since its inception, I tried to steer a large proportion of the funds to prevention, as recommended by the Centers for Disease Control (CDC). Although we never spent as much as the CDC recommended, we did much better than most states. Funding for TUPAC programs hit a high-water mark at $9.1 million a year in 2008 and, despite a tight budget, we still managed to spend $6 million in 2011. Larry Elmore and others at the DOH used an evidence-based approach, and they were not afraid to try new avenues: a media literacy program for young people to debunk tobacco ads; peer groups for Hispanic, Native American, Black, and gay teens; and a "Buck Tobacco" partnership with Caspar Baca, the owner of several New Mexico rodeos, to refuse smokeless tobacco sponsorships. There was "counter advertising" as well, to offset the industry's ads,

featuring startling billboards and TV ads from cancer survivors like Rick
Bender, an oral cancer survivor who lost part of his jaw, tongue, and neck
as a result of chewing smokeless tobacco. The name of his presentation:
"Half Off with Tobacco."

The counter advertising was a drop in the bucket in comparison to what
the tobacco companies spent on promotion and marketing to teens in New
Mexico, estimated by Tobacco Free Kids, a national advocacy group, to range
from $32 million to $75 million each year in the wake of the settlement.[6]

With advertising restrictions now in place through the MSA, the companies switched their approach to point-of-sale ads in convenience stores, discounts, coupons, candy flavoring, and reimbursements to storeowners
whose cigarette products (then placed in displays at a child's eye level) might
be stolen. At least that's what they hoped.

While the companies were beefing up the marketing, the DOH, often
using federal as well as state funds, was educating local communities about
the dangers of tobacco and laying down an infrastructure of grassroots
groups around the state that would come into play later when the legislature
tackled the next step in reducing tobacco deaths—banning indoor smoking
in public places.

Secondhand smoke had been recognized as a hazard for a long time, and
the evidence was becoming clear that it was not just a danger to children,
pregnant women, or those with asthma and other respiratory diseases. It
was a danger to everyone on the premises, even nonsmokers. During the
1990s, several towns in New Mexico had recognized this and banned smoking in public places. Albuquerque acted as early as 1989. The Las Cruces
ban took effect in 1995, Santa Fe's in 1999, Carlsbad's in 2000, Silver City's
in 2001, and Roswell's in 2002. All were political battles fought by bipartisan local groups, who would later join together in a coalition to fight for a
statewide ban.

But while cities and counties were clearing the air, the state capitol itself
was the scene of smoke-filled rooms, with curtains and carpets reeking of
tobacco. When I arrived in 1997 smoking had been restricted somewhat,
but it was entirely permissible in the Senate lounge and private offices. The
situation was particularly offensive to First Lady Dee Johnson, who thought
it sent the wrong message to school children and other visitors to the capitol—who were seeing important state officials, role models all, lighting up
and blowing smoke.

During her time as first lady, from 1994 to 2002, Dee Johnson waged a
campaign to make the capitol smoke free. Her efforts dovetailed with her

husband's dedication to health and physical fitness, but he was largely uninvolved. She carried the ball and her efforts were met with derision by the legislative leadership, many of whom smoked. Year after year she would present her proposal and, in the Senate, it would disappear into the void, without being taken seriously or heard in committee. Sometimes, like in 1998 and 2001, it would meet its demise in the Senate Public Affairs Committee, chaired by Sen. Shannon Robinson, famous for canceling committee hearings or just not hearing bills he didn't like. A dedicated smoker, Robinson was close friends with his Senate predecessor, Bobby McBride, lobbyist for Phillip Morris, and could often be seen taking a smoking break with his friend. Other times the bill would die in the House Business and Industry Committee, another black hole. Once, in 1999, the bill to ban was championed by smoker-in-chief Senator Aragon, who, coincidentally, attached a 13-cent-per-pack cigarette tax—about the same amount that had been vetoed by the governor the year before. The bill passed both houses and was promptly vetoed by the governor (see fig. 20).

When I became chairman of the Senate Public Affairs Committee in 2002, I vowed "the boys" would play games with Dee Johnson no longer. I promptly scheduled her, and the committee passed her bill, then sponsored by Senator Rawson. Together with co-sponsor Rep. Joe Thompson they made a great case and the bill was finally passed by the whole legislature that year. Smoking did not entirely disappear. There were scofflaws like Senator "Smokey" Robinson, but for the most part smoking now became an outdoor activity.

In 2002, with a looming Medicaid shortfall and the prospect of a new Democratic governor on the fourth floor of the Roundhouse, pressure began to mount for another cigarette tax increase. The state tax, still at 21 cents a pack, had not been changed since 1993, and it was one of the lowest in the region, ranking fortieth in the nation. A taskforce composed of legislators, insurers, medical providers, and outgoing administrators had recommended raising the tax. And a coalition of health groups, citing a telephone poll conducted by Research and Polling showing 63 percent supported a 60-cent increase, was beginning to organize, with the help of the New Mexico cancer, heart, and lung associations. The group, New Mexicans Concerned about Tobacco (NMCAT), had been gathering strength for the past few years, spurred by able organizers like Cheryl Ferguson from the Assist Program, Julia Valdez and Natasha Ning of the Heart Association, and Bianca Ortiz-Wertheim of the American Cancer Society. Cynthia Serna, now with the American Cancer Society, was the executive director. The advocates said a

60-cent increase would raise more than $54 million for state programs in the first year and would save the state $6 million in health care costs over the first five years.[7]

Alerted to the danger, the tobacco lobby stepped up its campaign contributions. Phillip Morris donated $65,700 to candidates in 2002, including $10,000 to gubernatorial hopeful Bill Richardson, then seen as a sure bet. The contributions made Phillip Morris the top donor that year.[8] From 1995 to 2003 the tobacco industry as a whole had given a total of $247,435 to all candidates.[9] The amount doesn't seem too great until it is combined with contributions from the industry's allies who also work to defeat taxes and smoking bans. Generally, these include the New Mexico Restaurant Association, the Retail Grocers, the Retail Association, and the Petroleum Marketers. These interest groups do not bear the negative stigma of the tobacco companies. From 1995 to 2003 these groups gave an additional $85,575 to state candidates.[10] As usual, the contributions went heavily to Democrats, who were in the majority and in control of key committees. Senate Public Affairs Committee Chair Shannon Robinson was one of the larger recipients, along with House Business and Industry Committee Chair Fred Luna, Sens. Phil Griego and Manny Aragon. Out of a total of 112 legislators there were only twenty-three members who did not receive any contributions from either the tobacco industry or its allies.[11] I was not among them. Even though I had vowed never to take a dime from tobacco, I had been fooled into accepting a contribution from one of their allies. Big tobacco was nothing if not inventive.

At first, it was hard to tell who was representing the tobacco companies, since the lobbyists, well aware of their clients' bad reputation, kept a relatively low public profile, often working through surrogates like the Restaurant Association. But I soon found out that tobacco lobbyists were among the most familiar faces at the Roundhouse. Former legislators Bobby McBride, Tom Rutherford, and Joe Laing served in the Senate. Joe Thomson hailed from both the House and the Johnson administration. Bob Barberousse, Luke Otero, Mickey Barnett, T. J. Trujillo, Mark Duran, Jeremy Rutherford, Jim O'Neill, Phillip Larraigoite, John Underwood, and Dennis Wallen all lobbied for various tobacco companies or associations.

"I always felt like I was going up against the very best, the most powerful lobbyists in the legislature," recalls Nathan Bush, now a regional director for the American Cancer Society Cancer Action Network, then a lobbyist, along with Linda Siegle, whose single, small braid made her a stand out among lobbyists.

The tobacco industry also got help from afar. More and more, the American Legislative Exchange Council (ALEC), a group of conservative legislators funded by tobacco and other corporations, worked closely with friendly legislators to introduce model bills that would undermine taxes and smoking restrictions and sabotage youth smoking programs.

But in 2003, the tobacco lobby was no match for a newly elected governor, now cooperating with a newly united Democratic leadership in the Senate to find fresh sources of revenue to kick off his administration. Senator Aragon, who had become majority leader after a mini-coup that toppled Sen. Tim Jennings from the post in the fall of 2001, was calling the shots. He put together a bill combining tax proposals from Senator Jennings, Senator McSorley, and me for a 70-cent-per-pack increase. Most of the revenue would go to the state's general fund, but a goodly share would be earmarked for the Cancer Center and UNM Hospital. UNM would use the revenue for a new wing of its hospital, later named the Bill and Barbara Richardson Pavilion.

The tax increase was supported by the Albuquerque Chamber of Commerce, usually no friend of tax increases. The chamber and its business allies saw it as a "user fee" that would cut down on smoking and reduce health care costs.

But New Mexicans Concerned about Tobacco was not exactly cracking open the champagne bottles. Part of the deal to raise revenue was a raid on the tobacco settlement permanent fund. To fill the Medicaid hole, the annual payments from the tobacco settlement (then about $40 million per year) would be deposited in the general fund for the next four years, rather than in the separate fund. As a result, the fund would not grow as anticipated and the temptation to use most of it for what I call the "crisis du jour" (then Medicaid) would mount.

Governor Richardson actually wanted to abolish the tobacco settlement permanent fund entirely and use *all* tobacco revenues for general government operations. The Senate went along, but the House came up with the compromise of a temporary raid—thus preserving the legislature's creation, the tobacco settlement permanent fund.

Even with this compromise, members of the Tobacco Settlement Revenue Oversight Committee were crestfallen. The leadership promised to channel the same amount of money into research and prevention as we had been recommending, but there were no guarantees that the programs we had started would continue. I was upset, like many other committee members who had come to view themselves as protectors of the fund. Unlike the other Democrats, I did not suck it up and vote for the raid. Nevertheless, the measure, along with the tax hike, passed handily, as part of that year's love fest between the Democrats and their new governor.

Although New Mexico's cigarette tax increase was the largest in the nation at that time, the tobacco lobbyists were not entirely dismayed since they believed there was a potential offset—fewer funds to prevention and cessation programs. Although still in their infancy, these programs were beginning to bear fruit, with adult smoking rates beginning to drop. The rate dropped by three percentage points from 2001 (23.8 percent) to 2007 (20.8 percent) as more and more smokers began to take advantage of cessation programs. Tracking the success of prevention efforts among young people, though, was a more difficult proposition. Peer pressure, word of mouth, and personal contacts (the preferred New Mexico method) take longer to bear fruit. It wasn't until a few years later that youth smoking rates would budge, responding to a combination attack: prevention messages, higher cigarette prices, and a ban on indoor smoking.

As always, the tobacco companies were watching what was happening in others states as well as New Mexico. And the evidence was clear. The more sustained and well funded the prevention efforts were, the fewer the number of new smokers. This was bad news for the tobacco companies who, acknowledging the drop in adult smokers, were fishing for "replacement" smokers—for those who died or quit.

Much to the dismay of the companies, the Democratic leadership made good on its promise. Cancer research and prevention programs were funded out of the general fund, with prevention funding reaching a high of $9.6 million in 2009. It was never as high a level as recommended by the CDC, but it put New Mexico in the middle of the pack when it came to states' efforts to address the nation's number-one killer.

By 2005 pressure was mounting to extend the ban on smoking in public places to restaurants and bars. One musician who played regularly at an Albuquerque restaurant where I occasionally ate called me about how, in order to make a living, he had to endure secondhand smoke and its health effects, even though he had quit smoking years ago. He didn't want to become one of the 2,100 New Mexicans who die each year of heart disease, lung cancer, or emphysema. His phone call was typical of a huge grassroots campaign focused on the legislature mounted by NMCAT. NMCAT had become a force to be reckoned with. A list of its supporters ran the gamut from the Clovis Housing and Redevelopment Agency to the Texico Conference of Seventh-Day Adventists—and beyond, to hundreds of community groups from around the state. The supporters went beyond the usual medical and wellness groups to the Municipal League, the Association of Counties, and individual cities around the state. Another poll that indicated that almost two-thirds of voters wanted a statewide ban on smoking in public places, including restaurants, created some tailwinds. With financing provided by a national coalition, The Campaign for Tobacco Free Kids, the group ran full-page ads in the *Albuquerque Journal* and *The New Mexican*. Its TV and radio advertisements, featuring a family dining at a local restaurant as others smoked in the background, attracted attention and won advertising awards. Its Brown Ribbon Wall of Remembrance in the rotunda of the state capitol displayed photos and personal remembrances from those who lost loved ones to tobacco. And its fact sheets provided evidence that indoor smoke was a killer that could not be contained by a separating wall in a restaurant or a high-powered ventilation system, two arguments used by Big Tobacco, which was now beginning to take the movement more seriously.

To combat the grassroots effort, the tobacco lobbyists turned to their friends and surrogates from restaurants and bars. They hastily organized groups of smokers in country and western nightclubs like Albuquerque's Midnight Rodeo and began looking for votes among those to whom they and their allies had contributed. Taking a cue from the NRA, the industry's main pitch was that this was a "rights" issue—the main right being the right to smoke wherever you wanted. For the Restaurant Association and the Albuquerque Chamber of Commerce, the main message amounted to "butt out of our business."

When the smoking ban (SB 515), sponsored by Sen. John Grubesic, finally came to a vote on the Senate floor in 2005, it went down to defeat 22 to 16. The Restaurant Association and the tobacco allies had prevailed. Swing votes were that of Sen. Mary Kay Papen, whose daughter is the lobbyist for the Restaurant Association, and tobacco users Sens. Phil Griego and James Taylor, two of the larger recipients of both tobacco and hospitality industry campaign contributions. A similar bill sponsored by Rep. Al Park passed the House handily but was never heard in the Senate, although it was on the calendar the last day of the session.

When the measure was heard again in 2007, the tobacco industry, knowing that the likelihood of passage was great, focused on gaining as many exemptions as possible. In 2005, much to the dismay of restaurants, stand-alone bars had been excluded. They were now included, thus neutralizing opposition from restaurants. But there were important exemptions: cigar bars (a favorite of cigar-smoking Gov. Bill Richardson), casinos and bingo halls, private clubs, certain hotel rooms, and Native American ceremonial locations. Park's bill, HB 283, passed the House unanimously. It then passed the Senate 27 to 9, with only a few tobacco loyalists holding out in opposition. The same special-interest pattern had repeated itself. Common Cause reported that in 2007 the tobacco industry and business groups had made larger contributions to senators who voted against the act than those who voted in favor. Corporations Committee Chairman Shannon Robinson, who received the largest total contributions from business, was not present for the vote. [12]

New Mexico was the sixteenth state to pass a clean indoor air law; now thirty-five states have them. In the end, the act was named the Dee Johnson Clean Air Act for the former first lady, who had died the year before. Everyone agreed that it was an appropriate tribute.

Floor of the NM Senate, March 4, 2010. Meanwhile, as I stood at my desk with the guys in suits behind me on the last day of the 2010 special session, the floor amendments to the tobacco tax bill kept coming. They were designed to wreck the side deals that had been cut to allow the House bill to finally cross over to the Senate and then come to the floor for a vote.

In order to get the bill out of the House, it had to pass Rep. Ed Sandoval's Tax and Revenue Committee. Sandoval was in favor of it, but two of his committee members, Rep. Sandra Jeff and Rep. Andrew Barreras, both close to the tobacco lobbyists, had gone rogue, joining with Republican committee members to kill a similar Senate bill that I sponsored during the regular session. But there was a deal and the representatives had agreed to vote for it if one-third of the revenue went to public schools, which were squeezed tight by the budget crisis. When it came over to the Senate side, however, it was apparent that there was a problem.

The chairman of the Senate Finance Committee, Sen. John Arthur Smith, who believed that education had not yet received its fair share of cuts, didn't like it. And the bill had to pass through his committee.

But there were larger forces at work.

To get it out of that committee, Republican Sen. Sue Beffort proposed that instead of one-third of the revenue going to public education, it go to early childhood education, which had suffered a disproportionate reduction. It was enough to garner passage through the committee, but it undermined the House deal and jeopardized concurrence (a vote that must occur for a bill to pass when it has been amended by the other chamber). And there were concerns it could be just the poison pill the tobacco lobbyists were looking for. The clock was ticking. And the tobacco lobbyists were swarming, desperate to derail the tax.

Although not permitted on the floor of the Senate during debate, lobbyists are allowed to roam the aisles of the chamber freely when the session starts late. And there they were, making final pitches to senators still on the fence or those disturbed by one of the side deals. At one point, they surrounded Sen. David Ulibarri, the Democratic caucus chair, who was wavering.

The previous evening, as the Senate Finance Committee met, the lobbyists had taken one senator out for drinks to try and persuade the legislator to introduce a last-ditch amendment. They brought the senator back to the capitol in an inebriated state. But the smell of liquor in the elevator attracted the attention of Sen. Michael Sanchez, who stormed into the committee room, pointed at Mark Duran, one of the tobacco lobbyists, and said, "You screwed up—come here now."

Outraged, Sanchez arranged for a ride home for his member and then started to work the bill in earnest, along with House Majority Leader Ken Martinez and Speaker Ben Lujan. It was, after all, the last piece to fall into place, and tomorrow, they knew, had to be the last day of the session, since the budget only covered three days.

Back on the floor that last morning, rumors were flying. The House would not accept this. The tribes were controlling things behind the scenes. The Senate had been sold out. This is a secret deal. Several House members were on the floor saying they had been promised additional funding for education through a controversial "sponge bond" that never materialized. They urged the removal of the early childhood amendment (see fig. 21).

But the fingerprints of the powerful tobacco lobby were clearly on most of the amendments, especially the one introduced by Sen. Phil Griego to impose a two-year—rather than a four-year—"sunset" on the tax increase. He said as much in his opening remarks. "This bill breaks faith with the tobacco industry that agreed to a 50-cent increase and a sunset," Griego said.

I hadn't heard of that deal, I responded, and, at any rate, going through all these tax revisions, dealing with the special stamps that tribal entities used on the reservations, would just not be worth it for two years.

My experts, to whom I turned for advice, agreed—unanimously. And there were eight of them on the floor sitting behind me—enough to, at least visually, match the overwhelming numbers of tobacco lobbyists.

When debate on the amendment had ended, Griego called for a roll call vote, then, as usual, he spit the remainder of his chewing tobacco into a plastic cup he kept for that purpose in between our adjoining desks on the Senate floor. I tried to keep track of the votes on one of the long, vertical tally sheets we use for this purpose in the Senate, but it was no use. I lost count until, after a pause in the general hubbub, the lieutenant governor said, "The House being evenly divided, the lieutenant governor votes in the negative."

The amendment was defeated.

Lt. Gov. Diane Denish rarely got to cast tie-breaking votes in the Senate, and I noticed that she did this one with some satisfaction. Since she was running for governor, some Senate Democrats had tried to protect her from voting directly on tax increases for political reasons and sometimes, I believe, even used her candidacy to prevent the passage of tax increases—all without consulting with her.

My experience with Denish is that she does what she thinks is right, without pulling punches. And here was an opportunity to do so. It didn't hurt, I guess, that in my opening statement I applauded her efforts to get the state to invest in early childhood education and pre-kindergarten. Both of those priorities stood to benefit from the amendment attached in the Senate Finance Committee.

Four other amendments were put forward, each agonizingly debated, as the opponents tried to wear down the bill's fragile coalition some way, somehow. Sen. Rod Adair, a Republican from the east side, asked me to provide a signed letter from each pueblo and tribe in New Mexico, proving their support. Earlier he tried for a one-year sunset, even though Griego's two-year sunset had just been defeated.

Taking the majority leader's advice not to talk so much, I replied sparingly, knowing that Sanchez must be confident that the votes were there.

And they were. After two-and-a-half hours of debate, the bill passed, without amendment, 25 to 15. Among the yea votes was one Republican, Sen. Sue Beffort, the Finance Committee member who had introduced the early childhood amendment.

Within minutes, the Senate adjourned "sine die." There would be no chance for a conference committee if the House refused to go along with the Senate amendment. But Speaker Ben Lujan and Majority Leader Ken Martinez had done their job, and the House votes were there, even after many members had already left. At 3:35 p.m., March 4, the House concurred 30 to 20.

Gov. Bill Richardson, well aware of the state's fading revenue and the persistent recession, signed the bill a few weeks later. He line-item vetoed the amendments calling for the automatic repeal (sunset) of the bill and the earmarking of a portion of the revenue it derived to early childhood education. Instead all the revenue would go to the state's general fund. New Mexico tribes, whose influence greatly affected the outcome, got to impose a tribal tax, which would help their nations as well.

New Mexico was one of six states to raise taxes that year. The year before, in 2009, sixteen states had likewise taken on Big Tobacco and won. The following year, in 2011, three others followed. All the increases were driven by budget shortfalls amid economic hard times.

The price of cigarettes in New Mexico went from $4.60 to $5.37, making it the eighteenth—not the thirty-first—highest in the nation. Phillip Morris's Bobby McBride and the tobacco industry's enlarged SWAT team had lost the battle against the Democratic leadership and governor's office. But in coming years, they would be back trying to exploit loopholes in the bill, which threatened the state's payments from the Master Settlement Agreement. The smokeless tobacco lobbyists would be there too, using the special status of the state's tribes to avoid taxation altogether. The battle would never be over, but the New Mexico legislature had won another round, more than holding its own in the face of Big Tobacco.

Late in the afternoon, after my triumph on the floor of the Senate, I was celebrating via text message with the bill's primary sponsor, Rep. Gail Chasey, the co-chair of the Tobacco Settlement Revenue Oversight Committee, when I got another call on my cell phone. It was Republican Sen. Allen Christiensen, calling from the Utah Senate where that very day they had passed a dollar-per-pack tax increase on cigarettes, despite many of the same arguments from the same tobacco lobbyists who had appeared in New Mexico. Christiensen, a pediatric dentist, had called me out of the blue the week before when the tobacco lobbyists said the New Mexico tax was dead as a doornail.

"Congratulations," he said, "to all of us."

CHAPTER 8

Taking a Bullet for the NRA

T HEY WERE MOTHERS OF TEENAGERS WHO HAD BEEN SHOT OR committed suicide. Mary Hunt lost her son Matthew in a triple homicide in the east mountains near Albuquerque. He, along with Viola Garcia's son Luis and Joan Shirley's son Kevin, were on their way home from a party on a May night in 1999 when their car was riddled with bullets at a quiet intersection in Sandia Park. A few years before the shooting that took the three teens, Gina Lujan's daughter, nineteen-year-old Emilia, depressed about her boyfriend and the suicide of a friend, used the loaded revolver her mother kept under the mattress to take her own life.

Now, in the winter of 2001, these moms were on a mission. They were standing together, telling their painful stories at a news conference in the Rotunda, at an event organized by the New Mexico Coalition against Gun Violence, a group of survivors, police officers, sheriffs, emergency room doctors, health advocates, and religious leaders. The news conference was being held to drum up support for the bills that three other women, Rep. Patsy Trujillo-Knauer from Santa Fe, Rep. Gail Chasey from Albuquerque,[1] and I were sponsoring in the 2001 session to reduce youth gun violence. My bill, the Children and Firearms Safety Bill (SB 131), required safety locks for every gun sold in New Mexico. Representative Knauer's Child Access Prevention Act (HB 250) established penalties for parents who did not safeguard handguns from possession by children. Representative Chasey's Handgun Safety Standard Act (HB 310) was aimed at getting a commission to look at new gun technologies, which would allow only their owners to fire them.

With memories of the Columbine High School shootings fresh in our minds and a growing awareness that New Mexico had a dismal record of gun violence, we believed that we could save young lives. Why should the

United States lead the rest of the world year after year in the number and rate of children dying from firearms? And why should we sit still while firearms became the second leading cause of teen deaths after auto accidents? We were careful to explain that we were not challenging rights to gun ownership but were just asking for a little commonsense regulation in an area that seemed to get an exemption from health and safety standards. Sixteen other states (and several major cities) already had laws requiring safe storage of loaded firearms, mostly through trigger locks. The National Rifle Association (NRA) had publicly supported these laws in California, Florida, Iowa, Maryland, and Wisconsin. Public polling showed widespread support, and we were optimistic.

Wearing t-shirts identifying themselves as Moms on a Mission, Mary Hunt and the other moms made the rounds of the committees to which the bills were assigned. They rattled off recent information compiled by the Department of Health's Child Fatality Review Board, a volunteer organization that painstakingly reviewed the cases of each child killed in New Mexico by a firearm.

The statistics for that time period were alarming:

› New Mexico ranked sixth in the nation in gun fatalities (1997).
› For children ages 1–9, half of all firearm deaths are unintentional, with most deaths from a loaded firearm that was not locked up.
› New Mexico has the seventh highest rate of youth suicide in the nation.
› 27.4 percent of students seriously considered suicide, and 47 percent of those made an attempt.
› Two-thirds of youth suicides are the result of a gunshot wound.
› The risk of a completed suicide increases five times in homes with guns; the risk is even higher for adolescents and young adults.[2]

But it was the moms' own stories, not the statistics, that made a difference. Matthew Hunt was already in a wheelchair when he was shot, we learned. Kevin Shirley and Luis Garcia were high school athletes. Emilia Lujan was taking college classes and left behind a three-year-old daughter.

At the turn of the century, in the wake of the Columbine shooting, gun control had once again become a national issue and the Brady Campaign to Prevent Gun Violence was active. A million moms marched on Washington on Mother's Day 2000, and national polling data showed a majority of Americans supported stronger gun control.[3] In New Mexico a new project, Not Even One, housed at the nonprofit New Mexico Advocates for

Children and Families (later known as New Mexico Voices for Children), got foundation funding to team up with the department of health (DOH) to run violence-prevention programs in schools, do media outreach, and search for policy alternatives. Bill Jordan was the primary organizer for Not Even One and the lobbyist for the safety bills. He was an AIDS advocate fresh off a victory in 1997 from a landmark bill to enable addicts to exchange dirty needles for clean ones (and hence avoid spreading AIDS and Hepatitis C).

During the course of the tumultuous session, which started with the overthrow of longtime president pro tempore Manny Aragon by Sen. Richard Romero, my bill did not attract much opposition—until it hit the floor. By that time the other two house bills were running into trouble, but mine was still alive. The ante was going up, and arguments that echoed the rhetoric of the NRA began to flow. Sen. Sue Wilson said she was afraid the bill represented an erosion of constitutional rights and could be a step toward registration and confiscation of guns.

The bill had nothing to do with that, I responded. It simply required gun dealers to provide safety locks (costing about $10) when they sold firearms. If a safety lock could not be attached, the dealer was to place the weapon in a locked box or container so only an adult could access it with a key. The move had saved lives in other states, I added.[4]

Opponents, however, belittled the bill as a "feel good" measure that would not accomplish anything because irresponsible adults would always be irresponsible, regardless of the law.

Frustrated, Sen. Leonard Tsosie, my seatmate on the floor of the Senate, said what I had been thinking. Tsosie often jumped around in his arguments, and this time his stream of consciousness led to the NRA. "Let us not bring Charlton Heston and pit him against our children," he said, referring to the actor and NRA president whose statue on horseback guards the NRA's shooting facility near Raton, New Mexico.

"This is about having the courage to say that the lives of our children matter more than the right of gun owners to store their guns in a manner that endangers the lives of children," I summarized.

"If this saves just one life in the state, it's worth it," added Sen. Michael Sanchez of Belen. It was a refrain repeated by several supporters, and it was enough to help the bill squeak by 20 to 17. With the help of Representatives Trujillo-Knauer and Chasey, the bill also squeaked by the House by three votes.

Moms on a Mission didn't have time to celebrate the narrow victory, though. Another gun bill, aimed in the opposite direction, was occupying center stage.

Sen. Shannon Robinson, one of the Senate's best-known mavericks, had been trying to pass a bill to allow the carrying of concealed weapons since the mid-1990s. New Mexico already allowed the carrying of loaded weapons in plain view and in a car's glove box, but Robinson and the NRA wanted New Mexico to join the ranks of thirty-two other states, which, at that time, had legalized the covert practice.

When I talked to my constituents in Albuquerque about guns, whether in my annual survey, at supermarkets, or local coffee shops, they assumed that gun ownership was already tightly controlled by the state. I thought so, too, until I looked into it. But nothing could be further from the truth—both then and now. New Mexico is what is called an "open carry" state. You can carry any kind of loaded gun as long as it is not concealed if you are not a felon and are over nineteen years old. No state permits, licenses, training, registration, or fingerprinting are required for the possession or purchasing of rifles, shotguns, or handguns. And if you have a gun, you can take it almost everywhere except federal buildings, courthouses, buses, bars, and inside schools.

As a rural state, New Mexico has a long tradition of gun ownership for hunting purposes. The fall elk hunt is often a family tradition, and children under eighteen are required to take a hunter training course. But the use of handguns and small arms for personal protection in urban areas had grown steadily during the last century—as had the crime rate.

Robinson, and other proponents of concealed weapons, contended that guns in pockets and purses were necessary to protect yourself—and others—from the bad guys packing heat. Rep. Judy Vanderstar-Russell, a Republican from Rio Rancho who was promoting her own concealed-carry bill in the House, emphasized that concealed-carry permits were particularly important for women as a defense against would-be rapists. "This is a women's issue," said Russell. "Women are the ones who are defenseless. Women are the ones who are preyed upon."[5] The argument was one of many that the NRA, acting through their lobbyists in the states, was encouraging.

But state police and local law enforcement groups weren't buying it, contending it would make it harder for the police to separate the good guys from the bad when they arrived at a volatile scene. "It's hard to accept that we've gotten to the point that to ensure people's safety we all have to be gun toters," Santa Fe Police Chief John Denko told the *Santa Fe New Mexican*. "We want people to be safe as much as anybody, but we don't feel that this is the answer."[6]

Voters in Santa Fe, where Denko was then the police chief, were over-whelmingly opposed to concealed-carry permits. The next year, when the issue was still pending, the city's daily paper, the *Santa Fe New Mexican*, commissioned a poll showing four out of five (80 percent) respondents op-posed. My own survey in 2001 showed that 71 percent of constituents who responded opposed the concealed carry bill. Albuquerque city councilors and Mayor Jim Baca were beginning to discuss a citywide ban on concealed weapons as well.

But thousands of NRA members were beating the drum in letters to the editors around the state, contacting their legislators via e-mail and phone. Momentum for the measure was mounting. For several years, Robinson, who represented a poor, heavily immigrant and crime-ridden area of Albu-querque, had been cultivating conservative rural legislators—joining them to decry gun control and support their hunting and ranching issues. Often he would raise his hands to his temples, forming mock moose antlers, to signal that this or that issue was a "Bull Moose" issue (see fig. 22). Supposedly, the Bull Moose issues were ones that Teddy Roosevelt and his dissident Republicans would have supported, although that didn't make much sense since the original Bull Moosers were progressive—and not advocates of the conservative values embedded in the issues Robinson was promoting. But Robinson had his own language, and it was usually very colorful.

After a prolonged debate, Robinson's bill (SB 148) passed the Senate; Vanderstar Russell's bill (HB 277) was making progress in the House. There were only a few more steps remaining for the bills to pass. Outgunned, op-ponents pleaded for common sense. "We have too many guns in this country and too many children shooting at each other," Gail Chasey told the House. "This will only add to the problem."[7]

"The use of guns is barbaric," said Santa Fe Sen. Roman Maes, who, one by one, asked a number of senators if they actually felt that they really needed to use a gun. All said no. "Anyone who has to carry a gun is in trou-ble," Maes continued. "The reality is that most of us do not need to carry aa gun."[8]

Robinson insisted that people need guns to protect themselves from criminals. Under the provisions of the bill, he said, those who wielded the weapons would have to be twenty-five, take a training course with periodic refreshers, pass a background check, and pay a $100 fee. These are the good guys, he emphasized, not the bad guys who carry weapons illegally.

Sen. Cisco McSorley, of Albuquerque, another opponent, mentioned that the reason concealed weapons were outlawed and visible ones permitted in

New Mexico was because carrying a concealed weapon had been considered cowardly throughout history. "The object of society is not to become more like the criminals," he said.[9]

With a lobbyist from the state police acting as my expert witness to counter the NRA lobbyist at Robinson's side, I brought up the specter of more accidental deaths, which we had just been discussing in a debate over my child safety act. "They're going to be storing these guns somewhere," I said, citing the high suicide and gun death rate among teens.

The thing that bothered me was that the call to allow concealed weapons was based on fear—fear that proponents were effectively whipping up. Once the fear took hold, and the bill passed, everyone would be arming themselves to the teeth in a death spiral of distrust.

"I don't want to be at a mall or a movie theater wondering if my neighbor is packing a gun. Wouldn't it be more dangerous in these populated areas with more and more people carrying concealed weapons?" I asked—to no avail. I was also worried that overzealous citizens would be more likely to become "deputy dawgs" and take the law into their own hands, for better and worse. Years later, in a famous 2012 case, Trayvon Martin, a young black man, was shot and killed in Florida by such a person, a neighborhood watch captain acting to defend himself (he said) under another law prominent on the NRA's national agenda: "Stand Your Ground."

Knowing that we could not defeat the House bill, which was now the nearest to passage, we attempted to amend it. During a three-hour debate, Sen. Michael Sanchez was successful in including a provision that would revoke a license if the holder was determined to be drunk while carrying a concealed weapon. Sen. Linda Lopez, from Albuquerque's South Valley, and I tried a series of amendments, which would have banned concealed weapons in banks, in hospitals, in churches, and in day care centers. Much to our amazement, they all failed, such was the zeal of the pro-gun forces. When Senator Robinson tried an amendment of his own, to remove a provision in the House bill that allowed cities to adopt their own ordinances, it failed too, presenting what would later become a pesky problem for the new law.

The Concealed Handgun Carry Act was passed in the final hours of the 2001 session, almost three decades after Albuquerque Rep. James Caudell, a Republican, first introduced it. Gov. Gary Johnson wasted no time in signing it—and vetoing my hard-fought Child and Firearms Safety Bill. I had tried to convince the governor that the two bills were compatible, but he was not persuaded. Doubly disappointed, I thought of the Moms on a Mission.

After their greater losses, this was nothing, I told myself. And then something I didn't expect happened.

In June, the New Mexico Supreme Court struck down the concealed-carry law as unconstitutional. Albuquerque's mayor, Jim Baca, had challenged the law based on a clause in the New Mexico constitution that stated, "No law shall abridge the right of the citizen to keep and bear arms for security and defense, for lawful hunting and recreational use and for other lawful purposes, but nothing herein shall be construed to permit the carrying of concealed weapons. No municipality or county shall regulate in any way an incident of the right to bear arms" (Article II, Section 6).

I'd always felt that the express prohibition on carrying of concealed weapons was pretty clear, but the court didn't strike the new law down on that provision. Instead it was that pesky inclusion of a local option to allow cities to ban concealed weapons. Baca never did get the city council to ban concealed weapons, but his lawsuit put a crimp in the style of the NRA, which was then in the process of adding notches to its gun as states passed more pro-gun legislation. That was OK with Baca, no stranger to showdowns with the liquor industry and cattle ranchers. He was not afraid of the NRA.

Baca, a former state land commissioner and liquor control director, owned dozens of guns himself, but he thought that allowing people to conceal them was "just nuts." Concealed-carry laws are just based on paranoia, he told me, and when people strap one on, they are usually looking for trouble. "I am surprised that the law hasn't led to more killings, road rage, and violence," he says. Baca, now retired, says it's all about the power of the NRA. "They have so much power, it's madness."

With approximately thirty thousand members in New Mexico, the country's largest shooting range (the Whittington Center, near Raton), youth programs, dozens of newsletters and blogs, the NRA presence in New Mexico is palpable. The state affiliate is called the New Mexico Shooting Sports Association. It has both gun industry and citizen support, and its political endorsements are important to politicians and members, who are vocal. Nationally, the NRA is an extremely conservative organization. Its president, David Keen, was the former chair of the American Conservative Union. Grover Norquist, president of Americans for Tax Reform, and Robert Brown, creator of *Soldier of Fortune* magazine, sit on its board, as does former rock guitarist Ted Nugent. In 2012, Nugent drew media attention for his remarks at that year's convention, saying that "Obama and his colleagues need to be shot like coyotes." Nugent's remarks were followed by others about riding into the battlefield and chopping their heads off in November, so I guess they were figurative, but they were enough to attract the attention of the Secret Service.

The NRA describes itself as a civil-rights organization with the main civil right, of course, being the second amendment—the right to bear arms. More Americans, it is now estimated, know about the second amendment than the first. This is important because fights over rights (rather than complicated facts or experience) are effective wedge issues that turn out voters. New Mexico candidates ignore the NRA at their peril; most seek its endorsement. Of New Mexico governors, Bill Richardson, Susana Martinez, and Gary Johnson all received NRA endorsements, as did Democratic congressmen Ben Ray Lujan, Steve Pearce, and Martin Heinrich. I was one of the few legislators who did not seek their endorsement, coming from a safe district where I had more freedom to vote my conscience.[10]

The good news about the court decision was enough to sustain me until the following year, when I picked up the newspaper and read an Associated Press story: "Four-year-old New Mexico Boy Shoots Neighbor Girl with Handgun." On Sunday afternoon, March 4, 2002, the boy got ahold of a Taurus .357 magnum that was hidden under the mattress in a bedroom of the Whispering Sands Apartments in Albuquerque's Southeast Heights. As the children watched *Shrek* the youngster shot and killed twenty-one-month-old Cierra Marie Gonzales. The parents of the children had been temporarily staying together in the apartment, and three of them were at home at the time of the shooting, in an adjoining room.[11]

I couldn't help thinking that it was a death that we could have prevented had the governor signed the trigger-lock bill. Our mantra had been, "If this saves the life of one child, it will be worth it." Now one child had died, and I feared others would follow.

By the time the 2003 session rolled around there had been a sea change in Santa Fe. The Democrats were now in control of both the legislature and the governor's mansion, and the new governor, Bill Richardson, was at the height of his popularity and power. Richardson was a friend of the NRA and a supporter of the concealed carry law that had recently been declared unconstitutional (see fig. 23).

Given the governor's support, it was almost a foregone conclusion that a reconstructed bill would pass—and it did. This time Senator Robinson was the proud sponsor and the measure (SB 23) passed the Senate (32–9) and House (50–19) overwhelmingly. Law enforcement was still opposed, but their opposition had become subdued. John Denko, the police chief from Santa Fe, was now Richardson's secretary of public safety. Not surprisingly, we didn't hear much from him in opposition. Others in the state police were gratified that at least the new law strengthened the training and required a criminal background check for licensees, who had to be at least twenty-five. And private businesses could still post a sign saying "No Weapons Allowed" if they didn't want to take any chances.

New Mexico Advocates for Families and Children, and Dr. Victor LaCerva, a Santa Fe doctor, sued almost immediately to have the law again declared unconstitutional on the grounds of the phrase, "nothing herein shall permit the carrying of concealed weapons." They were unsuccessful.

The NRA, which had tried and failed to intervene in the case, was overjoyed. Governor Richardson called it "a great day for the rights of gun owners" and said that he had worked diligently with the sponsor to craft a bill that would withstand constitutional scrutiny.[12]

In the years that followed, the NRA built upon its victory, attempting to increase the number of places where concealed weapons could be carried and to reduce refresher courses and training requirements. In 2007 (and 2012), they were successful in allowing those with concealed-carry licenses to carry their weapons into package liquor and convenience stores, lowering the qualifying age to twenty-one and extending the time period licensees could hold a license before retraining was required. In 2010 Sen. George Munoz, a Democrat from Gallup, passed a bill that allowed owners to carry concealed weapons into restaurants that served wine and beer (see fig. 24). Previously, bars were one of the few areas where concealed weapons could not be carried—but this prohibition was now fading into the gray line dividing restaurants from bars.

Rural Democrats carried many of the NRA's expansion bills, and some speculated that the party had simply thrown in the towel on any kind of gun control. The West was becoming a swing area in national elections and Richardson, who was a presidential candidate during much of his second term, wanted to build alliances with hunters, ranchers, and others who carried guns and wore boots in rural areas. And he needed the support of the NRA.[13] When Richardson was elected, funding dried up for grassroots gun-control advocates like Not Even One, and there was no organized opposition to the onslaught of bills that came later.

In 2011 Republican and Democratic legislators alike, sensing that the time was ripe, rushed to introduce a model bill supported by both the NRA and ALEC, a conservative legislative group with which it had longstanding ties. These "Castle" bills were based on the idea that a man's home was his castle and he or she had the right to shoot first and ask questions later, if his actions were in self-defense. Some of the bills allowed those with concealed-carry licenses to "stand their ground," even outside their personal residences. They would have no duty to retreat in the face of violence. And they could use their weapons to defend others, not just themselves.

New Mexico's statutes already included such rights, the legislative council staff told the eager sponsors—to no avail. In their zeal they introduced the bills anyway, although in 2011 they were not successful.

The West's longstanding romance with guns is a tough issue to tackle. "It's a force of nature you don't understand," said Jim Baca. Perhaps I should have known better than to pick a fight with people who are toting guns here in the Wild West. Who even knew who they were? They certainly seemed to be calling and e-mailing about anything that could be remotely related, although most were not from my district.

Because there is no registration or licensing requirement, except for concealed-carry permits (which now number about twenty-four thousand), no one knows how many gun owners there are in New Mexico. Nationally it is estimated that there are guns in one out of every three homes, which is actually a drop in ownership since 1980, according to the General Social Survey conducted by the National Policy Opinion Center at the University of Chicago.[14] Dave Heshley, a lobbyist with the New Mexico Fraternal Order of Police, estimates that in New Mexico 75 percent of those eligible to own a gun own one or more. And the NRA thinks it is about 50 percent of the population.

One of those gun owners is the current governor, Susana Martinez. Martinez, a former district attorney from the border city of Las Cruces, is licensed to carry a concealed weapon. In 2011, her Twitter page featured her perfect score on the renewal test she took for .38 and .45 caliber handguns. "Chuck [the first gentleman, as he is called in New Mexico, was also a rural sheriff] will never admit it, but I'm a better shot," the governor boasted on the page. And if you didn't believe her, there she was on video, hitting the target repeatedly and reminiscing about the .357 Magnum she acquired at age eighteen.[15]

One clue to the futility of gun control might lie in one of New Mexico's most rural areas—Catron County. Back in 1994 the county commission there *required* every head of household to maintain a firearm and ammunition needed to fire it.

When I heard about the old law, I saw why it might be time to move on to another issue, like health care or education, that was not the wedge those on the right end of the spectrum were hoping for.

But still, it scared me when on the opening day of the 2012 session, a year after the shooting of Rep. Gabby Gifford in Arizona, a number of people carrying handguns were milling around in the Capitol, eating lunch in the cafeteria, scaring the be-jesus out of staffers and many others (see fig. 25). The Tea Party had just held a rally on the west side of the capitol, and MoveOn. org was gathered on the east side. The Occupy movement was in its heyday. There were a number of outbursts from the Senate and House galleries during the session, and I thought about what easy targets elected officials were to those who were unhappy with our decisions. The previous year, I had to press the panic button provided under the dais where members of the Senate Public Affairs Committee sat, as several members of the audience, angry at our vote on a child custody issue, charged at us, shouting.

When the State Police told me it was perfectly legal to carry a gun into the Roundhouse, I couldn't believe it—although I should have, since it was now legal to carry a gun almost everywhere. So, in 2012, I sponsored a rule change to prevent guns on the Senate floor, in the gallery, committee rooms, and hallways. I knew that some senators had licenses to carry concealed weapons, and I wondered if they were packing heat on the floor. I couldn't find out exactly who they were (the drafters of the 2003 bill made sure to exclude the names of license holders from public information requests, except those coming from law enforcement personnel), but I wanted to hear what they would say.

I never got the chance. My rule change was not even heard in the initial committee to which it was assigned, the Senate Rules Committee.

It was not surprising. Even violent shootings like the one in 2010 that killed three employees and forced the evacuation of hundreds at Emcore, a high-tech Albuquerque company, did not spark discussion of the easy availability of guns. And armed robberies at convenience stores and restaurants continue to claim the lives of employees. Proponents of concealed carry claim that the possible presence of armed citizens actually deterred more incidents, like the one at a local Walmart where an armed customer shot another who was attacking his own wife, a Walmart employee.

More recently, the massacre of twelve moviegoers, and the wounding of scores of others in Aurora, Colorado, in 2012, by a young man armed with an AK47 and a magazine that carried one hundred rounds of ammunition did provoke some discussion. But not much. The NRA said even discussing the legality of using such assault rifles was an affront to the freedom of gun-loving Americans and exploitative of the unfortunate victims' deaths. The politicians, then on the campaign trail, largely complied with the gag order. The more recent school shooting in Newtown, Connecticut, has attracted more attention and has the potential to bring some changes.

Meanwhile, every year in the United States there are thirty thousand gun-related deaths and three hundred thousand gun-related assaults. Far more Americans have been casualties of domestic gunfire than have died in all of our wars combined—and it's costing us as much as $100 million a year.[16]

Here in New Mexico—in 2011—a Daily Beast study ranked our state sixth deadliest in gun deaths and sixth most lenient in gun laws.[17] The handgun suicide rate was over five times higher than the U.S. rate between 2001 and 2008; the handgun homicide rate was over three times higher during the same period. We have a lousy ranking for youth suicide, in particular, ranking fourth in the nation. About half of all our suicides are done with firearms, so easily available and unsafely stored in New Mexico.[18]

In January 2013 the shootings continued. Former senator Eric Griego's brother Greg, Greg's wife, and three of their children were killed by their fifteen-year-old son with guns stored at the family's South Valley home in Albuquerque. Greg Griego had been honored on the floor of the Senate the previous year.

"We have not carried out an effective prevention strategy in this area," Michael Landen, acting director of the department of health's epidemiology division, admitted to me when I called asking for a progress report. It's no wonder. There is no grassroots group like New Mexicans for Tobacco Control with whom to partner. There is no Tobacco Fund from which to draw, or even to protect. And there is no support from either the legislature leadership or the governor's office. Although the legislative leadership and the governor were willing to take on the tobacco companies, passing both tobacco tax increases and the Dee Johnson Clean Air Act, they are not willing to take on the NRA. Both special interest groups wear black hats, as far as I am concerned, when it comes to public health. But, with key allies in the governor's mansion and a hyper-active local membership, the NRA has been more successful than Big Tobacco in New Mexico. Perhaps in the Wild West its hat is not as black. Or perhaps it has just effectively used its huge national clout, campaign support, and its local advocates to leverage New Mexico's traditional libertarian streak. That's something that yields great rewards—for better or worse—in a small citizen legislature like New Mexico's.

PART IV   Patients and Patience
Turning Around the Battleship

L ONG BEFORE PRESIDENT OBAMA'S PATIENT PROTECTION AND
Affordable Care Act passed in 2010, states around the country were ex-
perimenting with health care reforms—struggling with high costs and the
unique health problems of their populations. Although the states partner
with the federal government to pay for services, the rubber meets the road in
local hospitals and doctors' offices where patients get their treatment and
cope with their diseases—for better or worse.

Health care is one of the biggest, most complex and costly issues state governments confront. For legislators, it is also the most personal, touching the
lives of every constituent. In New Mexico, the state's high proportion of citizens without insurance and the high incidence of chronic diseases, including
drug and alcohol addiction, especially among our Hispanic and Native American populations, have made this issue challenging for policymakers. Reforming health care, as well as changing our drug policies, has been a rocky road.
Presidential politics, personal rivalries, and, as always, special interests have
gotten in the way of big reform packages. But two unlikely coalitions, playing
on the personal stories of patients and taking advantage of some magic moments when the stars were aligned, won some significant early reforms. It takes
patience (as well as patients) to turn the battleship ever so slightly.

The following chapters show how some local heroes and mavericks learned
what former San Antonio mayor Henry Cisneros called the secret of governing, "the art of sighting that tiny sliver of daylight in the wall of obstruction
thrown up against change and squeezing through it to get something done."
Along the way these bipartisan allies passed incremental reforms like the legalization of medical marijuana and the protection of patients' rights, making New Mexico a laboratory for broader, national policies.

CHAPTER 9

The Rocky Road to Health Care Reform

Warning: Travelers May Experience Detours,
Speed Traps, and Road Rage

HEALTH CARE IS ONE OF THE KEY ISSUES ANY LEGISLATURE faces, and it was a personal focus during my time in Santa Fe. I often felt I was traveling a rocky road blocked by unforeseen obstacles and twisted by treacherous detours that took me far from my destination: affordable, quality health care for all New Mexicans. The journey to that destination is endless, it seems. Sen. Ted Kennedy called health care reform the great unfinished business of our society, a moral issue touching on fundamental principles of social justice and character in our country.

Nowhere does this ring truer than in New Mexico, a low-income state with a majority of Hispanics and Native Americans. For years, good health care has been out of reach for a higher proportion of its citizens than in other states, either because it costs too much or because it is simply unavailable in rural areas. For years, almost a quarter of the population has had no health insurance at all since the state's mostly small employers couldn't afford to offer it. When there is no coverage, there is usually no treatment, except in hospital emergency rooms. That means high death rates from chronic diseases and other medical problems that require regular treatment.

For years, it seemed like a hopeless situation, but by the mid-1990s a band of determined reformers began to chip away at a status quo that produced a huge gulf between the health-care "haves" and "have-nots." Health policy wonks call that gulf "health-care disparity"—the difference in health between those who can afford it and those who can't. In New Mexico the disparities run on ethnic and geographical lines, with huge Hispanic and Native American diabetes rates, higher infant mortality, and more obesity on the reservation and in the barrio. But poor health can simply be a matter of bad luck, too, with entire families inheriting the legacy of disability, mental illness, or alcoholism. To the reformers, and to me, it seemed like the worst kind of inequality.

EARLY REFORMS MARK MILESTONES ALONG THE ROAD

About two decades ago, Rep. J. Paul Taylor, a cultured and compassionate educator from Mesilla in southern New Mexico, and Rep. Ed Sandoval, a formidable teddy bear of a man from the North Valley of Albuquerque, wanted to do something about the lack of access to affordable health care. As members of a new Health and Human Services (HHS) Committee formed in the wake of a task force on health care reform in 1994, they had become weary of listening to troubling tales brought to the committee. They were stories told by parents of people with disabilities who were on a waiting list for decades, by seniors afraid to leave their homes, and by desperate relatives of people with cancer now impoverished because they did not have insurance coverage. The supplicants were people whom Ed Sandoval began to call "the folks"—the ones in every neighborhood who were poor, frail, homeless, widowed, or orphaned. They testified long into the night at every meeting of the HHS Committee, now at the center of reform activity.

"It was heartbreaking," Taylor said, especially since many of the committee's requests went unheeded by the larger legislature, "but it was so important that the real needs of New Mexicans be heard."

But not all of the recommendations of advocates and legislators in that era went unheard. Earlier in the decade, New Mexico had taken some significant steps to provide insurance coverage for its population. The state expanded its Medicaid program to include thousands more low-income children up to age eighteen, an early advance for which New Mexico even now receives kudos from national organizations. It also created insurance pools to keep down the cost of insurance for employers in the public and private sectors, including the Health Insurance Alliance (HIA) for businesses, and the Interagency Benefits Advisory Committee (IBAC) for state employees, teachers, and retirees. The initial idea was to share risk, purchase in bulk, and get more coverage at lower prices—common sense then, controversial now. There were other reforms as well, including the expansion of a high-risk pool established earlier by Roswell advocate Patty Jennings to cover families with disabled members rejected by private insurance companies and the establishment of a Health Policy Commission to collect data to inform health-care decisions and set priorities.

By the time I arrived in the Senate in 1997, there was another hot button issue: managed care. A program designed by insurance companies to coordinate care and cut costs through health maintenance organizations (HMOs), managed care had become the era's major health care reform. It didn't affect the growing number of people who had no insurance at all (a problem that would fester for years), but it sure caught the attention of people who already had insurance—and their doctors. HMOs now required patients to obtain prior authorizations and referrals. And many were denied treatments. I had heard all about it when I knocked on doors in the North Valley during my campaign the previous year.

In 1997, Gov. Gary Johnson abruptly put the state's expanding Medicaid program into a managed-care contract called the "Salud" program. The shift from the "fee-for service" model, where the state paid for services directly, was a monumental change, but the governor expected the cost-cutting move to be done quickly. Chaos ensued. The various insurers held enrollment fairs. Provider networks were shuffled. Medicaid clients, including many Native Americans, were assigned providers who were located across the state. The program was rolled out in different regions of the state at different times. The growing pains were severe. The cabinet secretary for human services resigned, and the governor appointed a new, more aggressive secretary, Duke Rodriguez.

Presbyterian's HMO, the Lovelace HMO, and Cimarron, a new insurance company headed by former governor Garrey Carruthers, competed for healthy children and sought ways to avoid paying for those who were sick or had special needs. The market was changing rapidly and tensions were rising between the Democratically controlled legislature, then led by Sen. Manny Aragon and Speaker Raymond Sanchez, and Republican Gov. Gary Johnson.

Even mild mannered Rep. J. Paul Taylor, then seventy-seven, was angry and upset. All these years he had been getting up before dawn to drive to Santa Fe to HHS Committee hearings from his home in distant Mesilla. But it was only getting worse. Now the pleas were coming from medical providers who were being paid less. Many of them were closing down their operations, leaving more children and others without medical services.

That was not the only thing that Taylor and the Democrats were worried about. A related matter—welfare reform—pushed legislators onto the warpath. Taylor was the lead plaintiff in a lawsuit about Johnson's veto of the welfare-reform bill passed by the legislature in 1997. Johnson had vetoed the bill and enacted his own policy, "New Mexico Progress," which had stiffer work requirements and fewer allowances than the federal law championed by President Bill Clinton in 1996.

Taylor and other legislators challenged the constitutionality of a governor vetoing a bill passed by the majority of the legislature and then going on to establish an alternative of his own choosing. Coincidentally, the New Mexico Supreme Court heard the case as the HHS Committee met in Santa Fe, and Chairman Taylor recessed the committee so we could watch the proceedings. Both Republicans and Democrats squeezed into the small courtroom to hear arguments. Things were so tight that I had to sit on Taylor's lap. But not for long. The justices heard brief arguments, and then told the audience to wait outside the courtroom as they deliberated. Coming back after about twenty minutes, the justices struck down the administrative program. A few months later, when the governor did not heed the court's decision, it held him in contempt, and the administration reluctantly gave up its plan.

$\backsim$

Republican resistance during this period also crumbled in the face of two other reforms. The Patient Protection Act (1998) and a bill requiring mental health parity (2000) were huge victories for health-care advocates, the medical community, and legislators.

Basically a patient's bill of rights, the Patient Protection Act was aimed at curbing the excesses of HMOs. From constituents, we had heard complaints about not being able to choose your own doctor, multiple referrals, long wait times, and denials of care—even for emergency services. From doctors, we had heard outrage about bean counters making medical decisions on treatment and complaints about declining reimbursements.

After the high salaries of HMO executives were made public and the Medicaid program began contracting with HMOs, the protests became louder. My phone began ringing and sometimes constituents appeared on my front porch. The practice of medicine was being fundamentally changed, the docs said, as incentives encouraged them to reduce care and, sometimes, even kept them from telling patients with serious diseases what their real options were.

The New Mexico Human Needs Coordinating Council, Health Action New Mexico, the New Mexico Medical Society, the New Mexico Nurses Association, New Mexico Protection and Advocacy, the Senior Citizens Law Office, and the AARP were but a few of the groups that brought tales of woe into the halls of the Roundhouse. The New Mexico Medical Association ran a large ad supporting the act, and more than four thousand letters and petitions poured in to both the governor and legislators.

It had become "profit before people," some charged, and the Democratic leadership agreed. Rep. Ed Sandoval had obtained the support of Speaker Raymond Sanchez and Pro Tem Manny Aragon, and he pressed the case in spite of his own persistent health problems.

On the other side of the issue were some of the most skilled lobbyists and the biggest contributors to both Democrats and Republicans: the health-care industry. Between 1997 (when the Patient Protection bill first passed) and 2006, the health-care industry's contributions accounted for 41 percent of total industry contributions to state officials. The state's largest HMO, Presbyterian Health Care, contributed $256,000, a large amount for that time.[1] Gary Johnson and most Republicans were initially allied with the industry, but as public opposition mounted, their support began to waver.

The Patient Protection Act provided certain rights: the right to a simple explanation of the benefits of the policy and disclosure of administrative costs so patients could compare policies. It also required timely services, an adequate provider network, no prior authorizations for emergencies, and clear grievance procedures. For providers, gag orders were outlawed, as were incentives for withholding care.

During the years-long process, Sandoval and other legislators had negotiated with the HMOs and addressed most of their concerns, especially language spelling out patients' rights to sue insurance companies—then a hot-button item in the Texas legislature's debate on the same issue. "We've long realized it doesn't do us any good if the HMOs don't support it," Sandoval told one Albuquerque newspaper. "Without their support, it won't have any chance of passing."[2]

In 1997, the measure, HB 350, passed the House 40–28 and the Senate 29–1. Shortly thereafter, at the behest of the insurance companies, the governor vetoed it. But in 1998, HB 361, a stripped-down version of the previous bill, passed the legislature (House 50–12 and Senate 23–8) and was signed by the governor with only a partial veto.

As we celebrated our victory, we realized that our persistence had paid off, and we had won converts from inside the administration—Health Secretary Alex Valdez, Medical Director Norty Kalishman, and Medicaid Director Chuck Milligan, all of whom had encouraged the veto-prone governor to sheath his pen. Insurance Superintendent Chris Krahling was especially instrumental in bringing the parties together, and the PRC's Division of Insurance would become more and more important in health care reform as time went by.

Health-care advocates knew that there was another problem that demanded immediate attention: the lack of adequate treatment and insurance for "the folks" with mental illness. Medicaid managed care was not helping. Fewer treatment dollars were making their way down to patients through a hierarchy of insurance companies and providers. Residential treatment programs were closing as a result of reduced and late payments. The state was rapidly losing psychiatrists and psychologists unwilling to work under the new regime. Since few treatment programs survived, children were placed in jails. Congresswoman Heather Wilson, Sen. Jeff Bingaman, and, especially, Sen. Pete Domenici were asked to intervene by desperate parents, providers, and judges.

Sandoval had long been an advocate of what the National Association for the Mentally Ill (NAMI) called "parity," or equal treatment of mental and other biological illnesses for insurance purposes. The discrimination against people with biologically-based conditions like schizophrenia, depression, and bipolar disorder were part of the stigma society placed on these folks, Sandoval said, and these folks deserve equal treatment.

Sandoval's mental health bills became as regular as his Saturday morning radio show, which featured local Hispanic music along with dedications to many of the ordinary "folks" he was concerned about. Unlike a number of other legislators, Sandoval did not have a family connection to the issue, but he was touched by the stories of advocates like Mabel Frary, of La Luz, NM, whose daughter was bipolar.

When Sandoval's bill was introduced for the fifth time in 2000, just when legislators thought they had heard it all, Sen. Pete Domenici—who had a family member with mental illness—addressed the legislature. He urged us to pass a parity bill like the one he was sponsoring with Sen. Paul Wellstone in the U.S. Senate—and we did.

The fifth time was the charm. The governor who had vetoed the bill in 1998 and 1999 signed it into law in March of 2000 after it passed unanimously in both houses. Republican Rep. Rob Burpo, of Albuquerque, had helped, co-sponsoring the bill and giving it a bipartisan flavor.

It would be eight more years before a strong mental-health parity bill passed the U.S. Congress. And a true patient protection act never made it at the national level until 2009, when it was incorporated into the Affordable Care Act.

But the holy grail of health care reform was still out there buried on the mesa somewhere—the one that would reduce health-care inequality and allow greater access through a system of insurance coverage for all New Mexicans. That would take a really big bill. One state—Massachusetts—had already taken the leap, and legislatures in Maine, Vermont, California, and Minnesota were taking a stab at it. New Mexico had nothing to lose but its escalating health-care costs and growing number of uninsured. It was time to go for it.

THE BIG SOLUTION

February 2008. Rep. John Heaton arrived at the Senate lounge early, ready to make his pitch for Gov. Bill Richardson's sweeping Health Solutions plan. Deep in the bowels of the Roundhouse, the Senate lounge, with its warm wood paneling, its couches, and its big screen TV, is a welcoming place where senators gather to take a break from floor debate or to chat about New Mexico sports.

But as the Senate Democrats gathered in caucus that day in 2008, the atmosphere was far from welcoming. An articulate and conservative Democrat from the far southeast corner of the state, John Heaton was well respected when it came to health care. A former pharmacist, Heaton had been an active player in health-care debates for ten years, often doing battle against HMOs and pharmaceutical companies who were shortchanging both the state and consumers. During this legislative session he had joined forces with Gov. Bill Richardson to expand insurance coverage to the roughly 400,000 New Mexicans without it. The bill he sponsored had just passed the House and now was in the hands of the senators.

"If we don't do something big like this, in the next five years we will continue to have another $1 billion increase in health-care costs," Heaton told the senators.

As Heaton explained the bill, which included many of the features later incorporated into the federal Patient Protection and Affordable Care Act in 2010, the senators sat patiently. More than a few had participated in the twenty-three-member task force that had studied the New Mexico situation for the previous nine months, hiring a D.C. consultant, Mathematica Policy Research, to price various coverage models. Others had met in a smaller bipartisan caucus to hammer out a compromise.

The need for a change was well known. The system was broken. New Mexico had the second highest percentage of people without health insurance in the country. Over the previous ten years, health-care premiums had doubled—with New Mexicans who did carry insurance paying the highest percentage of their income for it of any Americans.[3]

In 2008, reforming the unsustainable health-care system was a hot topic on the presidential campaign trail, from which Bill Richardson had just returned—empty-handed.

"We're already spending over $6 billion a year for health care in New Mexico, and leaving 430,000 New Mexicans without coverage," explained Heaton, looking around the room and trying not to reveal the impatience he often felt with those who knew so much less than he did. "For about the same amount we could cover everyone. There is enough money in the system—it's just that it's mal-distributed."

Sen. John Arthur Smith of Deming, the conservative chair of the Senate Finance Committee, was not convinced. He doubted the administration's $72 million figure on how much it would cost the state's general fund over five years and was amazed at the huge downward revision in the cost estimate made just before the session opened in mid-January. It might just have been a computer error, but it certainly didn't sit well with Smith, or with President Pro Tem Tim Jennings, both already angry at the administration for what they considered Richardson's presidential grandstanding.

Here's how it works, explained Heaton. Everyone in the state would be required to show they have insurance, with employers of six or more full-time workers required to offer it. Tax credits would help employers, but those who didn't provide insurance would pay a small amount into a state fund.

"You mean I would have to pay for health insurance for my waitresses?" asked Sen. Mary Jane Garcia, who, with her sisters, operated a bar outside of Las Cruces. Heaton replied that yes, she would have to either provide insurance or pay a small amount into a state fund, which didn't please Garcia, an otherwise avid supporter of all things Bill Richardson.

The plan would also expand the state's public programs, including Medicaid, to cover more low-income people and establish a health-care authority to help control health-care costs. Insurance reforms would be instituted to provide "guaranteed issue" (i.e., guaranteed coverage) for people with pre-existing conditions. "We've been negotiating 'a medical loss ratio' with the companies to ensure that 85 percent of premiums are spent on direct services and only 15 percent on administration and profit," Heaton continued.

As Heaton got into the details, heads began to nod—not in agreement but in slumber. The plush couches were just too comfortable for some senators, who, once lost in the details of any proposal, were difficult to revive. Those who remained awake were working on their Blackberries or leaving and reentering the room, preoccupied with other business.

I'm not sure exactly where he lost them, but it may have been with "guaranteed issue," a wildly popular policy (if explained in plain English) because it prevents insurance companies from discriminating against people with preexisting conditions—like cancer or allergies. A medical loss ratio? Community rating? What was this strange language, Sanskrit?

I sympathized with Heaton's difficulty in explaining the complicated recipe for reform—I had experienced the same kind of response a few years earlier in 2003 when I tried to explain a recipe to modernize the Medicaid program (the federal-state safety net for low-income children, the disabled, and elderly) in the face of a budget crunch. But Medicaid was only part of the ninety-six-page administration proposal for universal coverage that was the product of a huge task force composed of insurance companies, hospitals, doctors, laborers, consumers, and legislators. The Richardson administration often used task forces to create consensus around difficult but important issues. This one was the mother of all task forces. Chaired by Lt. Gov. Diane Denish and guided by Human Services Department (HSD) secretary Pam Hyde, a sharp, hard-driving health policy expert who was not used to losing, it had come to agreement on an amazing number of recommendations that had been kicking around state government for over a decade. These included the creation of a health-care authority to implement reforms and the creation of large insurance pools to bring down premiums. Everyone agreed that the state should expand Medicaid in order to maximize the handsome match from the federal government, since the federal government paid more than $70 of every $100 the state spent on the program (one of the highest matching rates in the country).

The recommendations built on the work of two other task forces set up by the administration starting in 2003 to build consensus on the tough issue. One of them, Insure New Mexico, also chaired by Denish, had successfully moved a number of reforms through previous sessions to increase the number of citizens with health insurance. These included allowing young adults to remain on their parents' insurance policies (which later became a provision of federal health reform) and strengthening two state programs to help employers cover more employees—the Health Insurance Alliance and the State Coverage Initiative. The administration also used executive orders to require state contractors to cover their employees. Health care reform was clearly a key policy objective of the governor, and the administration was creating pathways to broader coverage.

Richardson had a good relationship with the business community, particularly the Albuquerque Chamber of Commerce. He had come through with something on the chamber's wish list for years—a personal income tax reduction. His health-care team, spearheaded by chief advisor Michelle Welby, a veteran of the insurance sector, encouraged both businesses and private insurance companies to join in the reform effort and, for the most part, they did.

"Richardson used a lot of political capital on health care reform," recalls RubyAnn Esquibel, then a point person for the Human Services Department on the effort and now a staffer for the Legislative Finance Committee. "He got little in return. The major beneficiaries—sick and working people who can't afford insurance—provided little overt support, and often don't even vote." Yet each member of what Esquibel calls the "health industrial complex" had something to lose. As time went on, Esquibel recalls, the complex issue became tougher to advance. Although members of the health-care team went to great pains to include every stakeholder and to provide data on each alternative, the honeymoon between the legislature and the governor, now in office for five years, was ending.

REFORM TAKES A DETOUR INTO
PRESIDENTIAL AND PERSONAL POLITICS

The task force had formulated the plan in 2007, when Richardson was hot on the presidential campaign trail, boasting of being a bold, tax-cutting governor who was reducing driving while intoxicated (DWI), building a railroad, and launching a spaceport. His health plan for New Mexico was similar to the one enacted in Massachusetts a year earlier by Gov. Mitt Romney, and it was in sync with those of the other candidates, particularly Barak Obama and Hillary Clinton.

But legislators of both parties began to think the governor's big agenda that year was motivated only by his national ambitions. Throughout 2007 Richardson had been deep into fundraising for his presidential bid, operating several PACs and cashing in on two decades of service as a congressman from northern New Mexico, a UN ambassador, and a cabinet secretary under President Bill Clinton.

Richardson was easily the most formidable fundraiser in state history. He had amassed $21 million in his two races for governor. An additional $4 million had been donated to the two political committees he controlled (Moving America Forward and Sí Se Puede). He had raised $24 million in 2007–2008.[4] At the end of 2007 he began calling in favors from staff and fellow officeholders to join the campaign on the ground in Iowa and New Hampshire. He was out of the state even more often than when he chaired the Democratic Governors' Association two years before.

Tom Horan, chief lobbyist for Presbyterian Health Care Services, the state's largest HMO, and Richardson Health Advisor Michelle Welby joined his presidential campaign in Iowa during the bitterly cold month of December 2007, going door-to-door on Richardson's behalf. Rachel O'Conner, the governor's DWI czar, recruited her family to go with her to Iowa, and members of the environmental community, with whom Richardson was particularly close, formed part of his "ground troops."

Members of the health-care sector had always been big financial supporters of the governor, who they knew had big ideas—which just might include them. Reported contributions from the health sector for his two governor's races totaled $710,182,[5] and there was additional cash for his presidential bid in 2007. The company managing the state's newly reorganized behavioral health-care system, Value Options, contributed $50,000 to Richardson's 2006 reelection campaign; Lovelace/Ardent, one of the state's Medicaid contractors, gave $71,250. Evercare (United Healthcare) and AmeriGroup, two other national insurance companies who were selected to run a program serving seniors and people with disabilities, called COLTS, contributed substantially as well.[6]

Hard-pressed legislators were resentful that Richardson was sucking up so much of the campaign cash in 2007–2008, when the entire body was up for reelection.[7] It seemed to them that Richardson was using his position to give his friends contracts and to reward close associates.

Richardson still had a key ally in House Speaker Ben Lujan, but Sen. Tim Jennings was becoming an avowed enemy owing to Richardson's run-in with the senator's wife, Patty, over a pharmaceutical bill that would give a better deal to members of the state's high risk pool, which Mrs. Jennings had long administered. Jennings had taken to the floor many times to rail against the governor's profane and bullying tactics, which a shocked Patty Jennings had witnessed up close in a strategy meeting in the governor's office. Criticism of Richardson resonated with Republicans and conservative Democrats like Mary Kay Papen and John Arthur Smith. Now there were rumors of a new scandal.

In the previous two years, the state treasurer's office and the legislature itself had been rocked by political scandals, but the governor's office had remained out of the courts. True, Guy Riordan, a chief fundraiser and friend of Richardson, had been banned from the securities industry by the U.S. Securities and Exchange Commission (SEC) and fined $1.5 million for paying kickbacks to a previous treasurer, Michael Montoya. But now there was talk of a grand jury examining a larger scandal involving a key administration accomplishment, modestly called GRIP—Governor Richardson's

Improvement Program. Smith and Jennings had harbored doubts about the huge ($1.6 billion) municipal bonding program all along, and they were now horrified by the rumor that CDR Financial Products, contributors to the governor's presidential campaign, got contracts to advise New Mexico agencies on how to structure the bonds. The rumors were true. The media later reported that CDR's president, David Rubin, had given $110,000 to two of the governor's PACs.[8]

REFORMERS FACE CHALLENGES
FROM THE LEFT AND THE RIGHT

While the Democrats were sniping at Richardson, Republicans were stead fastly opposed to the Health Solutions Plan. Thanks to Speaker Ben Lujan, Heaton's bill had passed the House on a largely party line vote of 37 to 31. Republican opposition in the House foreshadowed later Republican opposition to Obama's Affordable Care Act. For House members like Keith Gardner, who would later become Gov. Susana Martinez's health-care advisor, the plan might as well have been called RichardsonCare. Republican legislators felt that their power was being usurped by the creation of a health-care authority to plan and control costs, which was stacked with the governor's appointees.

"Governor Richardson's version of the health-care bill basically enabled the governor to run the health-care business in New Mexico without the legislature," Rep. Paul Bandy, a Republican from San Juan County, told the *Albuquerque Journal* in February 2008. "The health-care authority will control the practice of medicine and reimbursements, under the control of the governor," Sen. Steven Komadina, a Republican doctor from Corrales, chimed in.[9] The opposition of Komadina and other senators was more virulent than Bandy's, shaped by an almost religious opposition to a single-payer health system that would create a centrally controlled system like Medicare.

The fact that the health care reform proposal now on the table was *not* a single payer system—but one based on private insurance and supported by a good portion of the business community—didn't seem to matter to the Republicans, who continued to muddle the issue and raise endless questions. Changing the composition of the health-care authority to include more legislative appointments didn't seem to matter to them.

As Heaton and the administration patiently answered their questions they were attacked from the left (see fig. 26). Mary Feldblum, the leading proponent of the New Mexico Health Security Act, which much more closely resembled an actual single-payer system, was hard at work on the Democrats. Members of her campaign testified at every committee and task force meeting. They corralled legislators during the summer and asked for commitments. A statewide coalition, Health Security for New Mexicans, had originated in the early 1990s, when Santa Fe Representatives Lucky Varela and Max Coll initially sponsored "NewMexicare." The previous year's task force, the Health Coverage for New Mexicans Committee, had analyzed the costs of various coverage systems and deemed the Health Security plan the least expensive. Although their plan was not recommended by the task force—and had been turned down repeatedly by the legislature—the group was pressing forward with its own bill, sponsored by Sen. Carlos Cisneros and Rep. Bobby Gonzales, both of Taos. For senators like Carroll Leavell, an insurance agent from Jal, and Sue Beffort, a longtime opponent of reform, the smell of socialism was everywhere.

The insurance companies themselves were supporting Richardson's Health Solutions plan, which actually enhanced their role, unlike the rival Health Security plan, which essentially eliminated them. But some of the insurance companies were hedging their bets. Blue Cross worked behind the scenes with the Restaurant Association, the Association of Commerce and Industry (ACI), and the Federation of Independent Businesses to defeat both plans.

Some of us on the Health and Human Services Committee, charged with vetting the proposals, saw the impasse coming and suggested a compromise. Rep. Danice Picraux and I each carried a stripped-down plan for an independent health-care authority, accountable to both the executive and legislative branches. The authority would be charged with developing a comprehensive financing plan, reorganizing public programs, cutting costs, and taking advantage of bulk-purchasing opportunities. Its membership would be carefully balanced but tilted toward the business community—the purchasers of insurance. Going into the session, the idea enjoyed widespread support from the New Mexico Medical Society and health-care advocates, who were themselves divided over whether the state should adopt a single-payer plan or the governor's.

But the administration wanted no bills to compete with the plan spearheaded by HSD secretary Pam Hyde, who was becoming more aggressive by the minute. The governor had made plain that he would veto any single-payer approach. When I pre-filed the health authority bill endorsed by the Health and Human Services Committee, the governor blew a gasket. One of his young staffers called me to say that he was withdrawing his support for my other bills and reassigning sponsorship of some of the alternative energy bills I was carrying for the administration. I tried to explain that this was a back-up plan in case the broader bill failed, but then the staffer burst into tears. The pressure she felt from the governor was just too much. My pragmatic style did not fit with his take-no-prisoners approach.

HEALTH REFORM FIZZLES

By February 7, with less than a week to go in the short session, both Heaton's bill and the alternative, establishing a health-care authority, were in the hands of the Senate. Compromises had been made along the way, and each bill had been rewritten to garner the votes to pass. Both easily cleared the committee I chaired, the Senate Public Affairs Committee, and with some significant concessions (the mandate had been removed in the House) the momentum was building. To fire up the senators, the administration, as it did for all its high priorities, had fielded a full court press, using almost every cabinet secretary, staffer, or surrogate who was friendly to individual legislators to keep track of them day and night—and make sure they voted for the bill.

But then came the final step—the Senate Finance Committee, chaired by Sen. John Arthur Smith and peopled by staunch opponents Sen. Sue Beffort and Sen. Carol Leavell, whom many regarded as an expert on insurance matters. Pressure from the advocates and the administration was mounting to either hear the bill in committee or move it directly to the floor to allow discussion and a vote. But Smith would not be moved. He never gave the governor's bill a hearing, and somehow Representative Picraux's health authority did not get a hearing either, although my bill for the same thing had passed the committee a week or so earlier. The roadblock was absolute.

I was frustrated and angry. By my reckoning, at least one of the bills could have gotten out of that committee had Smith allowed a vote. Years of consensus building, efforts by the New Mexico Medical Society, the Health and Human Services Committee, and other stakeholders—not just the administration—were going down the drain.

The next day, only hours from adjournment, I did what the Democratic leadership considers to be a cardinal sin—I tried to "blast" Representative Picraux's health-authority bill out of the committee and bring it to the floor for a vote. It had become apparent that it was a chip in the poker game between the Senate and the governor. "What's more important," I asked the senators as I made a motion to do so, "preserving the power of the Senate or providing health insurance for over 400,000 New Mexicans currently without it?"

Sen. Leonard Rawson immediately jumped to his feet and requested a Call of the Senate, a procedural move that, if backed by seven other senators, requires every senator to be present in the chambers for the debate and vote on the bill. Seven Republicans quickly raised their hands.

In the midst of the excitement, Majority Leader Michael Sanchez moved for a recess until the following morning, and the senators, weary from the end-of-session overload, quickly obliged, knowing that they would no longer have to deal with this difficult issue.

Immediately after the session adjourned on February 14, Richardson blasted the Senate in a capitol news conference as guilty of "theatrics and gridlock." "Unfortunately, a handful of senators, including certain members of the Senate leadership and the Senate Finance Committee," he said, "were more interested in regaining power they feel they have lost to me than working for what's best for New Mexicans. The result was no effective leadership in the Senate."[10]

Richardson said he would call a special session to deal with health care reform. A month later, in March, the senators felt the full impact of his wrath. The governor used his veto pen on the $348 million capital outlay bill to eliminate $7 million in projects for senators. No House members' projects were touched. Among the biggest losers were Sen. Leonard Rawson of Las Cruces, with $508,000 vetoed; Sen. John Arthur Smith, with a $500,000 renovation project in Deming vetoed; Sen. Sue Beffort, with a $450,000 middle-school track vetoed; and Sen. Tim Jennings, who lost $300,000 in capital outlay for projects in Chaves County.

Not surprisingly, when the special session was held in the fall, the gridlock continued. Senator Smith unearthed a new reason to distrust the governor and derail a scaled-down plan the administration had introduced. David Abbey, the director of the Legislative Finance Committee, which Smith chaired, appeared on the floor of the Senate with a letter charging the Human Services Department with withholding information from the Legislative Finance Committee on the state's Medicaid contracts. The secrecy was a pattern, he and Smith contended, and they were going to request an attorney general's opinion on whether it was unconstitutional. This and a negative analysis of the governor's health-care proposal, which was then carried by Sen. Mary Jane Garcia, was enough to make the senators strip down the bill even further, removing limits on the ability of insurance companies to turn down people with preexisting conditions and raise the rates on those who are sick, both key provisions. What remained was simply a Medicaid expansion to some additional children. Gone was the chance to

consolidate public employee benefits or create a central health-care authority. Another lost opportunity for health care reform.

As usual, I wondered what more I could have said or done to push the
issue over the finish line. Expanding access to affordable health care was
front and center during the presidential campaign, and I repeatedly shared
with the Democratic caucus polling data showing popular support. But the
issue was so complex that it was an ideal target for special interests, which are
most effective in killing (rather than passing) bills, especially during short
sessions. Senator Smith's blocking action had worked. Many of my colleagues threw up their hands, concluding that only the federal government
could address this complex issue. With so many pieces to the health puzzle,
and so little time, citizen legislators decided to do nothing, a dangerous default position given the skyrocketing cost of health care and New Mexico's
huge proportion of uninsured citizens.

I wondered whether Sen. Ben Altamirano's untimely death in December 2007 made a difference. Loved by both Bill Richardson and the Senate
as both the pro tem and the chair of Senate Finance, "Bennie," as he was
called, had brought the two branches together to pass some big items. Now
he was gone and, absent a united leadership, gridlock ensued. The status quo
remained the default position for a few more years.

"The hard issues, the big packages, they just don't work in a legislature
resistant to change," concluded Ruth Hoffman, a longtime health and human services lobbyist for the Lutheran Advocacy Ministry-New Mexico.
"We do things piecemeal."

MAGIC MOMENTS PAVED THE WAY

Why did the early reforms succeed while this one failed, even when the
same party controlled both the Roundhouse and the governor's mansion?
There's not one simple explanation for the successes of the 1990s and early
2000s. But a certain combination of key ingredients came into play. Personality, perseverance, party discipline, division among special interests
and opponents, a willingness to compromise, trained citizen advocates, and
good timing were all factors in one way or another. Other chapters illustrate how each of these factors figured in the defeat or passage of hot-button
issues like medical marijuana, tobacco, gun control, and a ban on the
death penalty.

The Patient Protection Act, which was debated for two years before its
passage, came at a time of great public discontent with managed care—a

discontent that affected providers (a major part of the health-care industry) as well as consumers. Although the governor was initially opposed, and the HMO lobby was strong, public pressure was intense. Proponents of the act were willing to compromise, and the industry was divided between the doctors and the insurance companies. The Democrats were united against the governor, with Pro Tem Manny Aragon and Speaker Raymond Sanchez active participants in pushing the issue. The time was ripe.

The National Association for the Mentally Ill and the families of people with mental illness mobilized, using personal stories to move legislators beyond the economic interests of insurance companies to pass the parity bill in 2000—after four or five unsuccessful tries. The influence of Sen. Pete Domenici, and his personal story that he shared with the entire legislature, the media, and then the reluctant governor, was crucial.

By and large, Republicans in the Senate (some of whom had a personal stake in the issue) voted for both bills, spurred by a spirit of compassion and compromise. They were influenced by advocates for the mentally ill, who used the tactics that had worked for the disability community in the previous decade. For years, the Albuquerque Retarded Citizens Association, Parents Reaching Out, and New Mexico Protection and Advocacy (now called Disability Rights New Mexico) had invested in training programs to teach people with disabilities how to become spokespersons. Photos and portraits of kids, grandkids, and real people with disabilities affected by the expansion or elimination of Medicaid or special education programs began appearing regularly on legislators' desks in the 1980s. Visits from families in their home districts and in Santa Fe became common. Sens. Manny Aragon, Joe Carraro, and others highlighted the presence of people with disabilities with introductions and testimony on the floor of the Senate. The results of these efforts included two landmark programs: one serving medically fragile children, the other funding early special education for three- and four-year-olds with developmental disabilities.

"Never underestimate the power of a compelling story," says longtime disability lobbyist Jim Jackson, of Disability Rights New Mexico, "and a personal connection."

Jackson says that it only takes a few legislators with skin in the game—family members with disabilities or mental illness—to make a big impact. Oft-repeated stories from the families of Sen. Tim Jennings (whose daughter Courtney has Down's), Sen. Mary Kay Papen (whose grandson is mentally ill), Sen. Clint Harden (whose grandson has autism), Sen. Rod Adair (whose son is disabled), or Sen. Kent Cravens (whose family was decimated by a drunk-driving accident), shattered the partisan divide. And, when it came to medical marijuana, Erin Armstrong made the difference; for the death penalty, it was the former death-row inmates.

The failure of some the larger health reforms later cannot be explained by the absence of some of these factors. Trained advocates had plenty of stories of people without insurance showing up at the emergency room. There was evidence aplenty of death and disease resulting from the lack of access to affordable health care. There was division within the industry, with some insurance companies and businesses supporting and some opposed. Many of the measures in the Health Solutions bill had been proposed before. Polling data showed overwhelming public support.

But the oversized Health Solutions bill was a big target, caught in the crosswinds between Senate leaders and the governor. The personalities and the hot air in the Senate in 2008 snuffed out the state's best chance in decades for overall health care reform. Presidential politics, Richardson's declining popularity and perceived (but unproved) corruption were major factors.

"There are certain magic moments, when the stars are aligned and openings allow big bills to pass," says Ellen Pinnes, a lobbyist who has worked for Health Action New Mexico and the Disability Coalition. For overall health care, 2008 was not one of the magic moments.

PICKING UP THE PIECES,
MOVING FORWARD INCREMENTALLY

In the years following the defeat of comprehensive health reform, reformers were able to squeeze a few measures through what San Antonio Mayor Henry Cisneros called "that tiny sliver of daylight in the wall of obstruction thrown up against change."[11] A "medical loss ratio" bill, limiting the amount that health insurance companies could spend on administration and profit, narrowly passed in 2010. Sponsored by Representative Heaton, it had been part of Health Solutions. A ban on gender rating, which had allowed insurance companies to charge more to insure women, was also adopted in 2010. Santa Fe Sen. Nancy Rodriguez sponsored it. A bill mandating a "medical home" pilot program for patients to more effectively coordinate care was passed at the behest of the Health and Human Services Committee. With the help of now congressman Ben Ray Lujan, Public Regulation Commissioner Jason Marks, and Insurance Superintendent Mo Chavez, I successfully sponsored a measure making it more difficult for insurance companies to rescind insurance policies for minor errors in application after someone got sick. In 2011, I was also successful in passing Senate Bill 208 to require more transparency and rigor in health insurance rate reviews by the PRC's insurance division. It was an important bill that required public justification of rate hikes, and the new governor, Susana Martinez, signed it.

Health-care advocates within and outside of the legislature have been persistent (see fig. 27). And, while not always successful in the way they hoped, Sen. Jeff Bingaman and others who had a hand in health care at the federal level were watching from afar. The Patient Protection and Affordable Care Act, signed into law in March 2010, incorporated almost all the piecemeal reforms New Mexico had made—and more. Poor, remote, and easily overlooked, New Mexico, again, had been a key laboratory for democracy.

CHAPTER 10

Patients, Mavericks, and Heroes

Behind the Smokescreen in the Legislative Drug Wars

All great truths begin as blasphemies.

—GEORGE BERNARD SHAW

T HIS TALE OF HOW THE NEW MEXICO LEGISLATURE OVERCAME
its conservative law-and-order mentality to legalize the use of medical
marijuana in 2007 is a chapter not only in this book but in a larger, unfinished story about the nation's changing attitudes toward marijuana and other
drugs. Drug policy—and the question of whether drug abuse should be
treated as a disease or a crime—has always been what pundits call a "third
rail" in politics, guaranteed to electrocute those who touch it. No other issue
reveals the great divide between those who are fearful of the murder and
mayhem drugs may unleash and those who want a more humane approach to
drug addiction, which they insist is an illness.

The great divide usually, but not always, runs along party lines. In New
Mexico the backdrop is striking. For almost twenty years the state has been at
the top of every national list for illicit drug abuse, and it now leads the nation in deaths from drug overdoses. The New Mexico Department of Health
(DOH) estimates as many as 200,000 abusers. Treatment programs are
scarce, and New Mexico spends less than all other states to address the problem.[1] The federal War on Drugs has filled the prisons but has not found a
solution to the ongoing epidemic.

But in the New Mexico legislature a group of determined reformers built a
bridge across the divide when it came to one drug issue, medical marijuana.
They built it with courage and with personal stories that allowed legislators of
both parties to see drugs in the broader context of treatment and illness, not

punishment and incarceration. There were many attempts to blow up the bridge. Opponents of the controversial change were even more vitriolic than those who successfully opposed health care reform in 2008. Partisan politics and federal drug laws have made bridge building difficult—but as other states begin to take action to legalize marijuana and enact broader reforms, New Mexico's early action is significant. But it could not have been done without the help of a few mavericks and heroes behind the scenes at the Roundhouse.

April 2007. The White House drug czar was aghast. He had warned Gov. Bill Richardson not to sign the long-debated bill legalizing the use of medical marijuana—and now the irrepressible Democrat was doing it. With a stroke of Richardson's pen, on April 3, 2007, New Mexico became the twelfth state to legalize medical marijuana and create a state program whereby patients could, under controlled conditions, use marijuana to relieve nausea, pain, and other side effects of chemotherapy and chronic conditions.

Czar John Walters, chief of the Office of National Drug Policy Control within the White House, had testified in legislative committees and visited the state to publicize anti-drug campaigns. Now he called the governor's signing "disappointing" and "irresponsible."[2] Walters said it was a political move (Richardson was then a candidate for president) that would garner him campaign contributions from the likes of Democratic philanthropist George Soros and the national Drug Policy Alliance, but would make New Mexico's problem of illegal drug use even worse and undermine the anti-drug message to youngsters.

But for patients like Erin Armstrong and Essie DeBonet, who for six years had suffered nausea and lost weight as they waited endlessly to testify before legislative committees, it was a day like no other. Now they were gathered around the huge travertine table in the governor's office as he handed out the red pens with which he signed bills. Crowded around with them were their legislative sponsors, public health advocates who had advocated this new approach of "harm reduction," and the local director of the Drug Policy Alliance (DPA), Reena Szczepanski.

"I hope that other elected officials take note," said Szczepanski. "Americans will stand behind those that believe in compassion and mercy for our most vulnerable, our sick and dying patients, struggling for relief."[3] The gratification of the dark-haired young woman, who had shepherded her flock of patients and spearheaded four separate bills through the process over the years, was nothing compared to the rush of relief that that the advocates felt upon the bill's tortured passage the previous month.

Essie DeBonet, a woman living with AIDS whose weight had shrunk to seventy-eight pounds during the legislative struggle, told the media, "For me medical marijuana is a matter of life and death. Today I can proudly say that my legislators showed compassion and took a stand to protect the sick and dying." Essie had so often been disappointed by the legislature that she could hardly believe it. And neither, at the time, could Reena. "I was shaking," she recalled, "and so tearful. My belief in the humanity of people and the legislature had been restored."

For Richardson, who had used his political muscle to win House votes late in the game, it was no big deal. Yes, it could be unpopular with law enforcement, but the program, after all, applied only to a few people for medical purposes. "My God, let's be reasonable," he had said earlier in the year.[4] Now he clarified, once more, that he did not support legalizing marijuana, but he did believe in alleviating suffering. "It's a humane piece of legislation . . . and, I must tell you, I was overcome by the personal stories of pain and the personal appeals I got."[5]

Richardson was no different from most legislators who, in the main, will respond to personal stories and repeated pleas for compassion, especially when the price tag is small. Medical marijuana was fairly small potatoes that year, one of many controversial bills the governor signed, including a ban on cockfighting and the Dee Johnson Clean Air Act. He was ready to move on to other issues he was trying to pass—domestic partnerships and ethics legislation, among others.

As legislators moved on to these issues, the DOH, which had championed medical marijuana since 2000, prepared to implement the new law. It was no easy task, since the possession, growth, or distribution of marijuana is illegal under federal law. But the New Mexico program was designed to be the most tightly regulated program in the country. Here's how it works. Patients with serious illnesses like cancer, HIV/AIDS, multiple sclerosis, epilepsy, spinal cord injuries, post-traumatic stress disorder, or those in hospice care can get a recommendation from their doctors and apply to the department to become a registered patient. The department considers each application and issues cards to those it approves. Only a small amount of marijuana is permitted (six ounces) over a three-month period; registrations must be renewed annually. In a feature that sets New Mexico apart from the eighteen other states and the District of Columbia, which now have similar programs, the department licenses producers, and patients obtain their medicine through a system of couriers and producers who have physical offices for pickup. There are no dispensaries or storefront outlets. Patients cannot use the drug in public places, school grounds, workplaces, or while driving. The usual penalties apply for trafficking or distribution of the drug.

Five years after the program began, there are over eight thousand certified patients and twenty-three active producers, according to Emily Kaltenbach, the current New Mexico state director of the Drug Policy Alliance. Repeatedly challenged by administrative obstacles, the program has survived—and thrived, says Sen. Cisco McSorley, who passed a bill to create a fund to provide funding for it in 2012. Now cited by many as a model for the country, the program has become less and less controversial over the years, says Kaltenbach. But the path to allow patients this new option was littered with political obstacles, and controversy was around every bend.

New Mexico's first brush with medical marijuana came in 1978, when twenty-six-year-old Vietnam veteran Lynn Pierson prowled the halls of the Roundhouse in search of relief from his intractable cancer pain. His haunted eyes and sad story brought together such ideological opposites as Republican Sen. John Irick from Albuquerque's Northeast Heights and Democratic Rep. David Salman from Mora to support—and pass—a bill setting up a research program at the University of New Mexico to test the effects of medical marijuana on cancer and glaucoma patients. The program lasted until 1986, when its funding ran out. Pierson didn't live long enough to be approved for treatment, but 250 others got relief.

In the decade that followed, New Mexico's drug policies were no longer focused on pain relief but on grappling with an epidemic of heroin and methamphetamine addiction in rural areas like Rio Arriba County. Drug addiction formed part of what the health department described in the late 1990s as the evil triad of substance-abuse problems, mental illness, and domestic violence, dragging the state down in almost every ranking. There were few treatment programs to take on the problems, which fed on one another. Criminal activity was spiking. In Albuquerque I was hearing about local gangs and heroin as I went door to door in 1996 campaigning for election to the Senate. The jails and prisons were so overcrowded that the courts ordered the state to build more prisons. The controversy then was not about drugs but about whether the prisons should be public or private.

Until 1999, that is, when an unlikely champion came out of nowhere. Well, not exactly nowhere. Gary Johnson had been in the governor's office since 1994, holding the line on state spending, vetoing one-third of all the bills the legislature sent him, and, above all, entertaining the state with his iron-man competitions, his marathon bicycle rides, and his relentless, competitive exercise routines. Now, shortly after he was reelected to a second term in 1998, the governor was suddenly everywhere, before the Taos Chamber of Commerce, the Albuquerque Rotarians, even the national TV show "Nightline," saying the unthinkable: the war on drugs was a miserable failure. Prohibition was not working. New Mexico and the nation were wasting millions of taxpayer dollars on attempts to imprison non-violent drug users who should be in treatment programs, not prisons. Marijuana, heroin, and cocaine should be legalized and regulated in a rational fashion. A whole series of reforms should shift policy from a criminal justice approach to a more medical model.

The blasphemy was quickly picked up by the state and national media and shockwaves began to shake the foundations of the New Mexico political establishment and the entire law enforcement community. Johnson's ultra-healthy lifestyle and libertarian philosophy took the whole debate in a different direction. Although Johnson said he had experimented with marijuana in college, everyone knew that the forty-six-year-old triathlete was a non-drinking, anti-tobacco health nut. Although he was always careful to say that drug use was a bad personal choice, that message was often lost in the eyes of university students, NORML (National Organization for the Reform of Marijuana Laws) members, and others who immediately jumped on the bandwagon.

What had happened? According to Joe Thompson, a former Albuquerque representative and Johnson aide who played a key role in the issue, Johnson had met with Ethan Nadelmann, founder of the Lindesmith Center, which, with the support of philanthropist George Soros, later became the Drug Policy Alliance. Johnson had conversations with Nadelmann, a Princeton professor who was writing about drug policy for periodicals like *Science*, *Foreign Affairs*, *American Heritage*, and the *National Review*. The governor brought back the ideas and sought input from his staff, the Department of Health and Republican officials.

Division and discord followed, with some admitting that this was an important issue that needed to be debated publicly and others believing it was a political liability *and* a wrongheaded policy. The leaders of the Republican Party—Chairman John Dendahl, National Committeeman Mickey Barnett, and Barnett's coterie of young Republican legislative recruits, including Reps. Thompson and Dan Foley—were on board. But other Republicans, among them Sen. Ramsay Gorham, Rep. Ron Godbey, Rep. Rob Burpo, Lt. Gov. Walter Bradley, and U.S. Sen. Pete Domenici, were not. Darren White, the governor's secretary of public safety, offered his resignation, which was accepted. "This was the biggest rift we ever had," recalled Joe Thompson, and it was growing. But Johnson plowed ahead, convening a Governor's Drug Policy

Advisory Group, hosting national drug policy forums in Albuquerque, and even challenging the then national drug czar Asa Hutchinson to a debate.

"My mantra is just say KNOW," Johnson told a drug policy forum in November of 1999 sponsored by the New Mexico Drug Policy Foundation. The debate was beginning. "Initially the governor didn't have a very sophisticated stance," recalls Thompson, "but we began to get a lot of advice." With the help of the New York–based Drug Policy Alliance, the Department of Health, and the newly formed Governor's Drug Policy Advisory Group, a coherent approach began to shape up.

The approach was based on some old public-health standbys: education, prevention, treatment, and something called "harm reduction," a pragmatic notion that it might be impossible to completely eliminate the sources of harm but that it was possible to prevent unnecessary death and disease. The advisory group added criminal justice reforms to the public health agenda, recommending that law enforcement focus on dangerous crimes like rape and murder rather than locking up nonviolent drug users (often women with children). The group's opening salvo was a recommendation that the state should restart a medical marijuana program based on "compassionate use" by eligible patients and decriminalize the possession of small amounts of marijuana. The Lindesmith Center opened a New Mexico office, directed by Katharine Huffman, and began grassroots organizing in preparation for the upcoming sixty-day session in 2001. To lobby the legislature, they hired former governor Toney Anaya to work the Democrats and former senator Mickey Barnett to work the Republicans. Dave Schmidt, an expert on children and the law, also became a lobbyist for DPA.

Over at the health department, Secretary Alex Valdez and Dr. Steve Jenison, who was with the New Mexico Infectious Disease Bureau, were already using the harm-reduction approach to prevent the spread of AIDS, reaching epidemic proportions in parts of the U.S. during the 1990s. A harm-reduction bill sponsored by Sen. Carlos Cisneros, of Questa, had passed the legislature in 1997, setting up a program of hypodermic-needle exchange. The program allowed addicts to exchange their dirty needles for sterile syringes without prosecution for drug paraphernalia. The counter-intuitive idea was that addicts would then be less likely to spread HIV or Hepatitis C. And when they exchanged their needles they could be steered into treatment programs. It was only a small jump from this approach to other public health measures, such as allowing the dispensing of Narcan (otherwise known as naloxone), a drug that can be used to stop heroin overdoses, in the same way that an "EpiPen" stops allergic reactions with an injection of epinephrine. Valdez also told the department's lawyer, Cliff Rees, to prepare a medical marijuana bill based on

Hawaii's and to get ready to usher it through the upcoming 2001 legislative session.

Democrats in the legislature were as perplexed as the Republicans. Many agreed with Johnson's position and were gratified that he had the courage to buck the trend and call for reform. But he had waited until after he was re-elected, they noted, which didn't exactly enhance his reputation for courage and sincerity. Twisting the accusation to justify his behavior, Johnson replied publicly that he was a living example of why term limits were a great idea. Later, he would say that even given his invulnerability he and his allies paid a huge political price. "I'm in the ground and the dirt is being thrown on top of me," he said.[6]

Sen. Cisco McSorley, who would soon become the Senate's champion on the issue, wondered how the governor's call for more treatment programs fit in with his well-known penchant for vetoing "excess" spending. In the years to come, McSorley, who was from one of the state's most liberal districts in Albuquerque's Nob Hill, would continually challenge the governor to put his money where his mouth was—and pour the millions into treatment programs.

Meanwhile, on the Republican side a bloodbath had commenced. Rep. Joe Thompson faced a primary challenge. Mickey Barnett was forced to choose between his GOP National Committee seat and his job as a lobbyist for the Center for Policy Reform, a group affiliated with the New York–based Lindesmith Center and the DPA. (He chose to maintain his committee seat, and another former Republican senator, Duncan Scott, became the lobbyist.) Rep. Ron Godbey took every opportunity to tell the public that the governor wanted to legalize heroin and cocaine and unleash unlimited drugs upon our children. Godbey (unsuccessfully) challenged Republican chair John Dendahl for his post on the drug issue in 2001. The party convention was hard fought. Dendahl opponents passed out pens shaped like hypodermic needles emblazoned with the slogan "Stick it to John." A few years later Godbey faced a primary challenger in his own district in the East Mountain area of Albuquerque—put up by the Republican drug reformers.

Godbey's rhetoric escalated even higher during the 2001 session when, after two years of crusading, the governor finally rolled out his drug-related bills. The package included decriminalizing the possession of small amounts of marijuana and legalizing its medical use. There were three harm-reduction measures as well. One bill allowed police officers to administer the antidote Narcan to reverse drug overdoses. Another allowed pharmacists to sell hypodermic needles without fear of criminal prosecution. Yet another appropriated $9.8 million for expanded drug treatment.

The $9.8 million was not the $40 million that Senator McSorley had asked for, but it was more than ever before. But for others the big package was too much, too soon.

In a rotunda rally, Godbey joined with Republican Sen. Ramsay Gorham, of Albuquerque; Rep. Martha Atkins, of Rio Rancho; and Sen. Shirley Bailey, of Hobbs. Before a backdrop of handmade posters reading "Just Say No," Godbey aimed his fire at the whole drug reform effort. "When out-of-state organizations spend hundreds of thousands of dollars to legalize marijuana in this little state, there's got to be something wrong."[7]

Godbey was brutal when Rep. Joe Thompson's Compassionate Use of Medical Marijuana bill came before the House Judiciary Committee, asking, "Does this [section of the bill] mean a patient using marijuana can go out and rape and pillage?"[8] He continued in the same fashion when Thompson presented the bill on the House floor. "I was so nervous, my hands were shaking," Thompson recalled. "Godbey tried to upset me, and he succeeded. I was not taking it well." But Godbey overplayed his hand, creating sympathy for the young representative, and House Bill 431 passed, 35–32. The Democrats had put it over the top. It was a huge surprise to almost everyone, especially since the Senate had already passed a similar bill, sponsored by Santa Fe Sen. Roman Maes—handily by a 29 to 12 margin.

When two nearly identical bills pass in each chamber, it's usually a foregone conclusion that, if time permits, one of them will survive. The very thought of the medical marijuana bill passing on the first try was driving the Republican opponents nuts. But they needn't have worried. The Democrats came to their rescue with stalling tactics that prevented either bill's passage. "Although they supported the bill, the powers that be in the Senate didn't want it to pass while Johnson could get credit," recalls Sen. Cisco McSorley.

Even though the key pieces of his package had failed, the governor said he was not "disheartened." Public support was growing, and a 2001 Research and Polling survey showed 81 percent of voters approved of a medical marijuana program for serious and terminally ill patients with cancer, MS, and AIDS. The governor would be back next year—and so would the opponents.

The following winter, as legislators considered Johnson's 2002 drug proposals and began to prepare for the fall elections, opponents unleashed a fury of radio ads in both Spanish and English on the state's most popular radio station, KOB-AM. The ads asked listeners to pressure lawmakers to reject the proposals to legalize marijuana, cocaine, and heroin and to send out-of-state drug reformers packing. A new group, Protect New Mexico, spearheaded by Albuquerque Sen. Ramsay Gorham, her husband Frank Gorham III (an oil and gas magnate), and former cabinet secretary Darren White sponsored the ads.

The radio campaign hinted that the legislature was trying to legalize heroin and that state employees would soon be harvesting marijuana. None of the proposals contained anything of the sort, the drug reformers countered in a new series of ads sponsored by a counter group, Improve New Mexico. But rumors flew as the ad war heated up, and Protect New Mexico rolled out new data from a poll taken by a conservative Republican group out of Virginia. The poll showed that 68 percent believed illegal drug use by children would increase if cocaine, marijuana, and heroin were decriminalized. When informed that drug use among teens increased in Nevada when penalties were eased, 67 percent of respondents opposed decriminalizing marijuana here.

The ads created a stir in the House, whose members faced elections in the fall. Rep. Joe Thompson was able to extract an admission from Rep. Ron Godbey that the ads were misleading, and that there were never any bills introduced to legalize heroin or cocaine.[9]

Whether as a result of the advertising campaign or the continued reluctance of the Democratic leadership to hand Johnson a victory on a signature issue, neither the medical marijuana bill introduced into the Senate by Sen. Roman Maes nor the decriminalization bill sponsored by Rep. Gail Chasey passed that session. But a few measures (including one to reduce prison time for nonviolent offenders) survived. The reformers were chipping away at the status quo, little by little—in spite of the election-year static. They got high praise from *Albuquerque Tribune* columnist V. B. Price, who thanked them for taking on an unpopular cause and rolling back what he called "Les Miserables" laws that hound people to the grave for stealing a loaf of bread or committing a minor drug infraction.[10]

Throughout the next few years the bitterness in the Republican Party increased. "We used to be so close, like a family," recalls former representative Joe Thompson, "but then everyone was forced to pick sides."

It was a no-brainer for Albuquerque's Rep. Rob Burpo, warming up for his gubernatorial campaign. Burpo tried (unsuccessfully) to drag Attorney General Patricia Madrid into the fray, asking for an opinion on how much it would cost to defend against federal lawsuits if medical marijuana was passed. "Instead of legalizing dangerous drugs we needed to strengthen the Boy and Girl Scouts, Little League . . . and take our country back, reestablishing moral and family values," Burpo said in a release he circulated to local press.[11]

Arch reform opponent Sen. Ramsay Gorham would eventually run against John Dendahl in a bitter campaign for Republican Party chair. Once again, the New Mexico Republican convention was brutal. Gorham won the contest in 2003, but was unable to unite the fractious Republican Party, which lost the governor's mansion to Bill Richardson. The following year, Gorham would throw up her hands and quit both the party post and her Senate seat. "It was so mean," says Thompson.

The first year after a new governor is elected in New Mexico is always a watershed year, and 2003 was no exception. A record 436 bills were signed by the governor, who was now of the same party as the majority in the legislature. Ironically, no medical marijuana bill was among them, even though the issue had been reframed as a legislative—and not an executive—initiative.

Rep. Ken Martinez sponsored the 2003 bill, now named after the original advocate, Lynn Pierson, the cancer patient who had so moved legislators on both sides of the aisle back in 1978, when Martinez's father, Walter Martinez, was in the House of Representatives. The Lynn Pierson Compassionate Use Act was ably presented by the Grants-area representative, who got some help from the bill's original sponsor Dave Salman, the House's former majority leader and member of the Mama Lucy faction. Salman told a House committee, "It was good legislation in 1978. It is better legislation today." [12]

But in the intervening year, opposition had mounted. The law enforcement sector and the district attorneys, led by Lemuel Martinez from Valencia County and Henry Valdez from Santa Fe County, had become increasingly active, contending that the reform would make marijuana more available to young people. Drug czars from the federal level were beginning to weigh in more heavily. In 2002 Czar Asa Hutchinson wrote a letter to the legislature saying that such a bill would violate federal law. In January 2003, as the legislature convened, Drug Enforcement Administration's John Walters made a preemptive visit to the new governor to warn against the new bill. At the same time, he rolled out a new anti-drug ad campaign featuring a ten-year-old Laguna Pueblo boy, Preston Chino. Chino was from Ken Martinez's district.

Martinez succeeded in getting HB 242 to the House floor, but it was defeated by a 46–20 vote. Many of the representatives who had voted for the 2001 bill changed sides. Some cited a provision that would have allowed patients to grow their own marijuana; others found a new fear of children becoming addicted to hard drugs.

The result was a surprise to former governor Gary Johnson, then returning from climbing Mount Everest. He told one observer he thought it would have sailed right through since he wasn't around to get credit for it. The result was also a surprise to the advocates, who had felt the momentum building, not crashing.

But while support for medical marijuana was dwindling in the House, and Speaker Ben Lujan was emerging as an opponent, support was growing in the Senate. My own committee, the Senate Public Affairs Committee, had heard the bill twice, passing it each time. Republican Sen. Steve Komadina, a doctor from Corrales and a former president of the New Mexico Medical Society, had become a proponent, and Sen. Cisco McSorley was busy building Republican bridges to his new bill in 2005. McSorley, whose own brother had died a painful death from liver cancer in 2002, had some new allies.

An increasing number of patients began to show up to testify for the bill, and their weary, pained presence began to be felt by legislators who were now coming to know them and their stories. Essie Debonet, an AIDS patient for twenty years, looked years older than she really was. As we saw her, year after year, she was shrinking before our eyes. We believed her when she said she didn't remember what it was like to sit and enjoy a meal without a wave of nausea (see fig. 28). But it was the entrance of Erin Armstrong, a young woman whose raspy voice was evidence of the thyroid cancer she had been living with since she was seventeen, that made a big difference.

Erin testified for medical marijuana from 2004 through 2007, sometimes deferring biopsies, enduring late nights in the gallery and grueling personal questions in committee. The daughter of the well-liked cabinet secretary for the Aging and Long-Term Services Department, Debbie Armstrong, Erin told her story and, in the process, turned the issue into a patients' rights issue—not a marijuana issue. "I'm here on behalf of myself and all other suffering patients who should never have to choose whether or not keeping down the next meal is worth getting arrested," she told one committee in 2005 (see fig. 29).[13]

The senators listened.

Erin was so calm, almost serene in her manner, Sen. Jerry Ortiz y Pino recalled. "She seems so fragile that her audience gets very quiet when she speaks, as if any noise it might make might startle her. A hush falls on the room and her voice can be heard by everyone."[14]

With the help of the patients, who had been organized by the Drug Policy Alliance's new director, Reena Szczepanski, McSorley's 2005 bill passed the Senate overwhelmingly 27–11. Then it passed through the House committees to which it was assigned and was poised for passage on the House floor. In the final few days, however, the bill was stalled due to a dispute between the Senate and the House. McSorley, then chairman of the Senate Judiciary Committee, was holding up a bill to allow tax increment bonding (under very favorable conditions) for a large development project on Albuquerque's west side. Several powerful members of the House tried first to leverage the medical marijuana bill to get the tax increment development district (TIDD) bill passed and, when that was not possible, to punish McSorley. It was Senate-House horsetrading—and the patients were held hostage.

"Oh how I cried in the basement," remembers Szczepanski, who was waiting there outside the House chambers to act as an expert witness if the bill was called up for final passage on the House floor. It never happened.

In 2006, the patients endured further torture as McSorley again tried to shepherd the measure through a now unpredictable maze of obstacles. At a hearing in the Senate Judiciary Committee, Erin Armstrong again told her story. It cost thousands of dollars a month for a constant dose of Zorn, an anti-nausea drug, she said, and she was in constant danger of losing insurance coverage every year. Armstrong was allergic to the cheaper alternative and wanted simply to have an alternative if she was accepted under the strict guidelines of the program. The senators had heard it before. But what came next was new.

David Murray, special assistant to the director of the White House Office of National Drug Control Policy, there to testify against the bill, said that proponents were engaged in a "manipulative and cynical" effort, using suffering patients like Erin and Essie to promote their agenda. Szczepanski and the DPA were snake-oil salesmen, he implied.[15]

Senators on the committee took umbrage. Sen. Michael Sanchez, by then the Senate majority leader, was furious. "This is the people's House and the people have a right to be here just as much as you do. I don't think you should ever come to a state and accuse the people of that state of being manipulative," he said. One committee member after another criticized this outsider who was telling the state what it could and could not do. "I think you are making statements that are completely erroneous," added conservative Sen. Lidio Rainaldi from Gallup.[16]

McSorley's bill cleared the Senate with an overwhelming majority (34–6), with more Republicans voting for it than ever before. But the momentary high felt by the advocates was short lived. Speaker Ben Lujan referred the bill to the House Agriculture Committee, where it was summarily tabled. "Why are you trying to kill us?" wailed Essie Debonet after an emotional hearing.[17] Outraged that a small group on a single committee could shelve the issue she had fought so hard for, Erin Armstrong appealed directly to the Speaker, recounting the amounts of scarce personal energy she had mustered in the effort and even quoting Eleanor Roosevelt ("When will our consciences grow so tender that we will act to prevent human misery rather than avenge it?").[18] Lujan relented, withdrawing the bill from the committee—too late to have it heard on the floor before the session adjourned.

Although Reena Szczepanski put a bright face on it, citing the $2.6 million in treatment funds that the drug reformers had embedded into the budget for methamphetamine treatment, 2006 was a tough year.

Meanwhile public support for medical marijuana had not dropped below

75 percent since 2001 when it was first tested by Research and Polling. In 2007, my own constituents favored it by 80 percent in my annual survey, with 89 percent saying the state did not have enough treatment programs. The *Albuquerque Journal* and other papers had editorialized in favor of the measure. But the system was not allowing the bill through, in spite of the personal stories and the overwhelming Senate support. True, a lot of incremental measures had passed. But the opponents' scare tactics still struck a chord. And the contradiction between a state program and federal law would not go away.

Faced with these difficulties, reformers adjusted their tactics in 2007. Senator McSorley would no longer be the prime sponsor but would, instead, work the bill behind the scenes. Sen. Jerry Ortiz y Pino would be the shepherd this time, a change that would avoid old animosities and give a new flavor to an old dish. The Senate president pro tem's wife, Patty Jennings, brought her clout to the issue. Then suffering from breast cancer, Jennings told committees that people who are not themselves patients don't always understand that patients need all the options open to them. As for the federal problem, Jennings said that unless states step forward and challenge the federal government, the federal policy would never be changed.[19] With the idea of states' rights powering the sails, Senate Bill 238 flew through the Senate (34–7) and moved quickly through the House committees. This time it passed the Agriculture Committee, but it faced new problems when it hit the House floor.

As is sometimes the case in the final days of any session, there were too many things happening simultaneously. Three major bills came up for their final, decisive votes on different chambers' floor on the same day: Senator Garcia's cockfighting ban (see chapter 11), Representative Park's Clean Indoor Air Act (see chapter 7), and Senator Ortiz y Pino's Medical Marijuana bill. Rep. Al Park was over in the Senate helping with his smoking ban when the House voted on medical marijuana. He dashed back to his chamber but missed the vote by a second, and after three hours of debate, the vote tied, meaning that the measure failed. A parliamentary move to reconsider the bill and then revote was immediately passed, but then the bill failed 33 to 36. Representative Park felt terrible; his own bill had passed the Senate but medical marijuana had been defeated. Erin Armstrong, Dr. Steve Jenison with the Health Department, and Reena Szczepanski had spent three hours on the floor with floor sponsor Rep. Moe Maestas as expert witnesses, suffering one emotional abuse after another. They thought they had the votes and now they were devastated—again (see fig. 30).

When word reached the Senate that *our* measure, a measure that had repeatedly passed the Senate by overwhelming majorities, had failed, we swung into action. And so, too, did the reformers, working with the governor to change some minds in the House.

In a rare parliamentary move, the Senate inserted Senator Ortiz y Pino's bill into another on the same subject sponsored by Sen. Shannon Robinson. Ortiz y Pino's thus replaced Robinson's bill. The substitute, Senate Bill 523, garnered even more support (only three members opposed) and sped back to the House, where it finally reached the floor. By that time, the governor had gotten a chance to talk to several House members. When the final vote was taken, the measure passed 36 to 31. Democratic Reps. Richard Vigil, Andrew Barreras, Ernest Chavez, Mary Helen Garcia, and Thomas Garcia changed their votes from no to yes. Rep. Nick Salazar was absent, but Rep. Al Park was there.

Rep. Moe Maestas, who carried the bill again on the House floor (this time debating for "only" two hours), rejoiced. "This is the most unlikely coalition in the history of this body," he said.

Maestas might have been right about his own chamber, but not about the Senate where party discipline is weaker and there are frequently bipartisan coalitions led by mavericks like Richard Romero and Les Houston, both from Albuquerque, and Tim Jennings from Roswell.

Over a number of years, Cisco McSorley, one of the mavericks, was successful in putting together the unlikely suspects in the Senate, sticking with it, and deferring to others when necessary. Reena Szczepanski calls him a champion. Former representative Sen. Joe Thompson says he was awesome, using his Senate Judiciary Committee to advance the cause. Even though he is a liberal Democrat, McSorley forged a practical alliance with the younger, more libertarian leaning Republicans in the House, trading off bills when the consequences were not too dire.

Immediately after the new law went into effect in July 2007, the medical marijuana program ran into trouble. Attorney General Gary King said that state workers implementing the new law in the health department could be prosecuted for their oversight of production and distribution of marijuana. It was the age-old problem—the federal government outlawed the production and distribution of the supply of marijuana on which the program depended. Health Secretary Dr. Alfredo Vigil then suspended the program—until prompted by the governor to go forth. Several months later the federal Drug Enforcement Administration and the Pecos Valley Drug Task Force in southern New Mexico burst into the house of one patient, Leonard French, a paraplegic licensed to use marijuana plants, to seize his supply. Reacting, Governor Richardson urged the DEA to not prosecute him, noting, "US Attorneys have their hands full with real drug cases and the border and can't afford to waste taxpayer dollars to prosecute individuals who are critically ill or suffering from debilitating conditions."[20]

Despite his run for the presidency, Richardson had become a champion of the program. Yes, he was a more careful, less maverick-like warrior than Gary Johnson, but he was effective. He didn't lose votes and, in fact, he got $50,000 in campaign contributions from the DPA and its allies. Just as the opponents had predicted!

"The people have been way out ahead of the politicians on this one," says Senator McSorley. "No politician has ever lost a seat because of a compassionate stance on this; I think we have proved that in New Mexico."

In 2012, McSorley was still fighting to make sure administrative obstacles don't swamp the program, and working with the Drug Policy Alliance to win important modifications, such as allowing patients to grow their own limited supply. During the 2012 legislative session he succeeded in getting law-and-order governor Susana Martinez to agree to create a special fund to be fed by licensing fees charged to growers. He is optimistic about the future now that two states (Colorado and Washington) have legalized the possession of small amounts of marijuana. And he often cites the Obama White House's advisory message that federal resources should be used to prosecute drug dealers instead of those who are in compliance with state laws on medical marijuana. Although now much less controversial, McSorley knows that, even with changing times, there is always the possibility of a political hijack.

McSorley credits Gary Johnson for kicking things off. "It was like Nixon going to China," he says. In a sense this *was* the camel's nose under the tent, as Sen. Ramsay Gorham had predicted, but in a different way.

Nineteen states now have medical marijuana programs, and many are looking at drug abuse from a medical standpoint rather than a criminal justice one. New Mexico now confronts a growing epidemic of overdoses and misuse of legal prescription drugs, and we still need treatment programs rather than incarceration. But the medical marijuana debate has changed our approach.

Over the years, the public has made a distinction between medical problems caused by drug addiction and the legal problems caused by the war on drugs. Americans want to treat and not incarcerate, says McSorley, but the legislature has yet to follow. Governor Johnson's overall package of drug reforms did not pass easily, just as Richardson's health care reform failed in 2008. But, over time, significant pieces of both have been enacted thanks to personal stories that stir compassion and the persistent efforts of behind-the-scenes heroes and mavericks in the governor's mansion and the legislature.

FIGURE 23

Gov. Bill Richardson (on the left) gets the endorsement and the help of the NRA's Wayne La Pierre (on the right) at an eastern New Mexico campaign rally for his re-election in 2006. AP Photo/Roswell Daily Record by Andrew Poetner, © Associated Press. Reprinted with permission.

FIGURE 24

Sen. George Munoz of Gallup confers with expert witness Steve Aikens, an NRA instructor, during a debate on his bill to allow licensed New Mexicans to carry concealed handguns into restaurants that sell liquor. Lobbyists are permitted on the floor as expert witnesses during debate. Photo by Dean Hanson, © *Albuquerque Journal.* Reprinted with permission.

FIGURE 25

Gun-toting activists held rallies outside the Roundhouse in Santa Fe to oppose gun control and carried guns into committee hearings during discussion of gun safety measures in 2013. Here Christopher Chase of Angel Fire holds up a sign on February 8, 2013. Photo by Jim Thompson, © *Albuquerque Journal.* Reprinted with permission.

FIGURE 26

Rep. John Heaton and Human Services Secretary Pam Hyde presenting the governor's omnibus health care reform bill Health Solutions in 2008. Patterned after the Massachusetts plan, adopted a year earlier, the complex bill failed in the Senate amid recriminations between Senate leaders and Gov. Bill Richardson. AP Photo by Adolphe Pierre-Louis, © Associated Press. Reprinted with permission.

FIGURE 27

Sen. Feldman campaigns for Obama Care in Albuquerque in 2009 in the wake of the failure of Health Solutions, the state's effort at health care reform. Feldman worked with the White House Working Group of State Legislators to shape the federal legislation, build support, and later to implement the law. Photo by Mary Ellen Broderick, Democracy for New Mexico.

FIGURE 28

Essie DeBonet, who suffered from AIDS, spoke in favor of medical marijuana before the Senate Public Affairs Committee in 2006. Year after year she testified, visibly diminished each time. But her story was key in passing the law in 2007. Photo by Kathy De La Torre, © 2007 *The New Mexican, Inc.* Reprinted with permission. All rights reserved.

FIGURE 29

"I know what it feels like to be a patient, and they needed that perspective," says Erin Armstrong, describing the reason she advocated in the New Mexico Legislature for legalized use of medical marijuana. Armstrong's raspy voice betrayed her thyroid cancer—and it was a key reason for the bill's passage. Photo by Katharine Kimball, © *Albuquerque Journal.* Reprinted with permission.

FIGURE 30

Rep. Antonio (Moe) Maestas, D-Albuquerque, speaks in support of a bill to legalize the use of marijuana for certain medical purposes, such as relieving nausea for cancer patients. With him on the House floor (left to right) are Reena Szcezepanski, director of the Drug Policy Alliance of New Mexico; Steve Jenison, medical director of the Infectious Disease Bureau with the New Mexico Department of Health; and Erin Armstrong, of the Drug Policy Alliance of New Mexico. Photo by Katherine Kimball, © *Albuquerque Journal*. Reprinted with permission.

FIGURE 31

Cockfighting supporters wait in the east lobby of the capitol in 2007 to testify against a bill to ban cockfighting in New Mexico. Photo by Adolphe Pierre-Louis, © *Albuquerque Journal*. Reprinted with permission.

FIGURE 32

Sen. Mary Jane Garcia greets Gov. Bill Richardson with gusto after his State of the Union speech in 2007. The governor announced he would support a ban on cockfighting during the session. Garcia had been pushing for the ban unsuccessfully for almost two decades. AP photo by Jeff Geissler, © Associated Press. Reprinted with permission.

FIGURE 33

Cockfighter Joe A. Parr, of Anthony, NM, wearing a jacket boosting his bird, Bad Boy, holds up a copy of the state constitution while expressing his opposition to a cockfighting ban in 2007. Photo by Luis Sanchez Saturno, © 2007 *The New Mexican, Inc.* Reprinted with permission. All rights reserved.

FIGURE 34
Actress Ali MacGraw (center) celebrates at the capitol with Allen Sánchez, director of the New Mexico Conference of Catholic Bishops, and Sen. Mary Jane Garcia, D-Doña Ana, after Gov. Bill Richardson signed Garcia's bill to ban cockfighting. Photo by Jane Phillips, © 2007 *The New Mexican, Inc.* Reprinted with permission. All rights reserved.

FIGURE 35
Members of the New Mexico Coalition to Repeal the Death Penalty gathered for a rally in the capitol rotunda in 2009 as the sixty-day session of the legislature approached its halfway point with bills to abolish capital punishment pending. Photo by Richard Pipes, © *Albuquerque Journal.* Reprinted with permission.

FIGURE 36

Rep. Gail Chasey asks the House Consumer and Public Affairs Committee in 2003 to support her bill to eliminate the death penalty. She is flanked by Michelle Giger, of Murder Victims' Families for Reconciliation (right), and Randi McGinn (left). Photo by Jerome Nakagawa, © 2003 *The New Mexican, Inc.* Reprinted with permission. All rights reserved.

FIGURE 37

Rep. Gail Chasey urges support on the House floor in 2005 for her bill to repeal New Mexico's death penalty and replace it with a sentence of life imprisonment without parole, as Speaker Ben Lujan (right) listens. Trace Rabern, a public defender, and Judi Caruso, director of the Juan Melendez Voices United for Justice, also listen in the background. The House passed the measure 38–31 and sent it to the Senate, where it was defeated that year. Photo by Jane Phillips, ©2005 *The New Mexican, Inc.* Reprinted with permission. All rights reserved.

FIGURE 38
Senate Majority Leader Michael Sanchez, D-Valencia, urges senators to ban the death
penalty in 2009. At right is the bill's sponsor Rep. Gail Chasey, Majority Whip Mary
Jane Garcia and Sen. Steve Fishman, both of Las Cruces. Photo by Jane Phillips,
© 2009 *The New Mexican, Inc.* Reprinted with permission. All rights reserved.

"GOOD NEWS! ETHICS REFORM IS JUST AROUND THE CORNER!"

FIGURE 39
New Mexico's round capitol building brings good news to those who want to avoid
ethics reform in the legislature. *Albuquerque Journal* cartoon, January 14, 2008.
© 2008 by John Trever, *Albuquerque Journal.* Reprinted with permission.

FIGURE 40

Bob Johnson, former Associated Press bureau chief and executive director of the Foundation for Open Government (FOG), shares a laugh on the Senate floor in 2006. The bill to open conference committees to the public was defeated that year, and I donned a Red Cross scarf to indicate the scale of the emergency for open government. I kept up the rescue effort until this and other transparency measures began to pass a few years later. AP Photo by Jeff Geissler, © Associated Press. Reprinted with permission.

FIGURE 41

A retired executive secretary and a 90-year-old great-grandmother of twelve, Doris "Granny" Haddock with me in the capitol rotunda after speaking about campaign-finance reform. Haddock, who became known as "Granny D," walked 3,200 miles cross country in support of campaign finance reform. She visited twelve states in fourteen months, ending on the steps of the Capitol in Washington, D.C., where she was embraced by Sen. John McCain, then promoting the McCain-Feingold campaign-reform bill. Photo courtesy of the author.

FIGURE 42
Getting things done in the New Mexico legislature is no easy task and, even for savvy senators, there's always the danger of rollbacks and slippage. Cartoon by the *Albuquerque Journal*'s John Trever, presented to Sen. Dede Feldman as an "E for Effort Award" by the Greater Albuquerque Chamber of Commerce, June 23, 2011. Reprinted with permission of the cartoonist.

PART V By Grit and Grace

WITH A HISTORY OF GUN SLINGING, MATANZAS, AND OTHER rural rituals, New Mexico could easily be taken for the Wild West. But by a bipartisan majority in 2007 and 2009 the New Mexico legislature ended two longstanding practices: cockfighting and executions. The bans came after years of testimony, which stirred the sympathies of senators, representatives, and finally the governor.

The following chapters are the stories of two very different issues: cockfighting and the death penalty. They are case studies of how courageous and persistent legislators can work with a coalition of advocates to educate the public and ultimately triumph over political and institutional roadblocks. There are stories of similar triumphs in all state legislatures. In New Mexico the roadblocks included uncooperative committees and a governor wary of alienating his conservative Democratic base as he ran for the presidency. In both cases, the Catholic Church, a potent ally or foe for any New Mexico legislator, may have turned the tide.

CHAPTER 11

Courageous Senator Closes Chapter on New Mexico's Dirty Little Secret

Cockfighting

T HE STATE POLICEWOMAN ESCORTING SEN. MARY JANE GARCIA back to her room at La Fonda entered first, checking to make sure that there was no one in the hotel room. The senator had been receiving death threats from the cockfighters since the beginning of the session. So had the animal protection lobbyists who had been working with her for almost twenty years now on a ban of the traditional blood sport.

This year, 2007, with the prospect that the bill could actually pass, the threats had intensified. One of the lobbyists, Danielle Bays, endured shots through her living room window. The family of Allen Sánchez, a lobbyist for the New Mexico Conference of Catholic Bishops, was harassed at home in Valencia County. The receptionist in Garcia's tiny office in the basement of the state capitol got calls pledging to dig a grave for Garcia and Sanchez. An official cockfighting website went further. Garcia, Bays, and Sanchez would have to dig their own graves.

In spite of the danger, the seemingly frail Garcia, now seventy years old, stood up straight by her desk in the corner of the Senate chambers. It had been eighteen years since she came to the Senate from a small Hispanic village in southern New Mexico. She had become the majority whip in 1996 in charge of rounding up votes for Democratic bills. She had suffered through close elections and leadership changes. She had recovered from breast cancer. She had donated a kidney to her sister. She was living with diabetes. She was not afraid.

"I will not be intimidated out of doing my job as a senator. Believe me," she said, "I am not chicken. The only 'grave' the vast majority of New Mexicans want to see is one marked 'Cockfighting, RIP.'" [1]

Garcia was not always so feisty. In 1989 when she first sponsored a bill to ban the practice of rooster fighting, she had few supporters at her side. She just knew that the practice was cruel, and she loved animals of all shapes and forms. She managed to get the bill through committees and onto the floor of the Senate. But once there, she was so embarrassed by sniggering comments of rural senators that she asked to have her own bill tabled indefinitely. One of the bill's opponents, Sen. Les Houston, egged on by other male senators, asked her to define a "cock."

"I wasn't going to stand there and be made fun of," she recalls. "I was just too green." Later, Garcia learned that it was sort of a good-ole-boys initiation process with the new senator on the block asked to carry the bill. It happened to former senator Joe Carraro, too. In 1984 he was approached by a group of senators. "They told me how bright I was and how well spoken, and how they really needed me to carry this bill they couldn't pass," he recalled. Later, Carraro realized how emotional an issue it was when an opponent came into his office and said, "This is my livelihood," as he stabbed a bowie knife in the senator's desk for emphasis. [2]

Christine Donisthorpe, another former senator from the 1980s, said that she could not recall any other bill that created that kind of emotion. The cockfighting debate was the only time in the Senate that she was really afraid, she remembered.

And that was just the beginning.

In its heyday, cockfighting was estimated to be an $80 million business in New Mexico, with ten thousand breeders and derbies held in Clovis, Jal, and Belen, among other rural towns. A traditional practice in Spanish-speaking countries like the Philippines, Puerto Rico, and Mexico, proponents say it also has deep U.S. roots. Don Bible, a cockfighting referee at Tommy's Game Fowl Farm near Hobbs, contends (preposterously) that cockfighters, including George Washington and Abraham Lincoln, freed America. He also asserts that President Lincoln got the nickname "Honest Abe" as a result of his fairness in judging cockfights. [3]

In a cockfight, two roosters with razor-sharp knives or "gaffs" attached to their feet are thrown into a pit where they fight until one is dead or incapacitated. The roosters are often given drugs to enhance their performance. Spectators crowd around, sometimes seated in bleachers, cheering on their birds, almost always gambling—illegally. Winners can take home as much as $80,000. Losing birds are not so lucky. At Tommy's Game Fowl Farm, the losers are thrown into wooden crates behind the stands. One night the dead roosters amounted to two hundred.[4]

Breeders like Ed Lowrey, from Chaparral, NM, celebrate the fierce determination of the roosters. "A gamecock shows what an American should be like," he said. "You defend to the death."[5] But to animal lovers like Garcia, the practice is brutal—the intentional killing of animals for money and entertainment.

From the very beginning of her efforts to ban the sport, Garcia hammered home its inherent violence. Her allies (not many in the early days) brought the actual razor blades, or "gaffs," used like spurs in fights, into committee rooms. Garcia and others said the inhumane treatment of roosters could be a precursor to domestic violence. Almost all other states, except for Oklahoma and Louisiana, had made it into a felony.

The Senate Public Affairs Committee had heard the bill repeatedly over the years, once viewing a video of a fight. Most of the members were aghast. So were most New Mexicans. The animal advocates started commissioning statewide polls in 2001, and support for a ban never slipped below 66 percent, with most years topping 80 percent. But as the bills began to make progress, more and more "cockers," as they call themselves, would begin to appear in the hallways and the gallery (see fig. 31). Their boots brought in mud, and their clothes bore the odor of the barnyard. Their conduct was disturbing to many. Now threatened, their voices got louder and angrier. The sergeants-at-arms were busier than ever before keeping the rowdy bunch in order.

The game fowl breeders contended that this was an urban vs. rural issue, and that they were upholding traditional, rural Hispanic culture. Opposition to the practice came mostly from outsiders, they said, animal rights activists from Hollywood and old white ladies who knew nothing about New Mexico. Let these people have their way, and soon our matanzas, our rodeos, and even hunting and fishing will go by the wayside, they said. Far from being barbarians, the cockers, who were largely Hispanic, presented themselves as a persecuted minority.

Garcia, for her part, was ready when the race card was dealt. "I know about being Hispanic in a rural community," she said. "Cockfighting has never been a part of my culture or my community."[6]

A trained anthropologist, Garcia had some credentials when it came to culture. For years she used her capital outlay funds to restore the historic plaza in her small, adobe village of Doña Ana. She organized mariachi contests at her family's bar, which showcased Mexican acts. A devout catholic, Garcia had a love of the world's helpless creatures, whether infants, seniors, or animals. While in Santa Fe, she never missed morning mass at the St. Francis Cathedral. St. Francis, she reminded everyone, was the patron saint of animals. My culture is not barbaric, she insisted.[7]

The cockers, for their part, insisted that the practice was enshrined in the 1848 Treaty of Guadalupe Hidalgo between Mexico and the United States, when New Mexico became a territory. Garcia asked for an attorney general's opinion from Attorney General (AG) Gary King, a device that is often used to see whether a measure follows the New Mexico constitution. The son of former Gov. Bruce King, the AG grew up on a ranch. But he had a history of passing animal protection bills when he was a state representative. King came back with a 2003 ruling that cockfighting was not mentioned in the treaty.

It was a momentary victory for Garcia. Momentum for the measure was building and a variant of the bill passed the House 45 to 21. Proponents had successfully made the argument that violence toward animals was often the precursor to domestic violence and other abuse. But the Senate was the stumbling block.

In 2005, Garcia's now-perennial bill to ban cockfighting was referred— as usual—to the Senate Conservation Committee. The committee's jurisdiction included water, environmental issues, and all things agricultural. It has always been populated by rural members and this year was no exception. In spite of the widespread public support for the ban, Garcia and her allies could only count on two votes out of the committee's nine members: Republicans John Ryan and Bill Payne, both from Albuquerque.

Things didn't look good, but they got worse when the major hearing, which had been moved to the Senate floor because of the huge crowds it was now attracting, was cancelled. Chairman Carlos Cisneros called it off because of a conflict—a cockfight that would draw many of the opponents away from the hallowed Senate chambers. Not wishing to offend the breeders, who had contributed to his campaign, Cisneros moved the date from a Saturday (hearings held on that day are well attended by the public) to one more convenient for the cockfighters.

When the hearing was finally held, cockfighters put their families front and center. One by one, teenagers walked to the rostrum and told the committee members seated at the front of the chambers that cockfighting had saved their lives, keeping them off drugs and out of gangs. To underline the point, a new crop of t-shirts had appeared in the gallery, proclaiming, "Cockfighting kept me off drugs." Former Washington state legislator Jack

Cairnes, who had moved to Hobbs, emphasized that cockfighting was a wholesome American family activity and continued the refrain. Those who did not understand this were racist.

Legislators who were not on the committee but who had come simply to see the show walked away shaking their heads. "Family values cannot be taught at the end of a razor blade," Rep. Jeff Steinborn later complained.[8]

Law enforcement officials, charged with enforcing the bans already in effect in thirteen New Mexico counties and thirty municipalities, had another picture. They had been at the fights themselves. Darren White, the Bernalillo county sheriff, was direct. "This is not about culture," he said, "This is not about urban vs. rural values. This is about animal cruelty."[9]

That year, the members of the Conservation Committee were unconvinced. They tabled the measure, along with the House version of the bill, sponsored by Rep. Peter Wirth, which had passed the House by a wide margin, 50 to 15. The committee system had worked again to hold back change.

In the world outside the legislature, however, New Mexico's determination to hang onto the practice was beginning to attract national attention. On the *Tonight Show*, Jay Leno ridiculed Gov. Bill Richardson, then at the start of his presidential campaign, for not playing an active role in banning the fights. Leno sarcastically quoted Richardson, who had said, "There were strong arguments on both sides of the issue." Bill Maher and Pamela Anderson, an animal rights activist who also starred in the TV show *Baywatch*, started calling the governor's office. It must have been a little uncomfortable for Richardson, who was then courting Hollywood for more movie business in the state. The cockfighters were squeezing him too. They contended that he had promised them in 2002, when he first ran for governor, that he would never ban the sport.

To make matters worse, in 2006, Sen. John Grubesic, a Santa Fe senator whose critiques of the governor were becoming more outrageous by the minute, introduced a memorial (nonbinding legislation) requesting that cockfighting be named as the official state disgrace. New Mexico has a number of "official" items including neckties (the bolo), vegetables (the chile), birds (the roadrunner), and jewelry (the squash blossom necklace). Cockfighting would fit right in, Grubisek said. The memorial went nowhere, but the message was sent.

January, 2007. Senator Garcia wanted to give the governor a big hug, she was so overjoyed. Her eyes twinkling, she practically rushed him as he left the podium set up in the House of Representatives for the opening day ceremony of the 2007 legislature (see fig. 32). Each year the governor gives a state-of-the-state address, outlining his priorities for the legislative session. This time the governor had gone out of his way to mention the issue that Garcia had been struggling with for years. "This year," Richardson said, looking at Garcia with her red dress and white corsage, "I am confident that we are finally going to ban cockfighting. New Mexicans don't want our state associated with this practice. I am ready to work with the legislature to get this done."[10]

Finally. The words were music to her ears. And there was even more good news: The New Mexico Conference of Catholic Bishops was entering the fray on the side of the roosters. Animal Protection Voters had done their homework. But so had the cockfighters, now cornered and fighting for their livelihood. Garcia and other high-profile animal advocates were put on a target list published in *Game Fowl News*, and the senator continued to receive harassing phone calls and death threats. The hallways were crowded with cockfighters in club jackets, with images of favorite roosters—Bad Boy or Red—emblazoned on the back (see fig. 33). But now the cockfighters were joined by animal rights advocates in their own t-shirts bearing cartoon roosters and the question, "Will the Fight Go On?"

Garcia knew that, once again, the Conservation Committee was the key stumbling block. But this time she had reinforcements. The proponents sitting on the Senate floor that day included priests from Española who pled for the lives of all of God's creatures. Archbishop Michael Sheehan asked committee members to imagine what St. Francis with his love of animals would think about strapping razor blades on roosters. Ali MacGraw, of *Love Story* fame, and Rue McClanahan, of the *Golden Girls* TV show, added their voices to the debate.

When the roll was called, Sen. Richard Martinez of Española, a close ally of Governor Richardson, was absent. His opposition to the measure would thus not be recorded. Two other Democrats, Sens. John Pinto and Ben Altamirano, changed their minds under pressure from constituents and the governor. Senate Bill 10 passed the committee 5 to 3. Sen. Phil Griego, a steadfast supporter of cockfighting, was peeved that the bill had passed the committee to which he had just been appointed chair. Opponents like Jim Nance of Socorro County had testified that the ban was part of an animal-rights agenda pushed by people who wanted a meatless, petless society where animals are equal to humans. These people were going around from state to state trying to disrupt rural traditions, he said. Griego agreed.

The bill still had a long way to go, but the proponents had crossed an important bridge. By the time the bill came to the Senate floor it had been amended by the Judiciary Committee to take out most of its teeth. The first offense was no longer a felony but a misdemeanor, and only repeat offenses were fourth degree felonies. Garcia acquiesced to the reduced penalties, but the advocates were wary. And they were right.

The floor debate on SB 10 lasted five hours. Garcia fended off amendment after amendment proposed by Senator Griego and Sen. Rod Adair, who represented Dexter, a hotbed of cockfighting. The penalties that finally emerged were weaker still: a petty misdemeanor for the first offense, a misdemeanor for the second, and a fourth degree felony only for the third and subsequent offenses. The debate got crazier and crazier. Sen. Shannon Robinson, whose father was a proud cockfighter, recalled a favorite rooster, Booger Red. In vivid detail he described looking into the eyes of sheep to be castrated in the farm operation. "It's really hard to look into their eyes when you cut their nuts off," he said. There was some connection to cockfighting there, but by this time it was lost on most of the senators.

Amid it all, between spitting his chewing tobacco into a paper cup located on the left side of his desk, Griego kept hammering away on the attack on rural lifestyle that the ban represented. "We're criminalizing customs. We're criminalizing traditions," he said, and the next thing would be banning smoking, rodeos, fishing, hunting, and the branding of livestock.

By the end of the debate Garcia began to wonder whether she really did have God on her side, as she had announced joyfully in her opener, referring to the endorsement of the Catholic bishops. But the bill passed 31 to 11. As Garcia collapsed into her chair with exhaustion, the animal lovers in the gallery rejoiced.

The bill's journey through the House was less eventful, punctuated only by the highly publicized eviction of a rowdy cockfighting booster (who turned out to be one of my constituents!) from a committee hearing. Rep. Tom Taylor introduced a much-needed note of levity into the debate, which everyone recognized was now drawing to an end. The Farmington Republican was worried that no one had considered what the roosters would do about retirement once the practice was ended. Taylor introduced a memorial to give the proud and mighty fighting cocks "twice weekly visits from the very best cage-free hens the state has to offer, one high definition TV for every six cocks, and a subscription to ESPN, Animal Planet, and CMT Pure Country—but not to the Food Network or FOX News." Sen. Tim Jennings went even further, bringing live chickens onto the Senate floor upon the bill's passage. He bemoaned the massive layoffs these chickens were now facing.

The cockfighters, now crestfallen, did not see the humor. After the bill had passed the House (49–20) and was on its way to the governor, they said cockfighting would continue anyway—and they would sue.

Governor Richardson wasted no time in signing the measure to ban the centuries-old practice; Louisiana then became the only state in which cockfighting was still legal. "It's history," Richardson told the standing-room-only crowd that had jammed into his cabinet room on March 12, 2007. The cheering crowd was led by Senator Garcia; Rep. Peter Wirth, who carried the bill in the House; actress Ali MacGraw; and the Conference of Catholic Bishops' Allen Sánchez. They flanked the governor around his huge marble table. Lisa Jennings, executive director of Animal Protection Voters, gave Richardson the group's signature t-shirt depicting a faux boxing match between two cartoon roosters, Rocky Not-So-Cocky and Joey the Chicken Rooster. She said his support was the turning point. MacGraw was glad New Mexico had acknowledged that cruelty to animals for recreational enjoyment is not OK. And Wirth was simply relieved that New Mexico's "dirty little secret" was now in the rear-view mirror. Garcia, for her part, was so happy, she said, she couldn't even express it (see fig. 34).

In the coming weeks, as the senator savored one of her greatest legislative accomplishments, the cockfighters were getting in their last licks before the ban went into effect on June 15. The New Mexico Gamefowl Association started legal proceedings for what was to become a long, drawn out, unsuccessful suit. To spite Garcia, they scheduled a special cockfight to pay tribute to La Malinche. Sen. Phil Griego distributed flyers advertising the match in San Jon a few weeks later in the Senate lounge where senators were gathering for a special session.

La Malinche is a well-known female figure in Mexico. Garcia explained that the woman is considered to have betrayed her people since her love for Spanish Conquistador Cortez in the 1600s led to the Spanish conquest of Mexico. Garcia knew the cockfighters were branding her as the new traitor to her race. It was highly insulting to a senator who prided herself as a champion of her people. "I just turned away as if I didn't hear about it," she recalls.

In retrospect, there were many reasons for the cockfighting ban's success in 2007. The proponents' powerful allies—including the Catholic Church and the governor—were a key factor in convincing the reluctant rural Hispanic men who had been a stumbling block in the Senate. Hollywood star power was appealing to Gov. Bill Richardson, then on the hunt for both campaign contributions for his presidential race and movie deals for New Mexico. Public opposition to cockfighting had become overwhelming, as revealed in poll after poll, and the national popularity of animal protection was on the ascent. Football star Michael Vick's conviction on animal cruelty charges showed that even the tough guys had to be accountable. Senator Garcia was willing to compromise to soften the penalties, but she would not give up, persisting even after repeated defeats. Finally—after twenty years—legislators realized that New Mexico, a state dependent on tourism, just couldn't continue as a laughing stock on late night TV without serious damage to its image—no matter what the cockfighters and their allies said about upholding rural values and Hispanic traditions.

"New Mexico is on the verge of having a modern culture," Heather Ferguson, the legislative director for Animal Protection of New Mexico, told the *New York Times* a few months later, as New Mexico assumed its position as the last state to ban cockfighting—save one, Louisiana.[11] But the year wasn't 1970 or even 1990. It was 2008 and it had taken almost twenty years of legislative struggle to overcome the grip of rural interests and a small Senate committee poised to block forward motion in many directions.

CHAPTER 12

Citizen Legislators Grapple
with the Ultimate Issue

The Death Penalty

B ACK IN 1997, WHEN NEWLY ELECTED REPRESENTATIVE GAIL
Chasey volunteered to take on the task of repealing the death penalty
in New Mexico, she knew it was an issue unlike any other.[1] Opponents of
the death penalty based their views on conscience and religion. Victims of
violence had strong feelings about justice and public safety. Emotion and
principles would be at the center of the debate, and she knew that it would
take years to sort out the stories, the statistics, and the political costs.

"My grandmother lived until she was 100," Chasey told the newly formed
Coalition to Repeal the Death Penalty when they came forward for the first
time, during an interim committee meeting in Santa Rosa that year. "So I
will be around to see it through," she joked.

The usual lobbyists, special interests, and tradeoffs so common in the
Roundhouse would not be involved in the issue. The debate would focus on
the basic question of the role of government and the value of a human life.
The stakes would be incredibly high since the death penalty is literally a
matter of life and death. It is the ultimate decision that a public official must
make. It would be quite a journey. Over the next twelve years the determined and respectful representative from Albuquerque's university district
would proceed with the utmost care.

It was an approach not often used in New Mexico. When Tony Hillerman
was a young *Santa Fe New Mexican* reporter he covered several executions
on New Mexico's death row during the 1950s. In one, he recalled, there was
sort of a Roman-holiday atmosphere, with about 110 drunken sheriff's posse

types celebrating right in the death chamber. "It was really a grisly kind of thing," Hillerman recalled in an interview with the *Santa Fe New Mexican* in 1999. "The politicos controlled the tickets. It was kind of like getting tickets to a Lobos-Utah game."[2] A few years earlier, in 1954, Hillerman had reported on the execution of another man, Spider Heisler, sentenced for a hitchhiking murder on Rt. 66. In that execution, Hillerman said, there was an overpowering smell of whiskey and, when the switch was thrown, smoke, sparks, and other smells. But the electrocution did not work, and Spider was still alive, prompting the executioner to mess around with the wire and do it again. "It was sickening," Hillerman wrote.[3]

By the time Representative Chasey embarked upon her quest, executions in New Mexico were rare. Only nine men had been put to death since 1933, a few years after the state took over executions from local governments. Although capital punishment for murder had been on the books since the Spanish colonial era, judges regularly requested commutations, and territorial governors complied. Juries were not eager for the death penalty either, according to former state historian Robert Tórrez, who wrote *The Myth of the Hanging Tree: Stories of Crime and Punishment in Territorial New Mexico.* Tórrez recounts how some territorial governors (George Curry and James Calhoun) even spoke out against capital punishment as uncivilized and ineffective as a deterrent. The Catholic Church may have had a big influence on the lenient approach at that time, and it still plays a potent role in the issue.

On the national level, the Supreme Court invalidated all death penalty laws in 1972, but then ruled in favor of a Georgia death penalty statute in 1976, opening the way for states to do their own thing. The move prompted the New Mexico legislature to act the same year, passing the law that stood until Chasey replaced it in 2009. The 1979 law restricted the death penalty to first-degree murder with aggravating circumstances. The circumstances included killing a law enforcement officer or a prison guard; killing a fellow inmate; killing while trying to escape incarceration; murder for hire; murdering to prevent a witness from testifying; and murder while committing rape, kidnapping, or child molestation. The new law caught a number of people in its net in the following years, but five inmates on death row had their sentences commuted by outgoing Gov. Toney Anaya in 1986. Since 1960, only one man has been executed, Terry Clark, who was sentenced to death shortly after Anaya left office. Clark, who murdered nine-year-old Dena Lynn Gore in 1986, was executed in 2001, after requesting that his appeals be dropped. Gov. Gary Johnson complied. He did not commute his sentence or declare a moratorium on executions as Illinois Gov. George Ryan had done a year earlier. He signed the death warrant, even though, as he revealed later, he was beginning to have doubts.[4] The night of Clark's execution on November 6, four hundred opponents of the death penalty held a candlelight vigil in the chilly Santa Fe night outside the Roundhouse. The demonstration reignited the debate over the death penalty in New Mexico and brought together opponents for numerous rallies during the following eight years.

The New Mexico Coalition to Repeal the Death Penalty grew from a handful of organizers in the legal and religious communities in 1997 to a co-alition of 140 organizations and about 3,600 individual members of different backgrounds and perspectives in 2009, says Viki Harrison, who was brought on as executive director of the coalition in 2008 (see fig. 35). Originally the core group consisted of Murder Victims Families for Reconciliation–New Mexico, the New Mexico Conference of Catholic Bishops, the New Mexico Conference of Churches, the National Association of Social Workers–New Mexico, the New Mexico Criminal Defense Lawyers Association, the NAACP, the American Civil Liberties Union–New Mexico, the New Mexico Public Health Association, and chapters of Amnesty International. The faith communities—Catholic, Lutheran, Quaker, Presbyterian, and Jewish con-gregations—made it an issue of conscience, invoking the power of redemp-tion. Key volunteers in the organization, like Cathy Ansheles, a criminal defense lawyer; Pat Tyrell, a social worker; and Michelle Giger, whose father was killed in Santa Rosa in 1984, were family members of murder victims. The family members for repeal were always up front before the cameras and the committees, says Harrison, to neutralize some of the anger around the issue. The family members described the cruel impact of the death penalty on them, which, far from providing closure, they said, reopened wounds with every new legal procedure (see fig. 36).

The coalition worked at the grassroots level, obtaining funds to hire a di-rector (three women over the course of twelve years) and to bring in spokes-people like Sister Helen Prejean, the U.S.'s leading advocate for abolition. A Louisiana nun, Prejean wrote *Dead Men Walking*, which was made into a movie in 1995. Susan Sarandon portrayed Prejean and won an academy award for the role. Prejean inspired, trained, and spread the word across New Mexico, along with a steady stream of now-skeptical law-enforcement officers. Death-row inmates who had been exonerated gave speeches as well. Coalition members learned how to contact and speak with their legislators.

The coalition conducted public opinion polls that showed that while a majority of New Mexicans supported the death penalty for murder, 64 percent of them favored replacing it with life without parole and redirecting the money saved to help victims' families. Armed with the data, kept up to date with e-mail, and coordinated through a website, the growing numbers of advocates began making their voices heard. They were ably assisted by four of the finest public interest lobbyists working the halls of the legislature—Ruth Hoffman of the Lutheran Advocacy Ministry–New Mexico, Diane Wood of the American Civil Liberties Union (ACLU), Holly Beaumont of the New Mexico Conference of Churches, and Allen Sánchez of the New Mexico Conference of Catholic Bishops.

Starting in 1999 the coalition began to introduce bills in each of the legislature's biannual sixty-day sessions. Repeal bills had been introduced before. In 1981, Chasey's predecessor in the House, Rep. Judy Pratt, also from Albuquerque's university district, sponsored a bill, but it—like most of Chasey's early attempts—did not make it out of committee. Some of the leaders in the House were unwilling to have their members vote on this hot potato, fearing that it would hurt them in an election year. Others, like Rep. Dave Pederson from Gallup, then chair of the House Judiciary Committee, felt that the discussion was long overdue. Sometimes the bill would progress and then be referred to another committee where it would meet its demise. Chasey often would couch her introduction as a plea for justice—not revenge.[5] The losses were painful, but gradually the bill began to receive more favorable hearings.

Coalition members worked to gain support from both Democrats and Republicans. Though it was more difficult to gain Republican support, because of the law-and-order bent of many party members, some Republicans were won over. Representative Chasey took Republican Rep. Dub Williams, a death penalty opponent from Lincoln County, with her when she took Sister Helen Prejean to call on Governor Johnson during the early days. Johnson began to move, especially when the issue was linked to mistakes made in the drug war, an issue he began to tackle in earnest after he was reelected in 1998 (see chapter 10). Republican Reps. Teresa Zanetti, Janice Arnold Jones, Brian Moore, Diane Hamilton, and Jimmie Hall became repeal supporters. Rep. Larry Larranaga was convinced by Archbishop Michael Sheehan.

Over in the Senate, our leader, President Pro Temp Manny Aragon, had no fear of hot potatoes. Long a supporter of repeal, the Albuquerque lawyer succeeded in bringing his repeal bill to the Senate floor in 1999, where it lost 22 to 10. In 2001, the momentum had increased and the bill now was not just a repeal but also a substitution of one penalty for another. Life without parole replaced the death sentence. Both senators and representatives were taking it more seriously. A four-hour hearing on the floor of the House held jointly by the House and Senate judiciary committees featured both sides of the issue. Bud Welch held up a photo of his daughter, killed in the bombing of the federal building in Oklahoma City in 1995, and asked the committee not to kill in her name. Prosecutors and police asked the committee to retain the ultimate penalty because it deterred police and prison guard murders.[6] Although Aragon's bill (SB239) passed the joint judiciary committees, opponents of repeal won a victory on the Senate floor when SB 239 was narrowly defeated 21 to 20. The "near miss" was due to the absence of a vital vote— Sen. Pete Campos, from Las Vegas, who had been a supporter of repeal.

With such a narrow loss, the repealers were convinced that the tide was turning. But the following years would test their faith. Although the cause was consistently picking up speed in the House (see fig. 37), it would take eight years to reach the Senate floor again. The stumbling block was the Senate Judiciary Committee, where one vote stood in the way, and Gov. Bill Richardson, then on the campaign trail singing the praises of the death penalty.

And then came 2009. It was the year Barack Obama began his presidency, and Democrats were gaining power in New Mexico, having picked up seats in both the House and the Senate. The budget crisis was beginning to hit. But there was no ignoring the issue that tugged at the heartstrings and tried the souls of legislators.

⌒

A big crowd was assembling outside the doors of Room 321, and the crowd was anticipating the hearing of Rep. Chasey's House Bill 285. It had recently passed the House and was now scheduled to be heard by my committee, the Senate Public Affairs Committee (SPAC). We were no strangers to wedge issues and controversial bills in SPAC and, to save time, I usually asked proponents and opponents to designate speakers on the issue, whether it be medical marijuana, cockfighting, stem-cell research, concealed weapons, or partial birth abortion. This time, the lead-up to the hearing was especially anxious. Although the repeal bill had passed the committee in 2007, with one Republican voting in favor, many of the members were new and had not heard the debate before. We were all receiving letters and visits from repeal supporters. A few days before the hearing, a huge rally of repeal supporters, many clad in yellow t-shirts, heard speeches from religious leaders, legislators, murder victims' families, and death-row inmates who had been freed just in time.

Several years earlier, one of my favorite constituents, Art Riffenburgh, had called on me at my home to share his experience with the death penalty and invite me to a special event. Riffenburgh, a former cop and federal parole officer, said he had seen too many politically motivated district attorneys and prejudiced investigations more interested in getting votes than obtaining justice. He said that almost all those on death row were penniless, represented by hard-pressed public defenders, and he wanted me to meet one man who was the victim of this system—Juan Melendez. I never did get to meet Melendez, who spent eighteen years on death row in Florida before he was found innocent and released. But it seemed as if almost everyone else in New Mexico had. Melendez made repeated road trips from one end of the state to the other, speaking to over two thousand people at events strategically staged by the Coalition to Repeal the Death Penalty in districts where legislators were on the fence. It was part of a sustained media and speakers' campaign that featured exhibits of death penalty photos from photojournalists, documentaries, power points, panels, and an original stage play—*The Exonerated*.

Melendez was just one of the 130 men who had been exonerated and freed from death row in the United States since the early 1930s. We had heard from another just before we convened our March hearing in SPAC. And his case was a lot closer to home. Ron Keine sent us a letter postmarked Sterling Heights, Michigan, reminding us of what we vaguely remembered: the Vagos gang. Keine was one of four members of the California motorcycle gang convicted by then district attorney James Brandenburg for the brutal 1974 murder of a twenty-six-year-old UNM student, William Velten. The highly publicized case rested on the testimony of a motel maid who had been coached by the prosecution and who later recanted. Yet Keine and the others spent nearly two years on death row in Santa Fe and had even ordered their last meals. They were ultimately freed when Kerry Rodney Lee, a Drug Enforcement Administration (DEA) informant, confessed the murder to his pastor in South Carolina.

Without the confession, Keine, then an out-of-work plumber and local Republican Party activist in a Detroit suburb, would have been the victim of the ultimate miscarriage of justice—in our names. The near execution of Keine and the three others lent New Mexico the distinction of having the highest rate of death-row exonerations in the nation. For me, Keine presented a strong argument. It spoke to several other legislators, I knew, including Sen. Phil Griego and Rep. Nick Salazar, who were not on my committee but who would have to vote on the issue eventually.

In case the innocence angle didn't convince us, the coalition had delivered to our offices the results of the most recent poll taken in late 2008.

Support for the death penalty was slipping, and a majority now favored life without parole instead.[7]

But when I banged the gavel to open the hearing on the death penalty in March 2009, the repeal advocates had shifted their focus. After heartrending testimony from Andrea Vigil, whose husband Carlos had been gunned down in the streets of Santa Fe, Representative Chasey introduced David Keys, a professor of criminology at New Mexico State University, who told the committee that it cost the state $2.75 million a year for a death penalty case—more than the cost of life imprisonment.[8] The practical emphasis appealed to legislators who made their minds up based on numbers, not emotions, and it was an effective tactic especially when ideological or religious beliefs divided the deliberators. In 2009, the cost-effectiveness case appealed to the fiscal conservatives, who just happened to be likely supporters of the death penalty.

With appeals, expert witnesses, longer trials, prolonged jury selections, and better lawyers, the state was spending a bundle, with few executions to show for it. New Mexico had executed only one person since 1960, although prosecutors had initially pursued two hundred death penalties. Of those, just over fifty actually went to a jury that decided on life or death.[9]

Given its costs, its errors, and its inability to actually deter crime, Chasey presented repeal as a practical step in a tight fiscal climate. The money saved (an estimated $2 million each year) could be better used to assist the victims' families, she said. When I asked audience members to raise their hands to show opposition or support, almost the entire room raised their hands in support of Chasey's measure. Only a few district attorneys, who were making the same arguments they had started with in 1997, raised their hands in opposition.

When committee members had an opportunity to speak, it was clear that Chasey had won the day. Newly elected senator Tim Eichenberg questioned Professor Keys closely about how much money could be saved given that there were then only two people on death row, but he seemed satisfied. Sen. Eric Griego said that everything he had read showed the death penalty did not deter crime and fell unfairly along racial and economic lines. Saying that the United States is out of touch with the rest of the world on this issue, he said cooler heads should prevail. Sen. Cynthia Nava, noting that the budget shortfall had focused everyone on what they *couldn't* do instead of what they *could* do, said, "This is a great thing we can do, and a positive step forward for New Mexico."

I hadn't spoken. I was raised Quaker and opposition to the death penalty, and all forms of violence, has been in my DNA since childhood, but I wanted to listen to what others said. And I really didn't know how I would react if one of my loved ones were murdered. Now, realizing that the votes were there, I made the motion for passage, saying, "We should never become the thing we hate." The bill sailed through on a party-line vote, with Democrats Mary Jane Garcia, Nava, Griego, Eichenberg, and Feldman voting yes, and Republicans Vernon Asbill and Gay Kernan voting no.

Unlike previous years, there had been few tears and little angst, only an honest discussion of the conflicting values and practical effects. Difficult debates had tended to provoke emotional reactions in the past, causing legislators to reach uncomfortable conclusions and sometimes switch votes. In 2003, Rep. Tom Anderson cried in his House committee when confronted with the cruel choice. "I am not a bad man," the Republican legislator from Albuquerque's west side said, tears filling his eyes. "This is not an easy job. It is difficult to do. I don't like this job."[10]

I felt for Anderson when I heard that story over in the Senate, because I knew that I had been there too, trying to weigh the conflicting values of safety, justice, compassion, and equality on other tough issues, sometimes without all the facts. That's what being a legislator is all about—and we had done it. As the crowds cleared out and we moved on to the next bill on the committee's long agenda, I was proud of my committee, proud of the New Mexico Senate and the high level of political discourse we had just completed on a high stakes issue.

～

Gov. Bill Richardson had always been a big problem for those who wanted to repeal the death penalty. On the hunt for the Democratic presidential nomination since 2004, the governor had not only announced his support of the death penalty but also sought to broaden it. Many believed he had used his power to keep the repeal, which passed the House in 2005 and 2007, from reaching his desk, forcing him to make the difficult decision in the middle of a presidential bid. How did he do it? The usual way—the committee bottleneck. In this case, the bottleneck was not the Senate Conservation Committee, as it had been for cockfighting, or the Corporations Committee, as it had been for the fireworks bill. Instead it was the Senate Judiciary Committee. Even though the committee was more heavily stacked with Democrats than most, the bill always lacked one vote—that of Sen. Richard Martinez, a retired magistrate judge from Española. Martinez had voted for the repeal when it was on the Senate floor in 2001, but he later blocked it in committee. Although Martinez denied it at the time, most legislators involved in the issue were certain that Martinez was acting on the governor's behalf. "He told me the governor would veto his capital outlay if he voted for the bill," recalled Allen Sánchez, the executive director of the New Mexico Conference of Catholic Bishops, who added that Martinez was not happy about the pressure. Sánchez believes Martinez was simply acting like many rural legislators who are dependent on "pork" projects (i.e., capital outlay projects for senior centers, water projects, etc.) for their reelection. Another Democrat on the committee, Sen. Lidio Rainaldi, a conservative who had always supported the death penalty, was also a stumbling block.

But now, in 2009, with the election in the rear-view mirror, the governor was leaving the door open, and he let it be known that he would not object if the bill reached the Senate floor. The "Obama sweep" of 2008 had placed new Democratic members on the Judiciary Committee, and this time the controversial bill had no trouble passing, in spite of the opposition from district attorneys who, the committee knew, used the tool to plea bargain with violent criminals.

When SB 285 finally reached the floor on Friday, March 13, Majority Leader Michael Sanchez acted as the floor sponsor with Representative Chasey at his side (see fig. 38). The gallery was packed with spectators expecting a good debate. They were not disappointed. The emotional three-hour marathon touched on the Bible, Navajo beliefs, and Quakerism as well as the more pragmatic problems of cost and mistakes. Sen. Bill Payne, a Republican from Albuquerque, echoed the concerns of police and law enforcement when he said that the men and women in blue would be at higher risk because the penalty was a deterrent. Sen. Kent Cravens, a Republican from Albuquerque, said that he believed only the death penalty—and not life in prison—put the "fear of God" into those who commit terrible crimes. And Sen. Rod Adair said that six thousand years of recorded history, as well as four hundred years of American Judeo-Christian tradition, affirmed that the death penalty was just.

Sen. Jerry Ortiz y Pino, on the other hand, argued that, "In six thousand years of history we've evolved, and we should not be relying on the lizard part of our brain. . . . We are the last Western society that holds onto it," he said, "and it makes us less than we should be." Sen. Lynda Lovejoy, one of the chamber's two Navajos, said that her culture put more stock in healing and restoring harmony than in retribution.[11]

For Senate President Pro Tempore Tim Jennings, one of only three Democrats opposing the repeal, the vote revolved around one person: Dena Lynn Gore, the Artesia nine-year-old who was killed by Terry Clark. "What chance did that girl have at life?" asked Jennings whose eastern New Mexico district was near the scene of the crime. "This vote, to me, is for her." The personal, again, was the political.[12]

The debate went on for over three hours, as it had in the House. In the end, the repealers triumphed, with HB 285 passing 24–18. In contrast to the House, there had been no Republican supporters of repeal. Chasey called the vote "momentous," and Catholic lobbyist Allen Sánchez said it was a big victory for forgiveness and love. "We're teaching our children that life is sacred," he said, echoing a familiar Catholic theme.[13] Turning around in my place, I could see the repeal advocates in the gallery above us, embracing one another and, after twelve years, crying the tears of the victory.

Newspapers in Germany and Europe were the first to carry the story. Reuters, the *Manchester Guardian*, the *Taiwan News* online, and the *Herald Tribune* were soon on the phone. The national media were not far behind. A news ticker scrolled across the bottom of MSNBC asking viewers to contact the office of New Mexico Gov. Bill Richardson—pro or con. The messages began to pour in. Opponents of the repeal, including the mothers of slain Bernalillo County Sheriff's Deputy James McGrane and Dena Lynn Gore, pleaded with the governor over the following weekend. The *Albuquerque Journal* opposed the repeal and prominently featured the opponents in news coverage.

But the Coalition to Repeal the Death Penalty left no stone unturned. For the previous month, the governor's office had been deluged by calls from celebrities like Martin Sheen, Susan Sarandon, Bianca Jagger, the children of Martin Luther King, and Cesar Chavez. Hispanic activist Dolores Huerta called, along with the president of Mexico Vicente Fox, John Corzine, the governor of New Jersey (which had repealed the death penalty a few years earlier), and former president Jimmy Carter. By Wednesday, March 18, the governor's office had gotten twelve thousand e-mails, calls, and visits, with three-quarters of them favoring repeal.

"We had to give him a graceful way to change his mind," said Viki Harrison, of the Coalition to Repeal the Death Penalty, who was nervous about what the governor, who was openly saying he had not yet made up his mind, would do. But Allen Sánchez, lobbyist for the Catholic bishops, had a good feeling. Over the previous months, he and the bishops had contacted numerous legislators. Richardson, a Catholic, had shared a number of dinners with Archbishop Sheehan and two other New Mexico bishops. At the last one, Sanchez said the bishops ran out of the usual moral arguments, which everyone had examined before. But then Sánchez tried a new tack with the governor, who, at the time, was under investigation for alleged pay-to-play contracts. "I thought he might be able to understand that ambitious prosecutors and investigators could be wrong. And with the death penalty consequences were irreversible. So I tried that argument. His eyes got wide," Sánchez recalled, "and I thought I had hit a nerve."

But victory was not at hand, not yet. The governor had three days to sign or veto the bill, since it had been sent to him before the end of the session, and he was searching his soul. On Wednesday, March 18, Richardson went to mass and then visited the death chamber in the state penitentiary. By 4:00 p.m. he had made up his mind, and he summoned clergy and coalition members to come to his office. Flanked by Archbishop Ricardo Ramirez, from Las Cruces, and Representative Chasey, Richardson said that regardless of his personal opinion about the death penalty he was signing the repeal because he did not have confidence in the criminal justice system to be the final arbiter when it comes to who lives and who dies for their crimes.[14] The governor said he was satisfied that dangerous criminals would not be out on the street because of the measure's requirement of life without parole, and he praised Rep. Gail Chasey for the courage with which she had carried the bill over so many years.

After the bill-signing ceremony he said that it was the most difficult decision of his political life, and he hoped that those who disagreed would realize he could only do what he thought was right. "I hope and pray it's the right decision," he said.[15]

"This has been a long process to come to this day," Chasey said, as the text messages, e-mails, and blogs from around the world began to spread the news. Chasey was numb and just beginning to understand the magnitude of what she had accomplished through grace, grit, and perseverance.

Fellow legislators, advocates, and constituents soon hailed Representative Chasey's courage and unwavering commitment to the issue. "People on both sides of the issue respected her ethics and moral fiber," said Viki Harrison, "and some changed their votes because of her character. She is the best advocate we could have ever had. She had an accordion file that she could dive into and find the answer to any question. She knew when to be flexible and when to stand firm."

Chasey had what I call a "passion for the possible." It had been my campaign theme. She had done even more, carrying the *impossible* across the finish line in this gun-loving, fireworks-friendly Western state, using a variety of allies and arguments to fit the ever-changing legislative circumstances.

For Chasey and the advocates, the best was yet to come. Days after the governor signed the bill, Chasey, the governor, Archbishop Sheehan, and key members of the winning coalition were invited to Rome for a special ceremony in their honor. The religious community of Sant' Egidio was going to light up the Roman Colosseum to mark the repeal of the death penalty in New Mexico as it had done for the state of New Jersey in 2007. The religious community was a leader in the international movement against the death penalty, and this victory was especially sweet in Europe. The amazing event featured over five hundred people, the mayor of Rome, bands, and speeches. In April 2009, the New Mexico group had a general audience with the Pope, who spoke with Richardson and blessed a silver olive branch, a gift from the religious community to the governor. Richardson accepted it, saying the Catholic Church is very influential in a Catholic state like New Mexico.[16]

There were other celebrations and awards for Chasey and the governor in the months to come, one of them in Hollywood where Mike Farrell, star of *MASH*, was among the celebrities who feted them. Supporters of the death penalty, including Bernalillo County Sherriff Darren White, threatened to launch a petition drive to allow voters to overturn the new law. The effort fizzled. The New Mexico Coalition to Repeal the Death Penalty and Representative Chasey, meanwhile, were now known internationally, and Chasey continued to make trips to Europe at her own expense throughout the next year. The group continues to this day to lobby for funds for murder victims' families in New Mexico and to assist advocates seeking to repeal the ultimate penalty in other states.

Part VI   Good People Trapped in a Flawed System

Ethics, Campaign Finance, and Transparency

E THICS AND CAMPAIGN FINANCE REFORM ARE TOUCHY SUBJECTS in every state legislature, but New Mexico is an extreme case. New Mexico is one of only eight states without an ethics commission. It was one of the last to limit campaign contributions and open up conference committees to public view. I found out the hard way that the mere mention of ethics, a hint about the undue influence of special interests, or simple questions about how public officials use money to get and stay in office were fighting words.

Ethics are, after all, personal affairs, values that are the products of up-bringing, religious background, personal discipline, and character. It's a particularly difficult subject for part-time, unpaid legislators who have no staff at any time other than the legislative session and are faced daily with conflicting interests that touch on their own lives and livelihoods. In a citizens' legislature where the members maintain their private occupations, conflict of interest is almost built in. But few like to discuss it beyond the one ethics training held every two years.

No one likes to talk about campaign financing either, despite public alarm about big money buying votes and elections. The system that brought legislators to power looks pretty good once they're in office.

At the beginning of each legislative session, senators raise their right hands and swear to refrain from using the office for personal gain and avoid any act of impropriety or any act that gives the appearance of impropriety. We acknowledge that it's a matter of honor to put aside personal and political interests and act in the best interest of New Mexico.

But during the decade of the 2000s, the honor system was not working, as the following incidents reflect:

› Former Senate president pro tem Manny Aragon is serving a five-and-half-year sentence in a federal prison in Florence, Colorado, for skimming over $600,000 from a courthouse project he had promoted while in the legislature. The bagman on the scheme (who delivered the money) was legislative lobbyist and former Albuquerque mayor Ken Schultz.

> Former treasurer Robert Vigil served over two years in prison and was almost impeached by the House of Representatives in 2005 for an extortion and kickback scheme involving state investments. Michael Montoya, another treasurer, served time as well.

> A federal investigation of a "pay-to-play" scheme centering on investment managers who were contributors to Gov. Bill Richardson's campaigns dragged on from 2008 to 2009. The managers won lucrative contracts but lost millions in state funds. Richardson was never indicted, but the highly publicized investigation scuttled the governor's chances for a post with the Obama administration and raised questions about the ethical climate in New Mexico.

> Former Clovis legislator Vincent "Smiley" Gallegos was indicted in 2009 on fraud, embezzlement, and money laundering charges related to a $300,000 loan from the Region III Housing Authority, which he directed. The case is still pending.

> The wife of former representative Richard Vigil of Las Vegas was convicted in 2009 of fraud in the misuse of state funds. Instead of going to the bilingual program she headed, the funds went for an after-hours party with an expensive band and for a forty-two-inch plasma TV, picked up at Sears by Representative Vigil and then somehow lost.

Meanwhile, the cost of campaigns escalated dramatically as big money flooded the state. Lax transparency, disclosure, and other accountability measures earned the Land of Enchantment a D- (62 percent) in the State Integrity Investigation by the Center for Public Integrity, Global Integrity and Public Radio International. Almost alone among the states, New Mexico still allowed unlimited contributions from corporations, and almost any source at all. It was the Wild West.

Despite the bad grades and growing public alarm, the New Mexico Senate dug in. The leadership led an energetic counterattack against all critics—including me. What follows are three chapters about how a bipartisan coalition of reformers fought for ethics, transparency, and finance reforms, often losing dramatically, but regrouping to make significant advances and reshape the political landscape.

CHAPTER 13

Ethics

Can Citizen Legislators Draw
Bright Lines in a Gray Area?

B Y ALL ACCOUNTS, IT WAS THE MOST DRAMATIC DAY IN THE HIS-
tory of the New Mexico legislature. Some called it the House of Representative's finest hour; others called it the worst. Over three hundred people
crowded into the House gallery for the four-hour debate that day in February 1992, as the body decided whether to expel one of its own, Rep. Ron
Olguin, a Democrat from Albuquerque's South Valley.

There was utter and complete silence as Sergeant at Arms Gilbert Baca
escorted Olguin to the front of the chambers. Once there, he was censured
publicly for a serious breach of ethical responsibilities as a legislator. Olguin
had sold his influence as a representative for a $15,000 contract to obtain
funding for a community corrections program, named, ironically, Staying
Straight Community Corrections. Olguin apologized for the dishonor and
disrepute he had brought upon the body, and the session resumed. His censure had no practical effect on his legislative work. He stayed in place on the
same committees and attended the same floor sessions as others.

But the lawmakers were shaken. They had originally planned to expel
him, a motion that was made by Rep. Max Coll, of Santa Fe. But instead,
after hours of draining debate in which representatives wept, quoted the
Bible, and referred to the ancient Greeks and lessons from their own fathers,
the House voted against expulsion 45 to 24 and for the lesser penalty 59 to
10. They chose compassion rather than discipline.

A number of legislators, including Rep. Barbara Perea Casey of Roswell,
the chair of the committee that reviewed the evidence (a criminal trial on the
indictment brought by Attorney General Tom Udall had not yet been held),

noted that the entire body had been compromised by Olguin's actions. Rep. Murray Ryan, of Silver City, said that with any decision "other than expulsion, we will be viewed as crooks, bums, or worse."[1] It looked like Olguin would surely be expelled, but then something turned the tide the other way, recalled Stuart Bluestone, then a staffer at the legislative council service who sat at the rostrum that day with Speaker Raymond Sanchez. It may have been the switch in position by Las Cruces Rep. J. Paul Taylor, widely regarded as the conscience of the legislature. Taylor said he had almost decided to vote for expulsion but could not because he felt compassion for Olguin.[2] Others felt that it just as well could have been them. Rep. Garth Simms, of Albuquerque, noted that it's common for legislators to promise various groups to get legislation through for them. Rep. Dominic Ferrari, of Gallup, said, "I'm concerned that if all were known about everybody, we may be in that same chair. That's a concern. Where do you draw the line? What's ethical? In a citizen legislature, there is a gray area."[3]

The gray area had always been problematic for lawmakers who were not full-time, salaried professionals working in Santa Fe day in and day out. The New Mexico constitution outlined a system of citizen legislators who kept their jobs as butchers, bakers, and candlestick makers. They naturally had divided loyalties, conflicts of interest between their personal and business ties and those of the state. It was an inherent part of the system, and for the most part it was left to legislators to decide what was right and wrong. Periodic calls for lobbying and campaign finance reform had been heard before Olguin's censure and later conviction for bribery. But the Olguin affair was a black eye that required action beyond a simple reprimand. The answer for the legislature, as always, was a task force.

The 1993 task force spurred a number of reforms—most of them laws requiring additional disclosures on the part of legislators, lobbyists, and political action committees. Legislators were now required to disclose the sources of gross income greater than $5,000, and describe business interests of more than $10,000. They were to list real estate they owned and memberships on for-profit boards. In addition legislators had to disclose the names of each state agency that was sold $5,000 or more in goods and services. Lobbyists were required to report expenditures, and PACs had to register with the secretary of state.

Most important, an interim Legislative Ethics Committee was set up to hear complaints lodged against legislators, conduct investigations into violations, and issue advisory opinions on ethical matters. The committee would be evenly divided between Republicans and Democrats from each chamber. House and Senate leaders would be committee members, along with a few others. The committee could recommend reprimand, censure, or expulsion. Or it could simply refer everything to the regular committees charged with ethics that met during each session.

Each body had its own rules (the Senate adopted new ones the same year as the Olguin censure) and the committee was the now the arbiter and enforcer. Guiding its deliberations was one underlying principle, spelled out in the Senate rules this way: "Full disclosure of real or potential conflicts of interest shall be a guiding principle for determining appropriate conduct of members."[4] But that was not all. The new Senate rules defined several danger zones:

› The acceptance of anything of value (other than campaign contributions!) that improperly influences an official act, decision, or vote
› The impairment of impartiality and independent judgment caused by a legislator's private employment
› Compensation or reimbursement outside of the usual mileage and per diem that a legislator gets from someone else for rendering services, advice, or assistance as a legislator
› Gifts or jobs offered with the intent to influence a senator's vote or performance of official duties

Many hoped the committee would enforce the rules, or at least apply them to specific situations, offering guidance to legislators trying to do the right thing. But with a few exceptions, the committee has been a disappointment. It has offered about a dozen advisory opinions in twenty years, mostly about the proper use of the state seal, legislative stationery, and calling cards. Complaints against legislators are not made public, and the committee had never found probable cause to recommend reprimands or other sanctions. The committee rarely meets. I didn't even know it existed until I had been in the Senate for a while, and I had never heard of the regular committees ever taking up a case—and for years I served on one of them, the Senate Rules Committee! If you were looking for action or enforcement, you'd have to look elsewhere.

Meanwhile ethical dilemmas kept popping up, and they continue. Almost every day legislators are called upon to vote on issues that have a direct financial effect on them—well beyond taxes or general regulations. Sen. Phil Griego, who was in the title insurance business for years, voted on a number of bills that would have removed title insurance companies' liability and made it tougher for people to sue them. Sen. Tim Eichenberg sponsored property tax bills even though his bread and butter was property tax appeals. Insurance agents like Sens. John Sapien and Carroll Leavell vote on plenty of insurance measures. Rep. James Strickler runs a small oil and gas production company, and Reps. Don Bratton, Bill Gray, and Bob Wooley have ties to oil and gas. They vote on environmental issues affecting that business. The spouses of county and state employees vote on their pensions and health benefits. Rep. Debbie Rodella, a Democrat from Española, once asked me to sponsor an amendment that would have exempted her husband, a county sheriff, and other public safety employees from a prohibition against "double-dipping" (getting a state salary and a state pension at the same time). A number of senators are educators or retired educators; any solution to the state's shrinking educational retiree fund may affect them directly.

In sixteen years I have seen only a few legislators excuse themselves from voting on these kinds of issues. One was Sen. Phil Maloof, whose family owned a liquor empire. The other was Sen. Sue Wilson Beffort, whose husband's University of New Mexico salary might have been affected by the outcome of one bill. On one occasion, Sen. Diana Duran tried to recuse (or excuse) herself from an issue involving a family member, but was discouraged by then president pro tem Manny Aragon. "We don't do that here," he said, according to several onlookers. For the most part, senators feel that their "impartiality is not impaired by their employment," but sometimes there is more than a shadow of a doubt.

New Mexico's unique and arcane system of allowing each legislator to appropriate funds for specific capital outlay projects in his or her district can also create conflicts. In 2008, Rep. Richard Vigil's appropriation went to a bilingual program his wife was operating in Las Vegas. A year later she was convicted of fraud and misuse of the funds. But what if the funds had not been flagrantly misspent but simply went to benefit a program she operated? Isn't that a conflict of interest?

Other appropriations made by the legislature have directly benefited senators' programs. The rugby team coached by Sen. Shannon Robinson in 2008 was funded through a $150,000 direct appropriation to UNM, although the team operated as a private club, not as an officially sanctioned university sport. The Albuquerque media covered the conflict intensively in 2008, revealing that prior to 2008 funding made by the legislature to the UNM Center for Regional Studies had been diverted to rugby. Robinson had sponsored legislation to fund the center. [5]

Contracts and outside jobs for legislators are even more problematic. Representative Olguin's problem stemmed from a contract he got to influence legislation at both the county and state levels. He got off without expulsion from the House, but he didn't fare so well in court. He was found guilty and served time. In 1998, Sen. Manny Aragon's contract with Wackenhut Corrections, a private prison company now known as the GEO Group, created a firestorm. Building on his national network of state legislators, Aragon was hired to provide lobbying and government relations work outside the state. He insisted over and over that it was not a conflict even though Wackenhut was then in negotiations with New Mexico to build and operate prisons in Hobbs and Santa Rosa. Aragon participated fully in the legislative deliberations but was finally forced by his colleagues to give up the contract. His former Senate colleague Les Houston continued to lobby for Wackenhut until 2011.

Sen. John Ryan, an Albuquerque Republican, currently has a contract to do federal lobbying for the City of Clovis, the Eastern New Mexico Water Utility Authority, and two electric transmission outfits—Tri-State Generation and Sun Zia. All seek funding and do business with the legislature as well as the federal government, much of it before the judiciary, water, and conservation committees, where Ryan is a member.

It's hard to believe that these legislators were not hired because of their knowledge and connections as legislators. I was approached several times by prospective public relations clients to lobby the Albuquerque City Council, where I would be lobbying those who shared constituents with me. I declined, thinking it was a conflict. But not everyone has a strict interpretation—or can afford to have one.

Consulting is one of the few occupations flexible enough to fit in with part-time legislating. But it presents other problems as well. I had to give up a contract with a small nonprofit, Law Access New Mexico, which operates a help line for low-income people who need legal advice. I was poised to help them publicize their program. But it turned out that the program had been authorized and funded in a broader bill that I had voted on to provide legal services to the indigent. A constitutional provision (Article 4, Section 28) prohibits legislators from having interests in contracts passed during their term. Contracting with state agencies or local governments funded by the state became more difficult to do as well, even if I bid for the project in a competitive process, and not as a sole source contractor. It's a problem faced by legislator/lawyers who have contracts with local governments to act as public defenders, or city attorneys, too.

One of the few ethics bills we managed to pass in 2007 clarified the Governmental Conduct Act and how it applied to contracts. Sponsored by then representative (now senator) Joe Cervantes, of Las Cruces, the bill was aimed at curbing the award of contracts to the friends and associates, the "political cronies," of public officials. As such, it targets the fuel that drives the bus in New Mexico—personal relationships.

The general public (and even some candidates) assumes that being a senator or representative will boost the profile and business opportunities for legislators. But, even before the new reform, public service closed many doors. As a consequence, legislators without a way of subsidizing their own service fall back on the money they receive in per diem payments for time in session or in committee and reimbursements for mileage. Increasingly they are using their campaign funds to pay for constituent services, committee expenses, and other activities for which legislators have no source of funding. They also rely on lobbyists for the stray meal, entertainment, and the maintenance of a lifestyle that befits their position—if not their pocketbook. It may be more difficult now to award a contract to a friend, but personal relationships, especially those with lobbyists, are still primary.

AN INCONVENIENT TRUTH

In the fall of 2005, the news of the indictment of former treasurers Robert Vigil and Michael Montoya hit New Mexico legislators like a slap in the face. Stunned by the evidence, which came out daily on TV and in the newspapers, legislators scrambled to respond. A defiant Robert Vigil professed his innocence and refused to resign. A trial date was still in the future. Meanwhile, a cloud hung over state government and the discussion turned to bagmen and $10,000 payments handed over in parking lots. Employees of the treasurer's office feared for their reputations and their jobs. So did legislators. Although Vigil was not one of our own, we grappled with our constitutional responsibility: impeachment.

The House of Representatives set up a special impeachment committee to review the evidence and begin the two-part proceedings. It was historic. The House would determine whether there was enough evidence to warrant a trial by the New Mexico Senate. Fortunately, amid the deliberations, Vigil decided to resign. He was later tried, found guilty of attempted extortion, and sentenced to twenty-six months. Montoya, who turned state's evidence, served forty months in a Colorado prison. Governor Richardson appointed Doug Brown, a well-respected banker and later dean of the University of New Mexico's business school, to serve as treasurer and clean up the mess. He also created an ethics task force composed of luminaries from the private and public sector to recommend remedies and restore confidence that this would not happen again.

Doug Brown was on the task force, which was chaired by former governor Garrey Carruthers and UNM Law School dean Suellyn Scarnecchia. So was former U.S. interior secretary Stewart Udall, former LFC director Maralyn Budke, lawyer Norman Thayer, accountant Leonard Sanchez, Matt Brix of Common Cause, and Stuart Bluestone from the Attorney General's office. Legislators and administration officials were there too. I was on it, listening carefully to the proposals and wondering how in the world we would ever get any of this through the Senate.

After months of testimony and deliberation, the group recommended a wide-ranging package of legislation for the 2007 session. It included limits on campaign contributions, which I would sponsor and agonize over, a gift act sponsored by Sen. John Grubesic of Santa Fe, and conflict-of-interest measures to strengthen the Governmental Conduct Act sponsored by Rep. Joe Cervantes of Las Cruces. It also included a new concept designed to address the fact that unsalaried legislators were using campaign funds for routine legislative expenses—contrary to state law.

The new idea was to amend the constitution so that legislators could be reimbursed up to $10,000 per year to cover legitimate constituent expenses (like surveys or a secretary to handle constituent requests). In return the law restricting the use of campaign funds for anything but campaigns would be tightened. The concept, which was translated into two companion bills, never went far although I introduced it several years later in response to our continued, destructive dependence on lobbyists and campaign contributions.[6]

By far the biggest idea from the task force was an independent ethics commission. New Mexico is one of only eight states that do not have an ethics commission with jurisdiction over state officials, employees, government contractors, and lobbyists. It does have a robust Judicial Standards Commission and a Legislative Ethics Committee that, as we have seen, rarely meets and has never taken action. But clearly the public wanted more. A poll reported in the *Albuquerque Journal* that year indicated that 90 percent of respondents wanted an ethics board and limits on campaign contributions.[7] Ninety percent is about as high as it gets in a poll.

Members of the task force proposed a bipartisan ten-member commission attached to (but not a part of) state government. The commission would have the power to investigate complaints and the ability to subpoena witnesses and documents. A whistleblower protection clause was included to protect employees and others bringing violations to light. The commission would also have an educational function, developing a code and conducting annual training sessions. It would, as former governor Garrey Carruthers said, "draw bright lines in a gray area."

The proposed commission was endorsed by the governor and highlighted in the press. But it was all but dead on arrival in the Senate, where it languished for over a month in the Senate Rules Committee and drew fire from Senate leaders.

The problem, once again, was not the message but the messenger, or, in this case, the dispatcher: the governor. At the time, Richardson was in full campaign mode, just reelected and swinging into presidential politics with aggressive fundraising techniques and two new PACs open for business. Rumors of a scandal involving highway bonds and investment advisors who had connections to Richardson were beginning to surface.

Majority Leader Michael Sanchez in particular was incensed at the hypocrisy of it all. And the more popular ethics reform became with the public and the House of Representatives (where it passed with only four opposing votes in 2007), the more he dug in. Sanchez argued the reforms were unnecessary in the legislature, which was being punished for the sins of one man (Robert Vigil) who was not even a member of the legislature. "What did the legislature do to warrant the push for the change?" he asked.[8]

He was not alone. Republican Minority Leader Stuart Ingle said you couldn't legislate ethics. "You either have ethics or you don't."[9]

Sen. Leonard Rawson said, "Ethics legislation would only trap people who are trying to be honest, and the laws can be abused. Just because you have an ethics commission or ethics laws, doesn't make someone ethical."[10] The argument that the legislature had done nothing to warrant change became harder to sell after the March 2007 indictment of the Senate's flamboyant pro tem, Manny Aragon. But that didn't mean the opponents didn't try. Even when the news of Aragon's indictment broke during the March 2007 special session, the leadership avoided dealing with the topic of the ethics commission, shifting instead to debate on public financing of judicial races.

In the next five years, legislators would introduce forty-nine bills proposing an ethics commission. Many would pass the House unanimously, or with few negative votes. But the Senate leadership was in no hurry. One commission bill in 2011 proposed a commission so weak that even advocates from Common Cause and the League of Women Voters backed away from it. Under the bill, a substitute engineered by Sen. Linda Lopez (SRC Sub for SB 164, 172, 293, 420), the commission would have limited subpoena power;

complaints would not be taken during campaign season, nor would they be made public. All meetings would be closed and no actions taken, with findings referred to the AG, the legislature, or other agencies. The only penalties prescribed in the bill would be for disclosure of confidential complaints by the press or members of the public.

Majority Leader Michael Sanchez continued his opposition, penning an opinion piece in 2009 that called out legislative supporters of ethics reforms as hypocrites who were all for ethics when the microphones and cameras were on but who themselves exhibited unethical behavior.[11]

News coverage of the Senate's opposition to ethics reforms had started on a negative pitch back in 2007 with the *Albuquerque Tribune*, a liberal afternoon paper, calling the Senate "obstinate and ego driven . . . a bunch of clowns tripping over their own oversized feet."[12] The *Albuquerque Journal* called upon the Senate to see the big picture. "It's not about buckling under to pressure from the governor . . . it's not about one bad actor in one elected position . . . or about targeting the New Mexico legislature," the *Journal* opined. "It's about setting up a system that limits influence peddling and targets officials who embrace the payoffs, the bagmen, the pay-to-play culture" (see fig. 39).[13]

For the Senate, over the next few years the coverage would only get worse, and with Richardson under a growing ethical cloud, the issue would become a partisan one. In the 2010 governor's race, Republicans jumped on the Democrats as corrupt and opaque. Republican gubernatorial candidate Susana Martinez (who was endorsed by the *Albuquerque Journal*) embraced transparency and ethics, calling for tougher criminal penalties for politicians and the creation of a public corruption unit in the Department of Public Safety. Martinez's opponent, Lt. Gov. Diane Denish, who had championed the sunshine portal (see next chapter) and investigations into the Region IV housing scandals, paid the price—losing the election.

As 2012 drew to a close, the Senate continued to hold out against an ethics commission with teeth. The hesitancy came at a cost. Independent PACs like Reform New Mexico Now, which is affiliated with Governor Martinez, are still beating the drum against Bill Richardson and the unethical Democrats. Campaign literature sponsored by the group in one hotly contested House race in 2012 charged Democrat Andrew Barreras with ethical misdeeds and harked back to "the Richardson Way."[14]

The facts seldom get in the way of a heated campaign. The fact that Richardson was never indicted for pay-to-play activities and was actually the promoter of an ethics commission was lost in a sea of negative perceptions.

The Senate's resistance to a strong ethics commission continued in 2013, when Rep. Brian Egolf's ethics commission bill passed the House with only one dissenting vote yet, like others before it, never emerged from the Senate Rules Committee. The perennial resistance to this measure as well as open conference committees and campaign contribution limits fuels the perception that legislators are above the law and quite content with policing themselves, thank you.

No wonder the public distrust of "self-serving" politicians has grown over the years. The American National Election Studies asks citizens about their trust in government biennially. The results indicate a steady decline in confidence from a rate of more than 60 percent in the early 1960s to less than 30 percent by the year 2000.[15]

In the first decade of the twenty-first century, public confidence is still dropping as candidates themselves bash gridlocked politicians as crooks, and the media finds stories that confirm this narrative. But this death spiral is based on perception, and not necessarily fact. The examples of corruption I've documented here do not validate the assumption that all legislators are corrupt. Unfortunately, the defensive reaction of the New Mexico Senate has made people think there's something to hide. The blind spot that Senate leaders have when it comes to ethics has fed this perception. Perhaps the blind spot is a natural, defensive reaction to the pressures brought to bear on unpaid, unstaffed citizens doing the best they can, given the confusing gray areas in which they must operate. I find it puzzling. Why is a body that has risen above the partisan divide to cope with a recession, reduce secondhand smoke, ban the death penalty, legalize medical marijuana, end cockfighting, and protect patients unwilling to address public perceptions of corruption?

The level of political corruption in New Mexico may not be worse than anywhere else in the United States. In fact, it may be better. The online newspaper *The Daily Beast* carried a study by Clark Merefield and Lauren Streib about public corruption in the states from 1998 through 2008. It ranked New Mexico forty-fifth lowest among fifty states and the District of Columbia. Likewise the *New York Times* ranked New Mexico forty-eighth for the number of convicted officials from 1998–2007.[16] But the perception persists that New Mexico state government is corrupt, and that is damaging and demoralizing for citizens and legislators alike. Of course, legislators find it challenging to police themselves or draw bright lines in a gray area. But they are the only ones with the authority to enact statutory changes or, at the very least, to take the issue seriously. Other states have stepped up to the plate, establishing independent ethics commissions, financing elections more fairly, tightening lobbyist restrictions, and providing broader, more transparent access for citizens and taxpayers. Sometimes the reforms that states make do not help. Sometimes they are preempted by federal laws or corruption arises in another area. But that is no excuse for doing nothing. Laws can be changed. Problems can be addressed. That is what legislatures are for.

CHAPTER 14

Transparency

Zero Visibility Possible

*F*EBRUARY 2006. BOB JOHNSON TOOK OFF HIS HAT AND CARE-
fully hung up his winter coat on the back of the door to my office in
the state capitol. He had come here for the perennial debate on opening
legislative conference committees to the public. The arcane issue had become symbolic of open government and transparency—and the Senate's
resistance to both.

As usual, Johnson arrived early, ready to get his teeth kicked in again.
Although he now walked with a cane, the eighty-four-year-old ex-Marine and
Associated Press (AP) bureau chief did not shrink from a fight. He was now
the executive director of the New Mexico Foundation for Open Government (FOG), a group begun in 1990 to protect the public's right to know.
Johnson built the organization with the help of Bill Dixon, an Albuquerque
attorney, and Kent Walz of the *Albuquerque Journal*. He reached out to newspapers and broadcasters in the state who had a vested interest in the first
amendment, but his group also included the general public. A freelance writer
and public relations practitioner at the time, I signed up, paying my dues of
$25, a small amount, I thought, to maintain freedom of the press.

Johnson didn't know much about running a nonprofit or an advocacy
group. His office was a mess. He'd worked for the Associated Press for
forty-two years, notably in Texas, where in 1963 he issued the first bulletin
on President John F. Kennedy's assassination. After rising to the top of the
AP hierarchy, Johnson decided it was time to prepare for retirement. He
moved to New Mexico in 1984, becoming the AP's New Mexico bureau
chief. He held the post until 1988 when he officially retired, not counting,
of course, his hobby—piercing the "fog" emanating from local and state

bureaucracies, sometimes taking police departments or public universities to court to enforce sunshine laws.

Politically, there wasn't much that the crusty ex-Marine and I agreed on—but there was one basic thing. It was that democracy rests on an informed public and that citizens must be able to know what public servants are doing in their name. My father was a newspaperman, and I came of age during the days of Vietnam and Watergate. This was a core belief for me—a belief that steered me into journalism and investigative reporting during the late 1970s and 1980s. But open government is not just for the benefit of journalists. It's a principle that is enshrined in the U.S. Constitution and New Mexico law.

New Mexico's Open Meetings Act was passed back in 1974, when Jerry Apodaca was governor and Bob Woodward and Carl Bernstein were uncovering secrets about the Nixon administration that resulted in the president's resignation. It includes this proviso: "In recognition of the fact that a representative government is dependent upon an informed electorate, it is declared to be the public policy of this state that all persons are entitled to the greatest possible information regarding the affairs of government and the official acts of those officers and employees who represent them."[1]

With each decade, more information about the workings of government has become available, although it is not always readily accessible. One vital piece of public information is the way officials get into and stay in office. For candidates and political committees in New Mexico, disclosure of campaign contributions dates back to 1912, when New Mexico first became a state. Even then, the requirements were detailed and punishments prescribed. But the reports, kept in files in the secretary of state's office, were open only to those who could travel to Santa Fe and copy the handwritten information by hand. I know, because as a reporter during the 1980s I followed this laborious process, guided by Bureau of Elections Chief Hoyt Clifton. He was very helpful, but it took hours.

The disclosure requirements were beefed up in 1993, in the wake of the censure of Rep. Ron Olguin by the House of Representatives (see chapter 13). Legislators and others had to file more frequent reports and could not accept contributions during the legislative session itself. Legislators were required to disclose sources of income over $5,000, a government oversight committee was set up, and penalties were increased. Political Action Committees had to register with the secretary of state, and lobbyists were required to disclose their expenditures.

For years, simple disclosure of campaign information was seen as an effective barrier to the influence of special interests. It did not interfere with anyone's rights to contribute or spend freely—which conservatives defend ardently as freedom of speech. And it allowed the public to "consider the source"—those who were funding a candidate—whether ordinary people who contributed $25 at a fundraiser or an oil and gas company that contributed $135,000.[2] This knowledge, it was assumed, was enough to sway voters. At least that's what I heard from the opponents of bills I sponsored with more stringent requirements—contribution limits and public financing.

Well then, I thought, let's make those records more readily available to the public by posting them on the secretary of state's website, so everyone can take a look-see. For three years at the turn of the century, I sponsored bills to do just that, encountering roadblocks from senators who said it was too difficult to switch to computers to file their reports and from the secretary of state (SOS) who said she didn't have the money or expertise to develop the kind of system other states had. To overcome the obstacles, I offered funding for the SOS and "hardship exemptions" for senators from rural areas who didn't have easy access to the Internet or who couldn't cope with computers. Finally, in 2003, I was successful in passing SB 22. Gov. Bill Richardson signed the bill, and the SOS set to work, contracting with a vendor to set up a searchable web system. The first electronic reports were due in 2006.

By that time the public was reeling from what it had found out had gone on behind closed doors at the treasurer's office. Although it hadn't been proven yet, state Treasurer Robert Vigil seemed to be selling contracts for cash. Disclosure was even more important, I thought, when it came to those seeking to contract with the state. And others agreed. With the help of the Attorney General, the governor's office, legislative council lawyer Jon Boller, and my own analyst Cliff Rees, I was able to pass one of the few laws on the books in this area (SB 344), later known as "pay-to-play." The law requires disclosure of campaign contributions and gifts worth more than $250 to public officials in a position to influence the awarding of contracts. It also prohibits all contributions during the actual procurement process. Bills to ban contributions from contractors altogether and enact more disclosure requirements were introduced in the next few years, but the alarm had sounded and they faced stiff resistance.

☞

Meanwhile, in 2006, Bob Johnson was still waiting in my office. Legislative conference committees—where the budget could be altered at the last minute to provide funding for this or that pet project—still remained closed to the public, despite about seven attempts to open them since 1994. Johnson thought that chances were better this year, since Governor Richardson had endorsed the concept and a big coalition had assembled behind the bills that Rep. Joe Cervantes and I sponsored. This time the coalition included the Albuquerque Chamber of Commerce, the Association of Commerce and Industry, the American Civil Liberties Union, and Common Cause, as well as the New Mexico Press Association and FOG.

Conference committees are small groups of legislators appointed by the president pro tem and the Speaker of the House to work out differences when the chambers pass different versions of the same bill and neither chamber is willing to concur with the other's changes. The state budget almost always goes to a conference committee, where final decisions are made and presented back to each chamber, whose members usually have little time to scrutinize the final bill. Sometimes entirely new additions are attached to bills in conference committees—little surprises that are technically against the rules.

More than forty states and the U.S. House of Representatives already had opened their conference committees and, with the recent scandal, we thought the time was ripe. My bill passed easily through committees but then faced a torrent of rhetoric on the floor. Opponents, including the leadership of both parties, had signaled their opposition earlier. They argued that adopting the bill would weaken the legislature and push decisionmaking further underground. The Senate is a deliberative body, they reminded us.

Both Sen. Michael Sanchez of Los Lunas, a Democrat, and Sen. Steve Komadina of Corrales, a Republican, agreed that legislators needed privacy to discuss delicate issues, and forcing transparency would make the committee meetings a charade, since the real decisions would be made elsewhere. "I don't think we have a transparent government," Komadina said. "Rather, government works based on relationships."[3]

Roswell's Sen. Rod Adair, a steadfast supporter of open meetings, said that this logic amounted to a threat that if you pass this law, "we will violate it." "I keep hearing the word protection," he said, referring to senators debating the bill on the floor. "Protection from what? The people of New Mexico?"[4]

Sen. Tim Jennings, as usual, picked up the microphone and started in on Governor Richardson, saying that if the legislature had to open up its meetings then the governor's meetings should be public too.

"This is one of the last rights that the legislature has in its own rules," said Sen. James Taylor, a Democrat who had been appointed to replace Manny Aragon as senator from Albuquerque's South Valley.[5]

Sitting next to me at my desk on the Senate floor, Johnson sighed. "I guess you won't be able to pass bills, confirm appointments, or override vetoes," he whispered to me sarcastically.

The bill was defeated 22 to 16. After the Senate chief clerk read the totals, I realized that this had become a crisis for open government. In a scene captured by an associated press photographer, I tied a Red Cross scarf on my head like a war nurse tending to the wounded on the battlefield. The Senate, with its defense of secret meetings and backroom deals, was wounding itself—and I thought it needed emergency rescue (see fig. 40).

But the worst was yet to come. Opposition to open conference committees and other ethics reforms reached a crescendo in 2007, the same year that a majority of senators tried to push back campaign finance reform by a thousand years (see chapter 15).

There were a number of bills to open conference committees in 2007, two in the Senate and three in the House. But this time, when Bob Johnson and I took to the floor to defend my bill (SB 288) the debate had shifted.

There's an old saying among lawyers and legislators: when you have a losing argument—change the subject. With the tide changing for reform, it was becoming harder to argue that government is best when conducted in secret. So opponents tried to change the subject—to the media itself.

Sen. Michael Sanchez said that it was only the press, not the public, that wanted this bill, and for Senator Jennings it was just a way to sell more newspapers. Sen. John Grubesic of Santa Fe said the press was "shoving this down our throat . . . bullying each one of us."[6] Speaking for many legislators who felt they had been burned by unfavorable or inaccurate coverage, Grubesic said that the press manipulated what happens in committees to serve their needs. "There's a reason that the words in the newspapers are called 'stories,'" he said. "Truth is secondary for the press."[7]

As so often happens in the Senate, the debate took on a life of its own, with the pitch rising as each senator tried to outdo the previous speaker. Sanchez and Jennings called newspaper editors hypocrites because they didn't open their own editorial board meetings to the public. Sen. John Arthur Smith, of Deming, asked me a series of questions about FOG, clearly designed to embarrass Bob Johnson, sitting next to me. He asked how much Johnson was making and what was the budget of the nonprofit, and he threatened legislation that would tax nonprofits like FOG. Jennings launched into his usual tirade against the governor.

On and on it went for three-and-a-half hours. Sen. Rod Adair, no fan of the press himself, said that to make this question turn on the press is intellectually dishonest. "It turns on us," he reminded everyone.[8] Adair said that in addition to the public blackout, closed conference committees kept other members of the legislature in the dark, too.

I thought Sen. Cisco McSorley, a liberal from Albuquerque, cut to the core, when he said, "If you can't stand for principle, then you want your vote secret, it seems to me. If you want secrecy, you create a wall between yourself and your constituents. When I stand on principle, I want my constituents to know it."[9]

During the whole debate, I just sat there in disbelief—and not just at the agreement between ideological opposites Adair and McSorley. How could the opponents not know that their vigorous opposition to this symbolic measure was making it look as if they were trying to hide something? That it would seem the Senate wanted secrecy at all costs, even with this public embarrassment? Once again, open conference committees went down, this time by the narrowest of margins, 20 to 19. Thinking that we could get one more vote, Sen. Joe Carraro and I engineered a vote on his nearly identical bill (SB 322) a few days later. It passed by one vote, but then, amid considerable scrambling, the opponents were able to reconsider the vote and overturn the decision—again by one vote. The switcher was Sen. Mary Kay Papen, a Democrat from Las Cruces, who said she wasn't paying attention during the first vote. Papen is now president pro tem, elected in 2013.

ONE STEP FORWARD, ONE STEP BACK

There's a road sign on the side of I-25 near Los Lunas where dust storms often stir up. For the next few years, it described the Senate perfectly: Zero Visibility Possible. And it was getting even darker with another victory for the opponents of open government in 2007. Senate Bill 363, passed by Sen. Michael Sanchez, succeeded in rolling back the 2003 requirement that candidates file their campaign reports electronically. The previous year (2006) was the first time that candidates had used the new system set up by the secretary of state, and legislators had been grumbling. The system was cumbersome, both for candidates and the public. With reports posted too late to be very useful and connections disrupted, the site had gotten an F in web usability from The Campaign Disclosure Project, a project of the UCLA School of Law, the Center for Governmental Studies, and the California Voter Foundation, which ranked all states' systems.[10] I had tried to work with the secretary of state's office to fix it, but to little avail. Sanchez took advantage of the situation, repealing the one mechanism that made campaign data accessible to the general public.

Fortunately, the governor quickly vetoed the bill, and the SOS finally got the message and started in earnest to improve its site. At least we were treading water, not going under, I thought.

SMILE, YOU'RE ON CANDID CAMERA

Meanwhile, Sen. Mark Boitano, an Albuquerque Republican, had jumped onto another transparency issue: streaming Senate proceedings on the web to allow unfiltered access to all who had a computer. It was an important idea, especially in a rural state where it cost so much just to show up in Santa Fe. Senator Boitano knew, of course, it would take money for the legislative council service (LCS) to develop a system, using their website as an access point. He started in 2005 with a simple appropriations bill for $75,000 to be directed to the LCS. When nothing happened, he tried again in 2006. Finally, in 2008, he sponsored a Senate memorial to express the will of the Senate to install a system. It passed, 27–13, along with the appropriation, and everyone thought that by the next session the cameras would be up and rolling. The LCS was working on it in the fall of 2008 and had started spending money, but then something strange happened. The contract was canceled. The Senate leadership, acting through the Committee on Committees, was not going through with it, blaming a budget crunch. The cameras had already gone up. The leadership ordered them taken down.

As the 2009 session got under way, both senators and the press corps noted that the maintenance staff was taking down the cameras for the start of what we had hoped would be C-SPAN–type coverage of Senate sessions. Many of us were amazed. We thought that—after years of discussion on whether the cameras would cause grandstanding in front of an enlarged public or maybe catch some senators asleep on the job—the webcast issue had been decided. It was a done deal.

Over on the House side, Rep. Janice Arnold-Jones, of Albuquerque, had forced the issue. Faced with opposition from the Speaker, who said that webcasting would "change the body," Arnold-Jones acted on her own and simply webcast meetings of the House Taxation and Revenue Committee through her own computer.

That's the thing about laptops—they usually have cameras. Newer models made it even easier to record events—a factor that made the Senate debate on webcasting even more kabuki-like.

The House adapted to these facts-on-the-ground and, in a week or so, passed rules for streaming live audio of its proceedings on the House floor and in some committees. But the Senate was stuck in denial.

Senators were now in open revolt, and the new, more progressive Democratic senators were flabbergasted. Albuquerque's Senator Ortiz y Pino expressed his frustration this way: "We simply need our leaders to do what we've asked them to do. The money is there; now get it done."[11]

Senators then voted (30 to 10) to call upon the leadership to rescind its decision and allow webcasting, which it did, putting forward a new Senate rule, drafted as narrowly as possible to allow the least amount of electronic access. Ever fearful of political use of comments made on the floor, the rule did not allow floor sessions' video to be archived. It also permitted only one camera, to be installed at the rear of the chamber, "to mimic the experience of onlookers from the Senate gallery." The resulting video provided a narrowcast of proceedings, but did give a great view of the bald heads of Las Cruces Sens. Steve Fishman and Jerry Ortiz y Pino, who sat directly in front of the camera.

It would take a few more years for senators to warm to the idea of a regular broadcast of Senate floor sessions and committee hearings, but it would eventually happen—with multiple cameras. The popularity of the web, plus the fact that more than forty other states provided the public with the service, finally made resistance futile.

"Transparency was kind of a revolution back then, especially since the idea didn't come from the leadership or from interim committees, but directly from the rank and file," recalled Senator Boitano. "It was bipartisan, too, which sparked some pretty wild coalitions and procedural moves in the middle of the night."

On the webcasting issue, the old arguments simply didn't work anymore, says Gwyneth Doland, former director of FOG, who covered the struggle for the *New Mexico Independent*. Doland says initially the new technology was seen as invasive. "But now everyone is Skypeing with the grandchildren and computer webcams are more a part of everyday life," she says. In other words, the ship had sailed, dragging the Senate along in its wake.

BOB JOHNSON'S REVENGE

Just like a bad penny, the open conference committee issue came up again in 2009. At the close of the dramatic 2007 debate, I had warned senators that this would happen over and over again until it passed. And sure enough, here it was again. Bob Johnson wasn't there. He had suffered a stroke in the summer of 2007 and died on his way into the FOG office. In 2009, he would have heard the same arguments from his opponents, Senators Sanchez,

Jennings, and Minority Leader Stuart Ingle. He would have endured the same glacial pace of the Senate Rules Committee. But this time, he would have seen a different result. The composition of the Senate had changed with many of the opponents (Taylor, Robinson, Rawson, Komadina) replaced by supporters. The pressure from the press intensified and the groundswell was too wide and too deep to ignore.

Rep. Joe Cervantes's conference committee bill passed the House rapidly, and I was able to persuade Sen. Michael Sanchez to schedule it, instead of mine, for a floor vote. In a change of pace, Sen. Linda Lopez, a previous opponent, carried Cervantes's bill, and even some former opponents, like John Arthur Smith, voted for it (although he couldn't resist speaking against it). Cervantes's HB393 passed 33 to 8. Bob Johnson could now rest in peace.

A few days after the bill passed, even before the governor signed it, we found out that open conference committees did not disappoint. On the last day of the session, Sen. John Arthur Smith invited the press to the first open conference committee, called to deal with Senate Bill 584, sponsored by Sen. Jerry Ortiz y Pino. A curious amendment had been attached to it in the House. The Senate did not go along with the amendment and the House refused to back down, thus triggering a conference committee.

Here is the backstory. The amendment was a last-ditch attempt by Speaker Ben Lujan to facilitate financing for a public-private project in Santa Fe's Railyard district. The Speaker's own bill to allow private developers to use the bonding authority of local governments (HB 820) had gone down to defeat on the House floor—twice—on a tie vote. But as the session drew to a close, and tired legislators lost track of details, Lujan was able to attach an amendment to Ortiz y Pino's SB 584 as it went through the House Taxation and Revenue Committee to do the same thing. SB 584 passed the House without notice. Smith, however, was on to the movida, which would have slid through a closed conference committee. But now, with a press-filled room, Smith said the amendment created a "cloud of suspicion."[12] The conference committee then stripped the Speaker's amendment off the bill and the House acquiesced, passing Ortiz y Pino's original bill just as the gavel fell, ending the session.

The first open conference committee had been historic. Sunlight illuminated a special interest that would have otherwise gone unnoticed. Bob Johnson had his revenge. The Speaker tried to get the last word, too, storming into the Senate chamber as reporters gathered upon adjournment, telling Senator Smith "he was full of shit . . . a racist SOB."[13]

As the confrontation unfolded, I was standing next to the two men, who had become adversaries in the previous few years. Representative Lujan looked terrible in the eyes of the media, and he later apologized. He said he was tired and offended by the implication that he was somehow profiting personally from the project.

In the next few years, sunshine became very popular with both the legislative and executive branches; everyone, it seemed, wanted to jump on the transparency bandwagon. Democratic Lt. Gov. Diane Denish joined with Republican Sen. Sander Rue in 2010 to push for a "Sunshine Portal" (http:// sunshineportalnm.com), a web page operated by the state to provide the public with an expanding array of information including budgets, contracts, and even some employee salaries. Transparency was a hot topic during the 2010 governor's campaign, with Martinez charging the Richardson administration with backroom deals and a culture of corruption.

A few months after her election in 2010, Martinez took to the podium in the House of Representatives for her first State of the State Address. Open government was a major theme. Acknowledging the erosion in public confidence, she said, "We must operate state government in an open and transparent manner." As a sign of her commitment, she said, she had signed an executive order preventing state agencies from frivolously blocking open records requests through executive privilege. "The public has a right to know exactly what their government is doing."[14]

By the summer of 2012, the Martinez administration was embroiled in a scandal of its own that strained its commitment to open government. "E-mailgate" was uncovered by a liberal group, Independent Source PAC, and confirmed by members of the media. They discovered that members of the administration were using private—not public—e-mail to discuss state business such as the controversial contract to operate a racetrack/casino at New Mexico's State Fair.

By law, official business must be conducted on state e-mail accounts, which are subject to the Inspection of Public Records Act. Instead, members of the executive were using campaign e-mail accounts to plan strategy with Jay McCleskey, the governor's political advisor. Martinez's Chief of Staff Keith Gardner was caught on a hidden recorder telling a Roswell friend he never used his official e-mail because it was "discoverable."

The governor responded to the scandal by ordering her staff to use government e-mail for state business, but she also accused the Independent Source PAC of hacking the private messages. And she vigorously resisted charges that the negotiations for the Albuquerque Downs contract looked a lot like what she had called pay-to-play in the previous administration.[15]

New technology—e-mail, Twitter, Facebook, all of it—will pose new challenges as public officials, advocates, and the news media work out proper balances among efficient, deliberative, and open government. New Mexico's new generation of diggers, bloggers, investigators, and watchdogs are currently opening the windows of the halls of government and letting the light shine in. For homegrown democracy here in New Mexico, that gives me hope.

CHAPTER 15

Campaign Finance Reform
Navigating the Endless Minefield

*M*ARCH 13, 2007. IT WAS A "POISON PILL." THE MEDICINE, dished out by Sen. Leonard Lee Rawson, of Las Cruces, nearly killed me as well as my bill to limit campaign contributions. Standing at my desk in the middle of the chamber, I couldn't believe it. Rawson, the Republican whip, had a simple amendment to my bill, he said. All he wanted to do was delay the enactment of my legislation—for a thousand years, until July 1, 3007.

Senate Bill 800 was the capstone for a package of ethics and campaign reforms designed to restore public confidence in government after the scandal involving Robert Vigil, the state treasurer. At that point, I had been defending the bill for two hours. I had deflected amendment after amendment, poison pills designed to render legislation unworkable. But when I read this one, I realized that the opponents were stepping the fight up to nuclear war. They were trying to make a mockery of reform.

And they were succeeding. Amid snickering and audible expressions of disgust on both sides, the amendment passed. I asked for a pause in the action, and appealed to Majority Leader Michael Sanchez, an opponent of the bill, but someone who could persuade the Democrats to base their votes on reason and not sarcasm or spite. I consulted with my expert witnesses from the attorney general's office and Common Cause. Moments later, the amendment was reconsidered and repealed. The bill then passed the Senate 25 to 12, with four other amendments, and went on to the House. The campaign finance reformers had lived to fight another day, but the battle was far from over.

A SHORT HISTORY OF CAMPAIGN FINANCE REFORM

My efforts to control the influence of big money on state campaigns began when I was elected to office in 1996. I saw what was going on around me then—casinos bankrolling entire campaigns; oil and gas fueling east-side candidacies; unions, trial lawyers, and other big groups crowding out the little guy. But I had worked hard to get that guy's support. I was determined that his (or more likely her) vote would count as much as those $10,000 contributions. I was only too happy to team up with Attorney General Tom Udall and Sen. Richard Romero in 1997 to sponsor a bill much like the one Senator Rawson attempted to poison ten years later.

SB 112 limited contributions from individuals and groups to $1,000 for statewide candidates and $500 for legislators. It was actually sponsored by Sen. Richard Romero, but he asked me to take the lead and thereby learn the ropes. Fred Nathan, the director of Think New Mexico, who was then Udall's special counsel, helped Senator Romero and me present the bill that year. We emphasized that the limits would level the playing field by slowing down the escalating cost of campaigns. New Mexico was one of only five states that placed no limits on contributions, we said, and the bill was a good way to address the perception that office holders are beholden to special interests.

The bill met opposition in every committee it was sent to but, amazingly, made it to the floor, where it passed 26–12 on a party-line vote, with Republicans offering amendment after amendment. But when the bill came up in its first House committee, it hit a brick wall. We soon discovered why. House members said what senators, who knew that either the House or the governor would likely kill the measure, would not: It would make it more difficult for incumbents, who have an advantage over challengers, to raise money.

I began to suspect that the Democratic leadership and the unions were behind the defeat when I received a visit from Jeep Gilliland, then the director of the AFL-CIO. This powerful group felt the limits would diminish the power of unions and of the Democratic Party. House Speaker Raymond Sanchez, too, had expressed concern that supporters of the bill were implying that lawmakers' votes could be bought.[1] It was the first hint I had of the umbrage that legislators took at the very suggestion that our elections had become more like auctions, with some bidders able to buy all the items. It was information that served us well in the next few years as we put together a more broad-based coalition and developed a more nuanced strategy.

In the late 1990s, campaign reform was becoming popular nationally, with our neighboring state of Arizona leading the way. Sen. John McCain pushed for federal controls on independent campaign expenditures in advance of his 2000 presidential campaign. Arizona, Maine, and Vermont adopted public financing of state campaigns, and candidates from both parties in those states began using the new system. A dozen other states operated partially public-financed campaigns, including Minnesota, where ex-wrestler Jesse Ventura—a good buddy of New Mexico Gov. Gary Johnson—had used the system.[2] The reforms were the result of citizens' initiatives, where ordinary people passed the measures on election day in the name of "clean money." But in New Mexico, since we do not have an initiative mechanism, we had been trying to get more incremental reforms like contribution limits through the legislature. And, so far, we were running into a brick wall.

In 1998, we began laying the groundwork for a sustained campaign. I passed a memorial to create an interim committee to study campaign finance laws and regulations in other states. Usually passing memorials is a piece of cake, since they are mainly ceremonial without the effect of law. But this one was tough. Republicans kept saying this was not an issue the public cared about. Even after the measure passed, I had to beg Speaker Raymond Sanchez and Sen. Manny Aragon to appoint a committee and get going. They finally did. Rep. Ed Sandoval, of Albuquerque, and I acted as co-chairs. The committee heard testimony from experts from the National Conference of State Legislatures, legislators and secretaries of state from states where reforms were in effect. They reported that the sky had not fallen as a result. Mission accomplished. We had kept the issue alive.

Support from New Mexicans for Campaign Finance Reform, a new group formed to supplement the efforts of the usual suspects, Common Cause, and the League of Women Voters was crucial. The new coalition included twenty-six different organizations, including public health groups like the American lung and cancer societies and the Alcohol Issues Consortium—groups long stymied by well-connected lobbyists and special interests. A broad coalition of religious groups joined in—Catholics, Jews, and Protestants—all making moral arguments about the injustice done to ordinary citizens whose voices were drowned out by the huge cash influx. The new attorney general, Patricia Madrid, became a key supporter, and Secretary of State Rebecca Vigil and her lieutenant, Denise Lamb, said the state could—and would—implement a new system if such a bill passed.

The most important members of the new coalition were labor unions. After the contribution-limits bill went down to defeat, the activists had worked with the unions, big contributors to Democratic campaigns. The unions came to see how campaign reform—especially public financing— would level the playing field, allowing ordinary people without deep pockets to run for office and win.

We had a new message as well. We did not suggest that politicians and their campaigns were dirty (a message that had worked in states with popular initiatives). We simply suggested that elected officials were good people trapped in a flawed system. The success of our cause, after all, would depend largely on legislators who had come to the dance courtesy of their donors and now were unwilling to change partners.

To give the legislators courage, Re-Visioning New Mexico, an activist group leading the coalition, commissioned a poll from Brian Sanderoff's Research and Polling. It showed that 92 percent of the registered voters sampled believed that special-interest contributions affected the way elected officials voted, and 59 percent would support a public financing system.[3]

In 1999, after weeks of coalition meetings, Richard Romero and I introduced SB 618, the Public Campaign Finance Option Act, New Mexico's first stab at public financing. The bill outlined a voluntary system based on one that was used in Arizona and Maine whereby participating candidates collect small donations from a certain percentage of voters in their district in order to qualify for a public stipend. They cannot accept private donations or use their own money, and their spending is capped at the amount of the stipend. If they are outspent by a nonparticipating candidate, they receive matching money (up to a point) from the fund established for this purpose.

The new system did not address independent financing or political party spending—but it was a start. Over time, we said, it would slow campaign spending, level the playing field, and relieve candidates of some of the time they spend on the phone raising cash instead of talking to voters. The basic idea would be replicated and refined in many later bills—eight as of December 2012.

In spite of good press and grassroots support that year, the bill never emerged from the Senate Finance Committee, where it foundered on its funding mechanism. The next year, we tried a constitutional amendment, the one mechanism in the state constitution that allowed direct votes on issues. It had the advantage of bypassing the governor's office since resolutions to amend the constitution do not require the governor's signature. The amendment passed both the House and the Senate but failed when the two bodies could not concur. Rep. Ben Lujan, of Santa Fe, sponsored it.

Rep. Ben Lujan was an early believer in public financing and his support was crucial, particularly since he had just been elected Speaker of the House. Lujan ascended to the post unexpectedly upon the defeat of Raymond Sanchez in one of the most expensive legislative races ever. The vicious campaign, waged in Albuquerque's North Valley, cost a combined total of $500,000—an unprecedented amount.

Undaunted by the narrow defeat of the constitutional amendment in the legislature, New Mexicans for Campaign Finance Reform pressed on, with bills in 2001 and 2002, gaining public support each time but falling short of the votes needed for passage. The bills drew increasing fire from Republicans like John Dendahl, then chair of the New Mexico Republican Party, who said they were proposals "only a communist would love."[4] Immersed as I was in battles over prescription drugs and gun control, my enthusiasm for campaign finance reform was beginning to wane with the repeated defeats. And there were other things happening—like the overthrow of President Pro Tem Manny Aragon by Sen. Richard Romero. But then something unexpected happened.

Ninety-year-old Doris Haddock agreed to appear at our January 2001 news conference to help promote that year's bill (see fig. 41). She was just passing through, she said in her grandmotherly New Hampshire accent, just as she had passed through the state the year before—on foot.

She'd walked the continent the previous year to draw national attention to the issue, which she said was the greatest threat to democracy. The retired secretary started her journey in Pasadena following the Rose Bowl parade, and then kept walking east on her own, ten miles a day, with a twenty-nine-pound pack on her back. By the time she reached the steps of the U.S. Capitol fourteen months later, everyone knew her as Granny D, including Sen. John McCain, who hailed her as a valuable ally in the passage of his bill in 2002.

Granny D had stopped at rodeo grounds, spoken at elementary schools, and dropped in at biker bars, preaching the gospel, as she was now preaching it to us gathered in the capitol rotunda. Wearing her trademark straw hat with a feather stuck in the brim, she did not mince words. The current system was nothing short of bribery—a cruel hoax on soldiers throughout history who had died to protect democracy, not special interests.[5] Those in the small audience—representatives of labor; the AARP; Attorney General Patricia Madrid; Speaker Lujan; Fred Harris, the former Oklahoma senator who was then serving as the chair of Common Cause New Mexico; and Stuart Bluestone, the AG's chief deputy—all applauded. The reporters scribbled their stories. But something more happened to me. I was inspired to continue the struggle no matter what it took. I'd always joked about how my ambition was to become a little old lady in tennis shoes, giving them hell until my dying day—and here was Granny D, doing just that. If this ordinary citizen, with no public office and no independent source of funding, could do it—so could I. My determination would not go untested.

In 2003, the legislature finally passed a public financing bill, a pilot project that would apply to candidates for the Public Regulation Commission (PRC). Newly elected governor Bill Richardson signed it—as an experiment.[6] Meanwhile, Tucson and other cities were beginning to use public financing in municipal campaigns. In Albuquerque, the state's largest city, the costs of mayoral campaigns, once limited by a spending cap, were skyrocketing. The spending cap had been overturned in court. But voters had recourse. City charter amendments went to the voters, and in October 2005 city councilors voted to place public financing of municipal campaigns on the ballot. Then city councilor Eric Griego (who later became a state senator) was the sponsor, but even he was stunned by the scandal that rocked the state a month before the election.

On September 16, 2005, State Auditor Robert Vigil and Treasurer Michael Montoya were arrested for extortion and federal racketeering and for pocketing hundreds of thousands of dollars from investment advisors. Prosecutors released plea agreements from two men who were paying the officials to gain investment contracts in what became known as a "pay-to-play" scandal. The nightly news began to feature videos of cash changing hands—as much as $10,000 at a time. Vigil's justification was that the cash was a perfectly legitimate campaign contribution.

By October 26, under threat of impeachment by the New Mexico legislature—then meeting in special session—Vigil had stepped down. In the meantime, Albuquerque voters voiced their opinion. The "Clean Elections" charter amendment, providing for a voluntary public financing system for city elections, passed by 69 percent.

Politicians scrambled to pick up the pieces. Governor Richardson appointed an ethics and campaign finance task force to come up with a package of bills to address the serious breach in public confidence that followed the scandal (see chapter 13).

HARD KNOCKS IN 2007
OPENS DOORS FOR LATER REFORMS

For the 2007 session, the governor endorsed the group's recommendations for limits on campaign contributions and a system of public financing for statewide officials and judges based on the successful PRC experiment. The two measures were part of a huge package parceled out to various legislators by the administration. My assignment (and that of Rep. Mimi Stewart, of Albuquerque) was to pass campaign contribution limits for state candidates, parties, and PACs based on the federal limits. It was essentially the same bill Richard Romero and I had passed through the Senate ten years ago, only now with contributions from individuals and political committees limited to $2,300 per election instead of $500. There were additional reporting requirements as well, some of them directed at independent expenditures.

With the public galvanized by a major ethics scandal, and with the support of the governor and House leadership, the prospects for reform looked good. But it wasn't long before I recognized the old game of Senate slow ball.

The chair of the Senate Rules Committee, which is charged with hearing elections bills, hadn't held hearings on any of the bills, and it was already the first week in March, with only ten days to go in the session. Meeting after meeting droned on, with reform advocates endlessly waiting in the audience, learning more than they ever wanted about Senate confirmation of the governor's appointees, another job of the committee. I was a member of the committee at the time, and at every meeting I pushed for a hearing on the bills with the best chance of passage. Chairman Linda Lopez refused, for one reason or another, and she would not allow bills to be heard in her frequent absences, caused by her mother's illness. Finally, Senator Lopez allowed two bills in the package to escape: Senator Grubesic's gift ban and my contributions limits.

The narrow escape allowed my Senate Bill 800 to make it to the Senate floor, where Senator Rawson and others tried one method after another, including the poison pill described earlier in this chapter, to kill the popular measure. But it survived, sped through House committees rapidly, and passed the House on a bipartisan basis with only five dissenting votes. But time was running out. And the bill had to come back to the Senate for concurrence on the changes made by the House removal of some of the damaging amendments that senators had stuck on the bill earlier.

The last days of any legislative session are a madhouse, with legislators scrambling for the last chance to move their bills off the daily calendar, get them put up for a vote, and get them passed into law. The Senate majority leader calls the shots, deciding which bills will be heard and when. And sometimes he is reluctant to schedule controversial—but important—bills for fear of prolonged debate. The waiting, particularly if your bill is not heard before the last morning, is agony. And every little distraction is galling. The 2007 session had featured plenty of distractions, taking up valuable time. Football great Brian Urlacher had visited; a soprano from the Santa Fe Opera had sung an aria. The Duranes Elementary School Character Counts chorus had sere-naded us with their version of "Eres Tu." The Department of Transportation's Buckle Bear had taught us how to buckle our seat belts, and we had debated the Official Answer to the Official Question—Red or Green (Chile)? (The Official Answer is Christmas, that is, both.) Now on the last morning of the 2007 session (March 17), the Democratic caucus called for a recess—with only an hour or so to go and the concurrence calendar containing SB 800, the campaign finance bill, lying on all our desks, waiting for a vote.

When we returned from the lounge, with only ten minutes to go in the session, Majority Leader Sanchez turned to the concurrence calendar, and senators voted on my recommendation to concur with the House amend-ments to SB 800. Now alone at my desk, amid a divided chamber, with no support from my usual ally from the AG's office, Stuart Bluestone, I called for a roll-call vote. It would be close, but I thought I had a majority. In the end, the nays had it—by one vote. A number of senators switched their votes from the bill's initial floor hearing, including Republicans Clint Harden and Joe Carraro and Democrats John Arthur Smith, Linda Lopez, and Michael Sanchez.

Within a minute after the vote was tallied, the gavel fell on the 2007 ses-sion. Crowds of staffers, family, lobbyists, and onlookers began to crowd into the chambers to hear the congratulations and the goodbyes that followed. Shattered, I could not think of anything but Granny D and another lost op-portunity to fix our wounded system.

But I did not have time to mourn. Suddenly Sen. Pete Campos was call-ing my name from the front of the chamber. He was beckoning me to come forward and accept the Milagro Award, an award given annually to one senator who has been particularly impressive. Campos read the certificate, praising me for withstanding "arduous and meaningful debates on import-ant social issues, and bringing forth leading-edge legislation." Everyone was applauding. I gave the obligatory thank-you speech and returned to my seat, thinking that with the one-vote loss of both the contribution limits and the open conference committee bills, this was the worst session ever. And now, as if I were in the old Miss America Pageant, I had won Miss Congeniality. Even after ten years in the Senate I still felt like Alice in Wonderland.

Public reaction to the Senate's failure to pass most of the ethics package was strong, with the print media leading the way. In early March the *Albuquerque Tribune* accused the Senate of making a "mockery of ethics reform,"[7] and the *Albuquerque Journal*, citing a September poll showing that 90 percent of voters wanted contribution limits and other reforms, asked, "What Will It Take To Get Ethics Reform?"[8] Gov. Bill Richardson thought he knew. Almost immediately after adjournment he called the legislature back into special session to deal with the unfinished ethics agenda and other items, including tougher penalties for domestic violence and a registry for former methamphetamine lab sites. The Senate was not pleased.

Under Senate rules, a majority of the members can adjourn permanently using a Latin phrase, sine die. Senators did so twice during the special session in an effort to thwart Governor Richardson's agenda and protest his out-of-state electioneering. But the session continued anyway, since the House never left Santa Fe, sometimes meeting throughout the night to come up with a palatable version of an ethics commission, a highway bill, and other leftovers.

One of the leftovers was Speaker Ben Lujan's bill to publicly finance state-wide campaigns, now pared down to just statewide judicial races. Campaigns for the state Supreme Court had been increasing in cost in almost every state as the atmosphere became more partisan and out-of-state groups entered the fray. Lujan's bill, HB 6, was one of a list of bills subject to horse trading between the stubborn Senate and a governor who, with his veto pen, held the fate of all the bills just passed in the regular session in his hand. One of the concessions made by the Senate was to hear Lujan's bill, which, at that point, was less controversial than two others that had failed to pass—my contributions limits and the domestic partners bill, which for civil rights advocates was the most important bill of the session. In addition, the governor also got funding for the second stage of his transportation project—GRIP 2, but that was all. Senators, whose numbers were dwindling as the session went on, were willing to go no further.

But public financing of judicial elections was pretty far—and there was opposition aplenty as I presented Lujan's bill on the Senate floor. Senator Rawson, the detail-oriented Republican whip, came up with another poison pill. This time, the amendment he offered made the whole system contingent on abolishing judicial retention elections. "Retention" elections are a key component of New Mexico's hybrid judicial-selection process, which includes an initial partisan election and then, for the winner, a retention election every four years. Opinions differ on whether judges should be appointed or elected, and the hybrid system constructed by the legislature was a compromise offered to the people as a constitutional amendment. It was passed by the voters in 1988.

Much to my dismay, Rawson's amendment to HB 6 passed by one vote, and this time it stuck. Judicial public financing—which finally passed on a bipartisan basis 20 to 15—would not go into effect until voters approved a constitutional amendment nixing retention elections. That might never happen. The session ended with the new poison pill stuck in my throat.

It was déjà vu all over again, complete with the one-vote margin and the bittersweet finale. But much to my surprise we discovered a solution. A group of us were out in the hall, debating whether we should ask the governor to veto our own bill, when lobbyist Tom Horan breezed by. Pointing to the bill's title he said, "Oh, that's an appropriations bill, creating a fund." As such, it was subject to a line-item veto; that is, a portion of the bill could be struck without affecting the substance. The governor, Horan hinted, could veto the poison pill and allow the system to go into effect, which is exactly what he did a week later. The victory was sweet. But the big banana, campaign contribution limits, would have to wait until 2009.

By that time, the Senate contained a new cast of characters.

Although campaign finance reform opponents remained in the leadership, the Democratic rank and file now contained more progressives, including Sen. Eric Griego, who spearheaded the Albuquerque charter election; Tim Keller, who defeated Sen. Shannon Robinson; and former Rep. Peter Wirth, of Santa Fe. The negotiating skills, the patience, and the good relationships that Wirth, a lawyer, enjoyed with both Democrats and Republicans were key factors in the final passage of contribution limits in 2009. The final bill, SB 116, was hammered out by the Rules Committee, whose chair, Linda Lopez, finally acquiesced and combined my now perennial bill with Wirth's and several others. Lopez, the former opponent, could then claim credit for fixing what had become New Mexico's embarrassing status as one of six states with no limits on campaign contributions.

New Mexico's lack of limits was beginning to attract national attention, in the same way that the state's last stand for cockfighting had. "We're the Wild West out here," I told the *Wall Street Journal*, a theme that was repeated by others and picked up by the *New York Times*, especially as new scandals implicating Bill Richardson surfaced.

When SB 116 passed the Senate on March 12, 2009, it contained limits on contributions to individuals, political committees, and political parties. The limits mimicked the federal law, but did not go into effect until after the 2010 gubernatorial election. The delay made the medicine go down a lot easier. In the end, the bill received only one dissenting vote in the Senate, from Sen. Rod Adair, from Roswell, who works as a consultant to Republican candidates.

A few years later, in the wake of the landmark Supreme Court decision in Citizens United, Adair would join with Republican lawyer James Bopp to overturn the New Mexico law. The Republicans, they said in the official complaint, were prepared to spend much more than the $5,000 limits on contributions to political parties and PACS who spent money independently of candidates. In the name of free speech, they wanted to purchase a larger megaphone, and the federal district court in New Mexico ruled they could, paving the way for a new generation of state super PACs like Reform New Mexico Now (funded by oil and gas companies) and Independent Source PAC (funded largely by unions). These groups could accept unlimited donations and spend unlimited amounts as long as they did not coordinate directly with individual campaigns.

In the 2012 election, they played a bigger role than ever in legislative campaigns, sending direct mailers and sponsoring advertisements, polls, and other activities. And they were not alone. With direct contributions now limited to $2,400 to candidates and $5,000 to regular PACS, a proliferation of political action committees sprang up. Where once there was one Senate majority leader's PAC, now there were six or seven, sponsored by individual senators, each accepting contributions up to the limits. Add these to the regular PACS run by interest groups like realtors or plumbers, plus the party committees and nonprofits, and you had a veritable torrent of special interest funds.

Suppressed in one area, money, the mother's milk of politics, spurts up in another. The reformers too will have to regroup and continue to navigate the endless minefield.

Tackling the Unfinished Agenda

A Handbook

Unfolding the roadmap of the New Mexico Senate, tracing the twisted paths that advocates for change must follow—from committees to floor sessions, through the offices of cowboys and lawyers alike—has been tricky. Actually *using* the map to reach a grand destination, like health care or campaign finance reform, has been even harder. As you may have noticed, armed guards are stationed at every pass to bar the way (see fig. 42).

It took me years to understand a system fueled by special interests, personal loyalties, and maverick leaders. It took citizen activists taking on Big Tobacco, the NRA, Big Pharma, and, yes, "the powers that be" in the Senate even longer. This has been their story, as well as mine. It is a New Mexico story, but it shares its themes with many other states.

I've devoted the last section of this book to ethics and campaign finance reform because I believe they are the keys to curbing special interests and restoring the public's trust in the New Mexico Senate. Progress in this area has been painfully slow in the past sixteen years. With so much at stake, it's easy to see why. But that doesn't change the results.

It's no coincidence that a ban on fireworks sales during extreme fire danger in 2012 was stopped in a committee chaired by a big recipient of industry contributions and a key ally of fireworks lobbyists. And it's well documented that senators who voted against tobacco taxes got more from the industry than those who didn't. Ditto for senators who voted with the pharmaceutical industry against a simple requirement that drug companies disclose gifts to doctors of more than $75. They received, on average, more industry cash than those who voted for the requirement.

But, as you have seen, advocates sometimes have succeeded in fighting off special interests and even hardened partisan opposition, going on to win against all odds. They have done it by telling human stories that elicit compassion. These are the stories of Erin Armstrong and Essie DeBonet, who convinced both Republicans and Democrats that legalizing medical marijuana was safe even though it conflicted with federal law. These are the stories shared by Juan Melendez and Ron Keine, two men who were almost executed for crimes they did not commit.

Legislators like former Sen. Mary Jane Garcia and Rep. Gail Chasey have fought special interests with grit and grace, persevering over a decade to end cockfighting and the death penalty, two practices that they believed were inhuman. I too fought for years for campaign finance and healthcare reform before finally scoring some partial victories. Even though the issues were near and dear to our hearts, all three of us were careful not to burn our bridges or create permanent enemies, knowing that today's opponent might be tomorrow's ally on another issue.

TIPS FOR REFORMERS

Alice in Wonderland finally figured out how to navigate the strange land into which she was thrust—with a little help from her friends. And so did I. Like Alice, I joined forces with allies wherever I could find them lining the crazy, circular hallways of the Roundhouse, down the street at the First Christian Church, at receptions at La Fonda Hotel, wherever. Here are a few lessons for other reformers that I've learned during my adventures with boots, suits, and citizens in the New Mexico Senate. If you've read the previous chapters they will seem familiar.

The Perfect Is Often the Enemy of the Good: Big Packages Fail

Some of the big ideas that reformers have for change have failed, especially when they were presented as one huge package that would solve all problems in a certain area. Gov. Gary Johnson's drug-reform package in 2001 contained a number of bills to do everything from decriminalizing marijuana to allowing new ways to treat overdoses. Gov. Bill Richardson's 2008 Health Solutions package was almost as encompassing as Hillary Clinton's "managed competition" plan back in 1994 or "Obamacare," which was passed in 2010. The ethics package introduced in 2007 in response to the treasurer's office scandal was also comprehensive, ranging from public financing to a gift act.

All of the packages were introduced with great fanfare based on recommendations from task forces asked to solve complex problems. But, legislatively, all the big packages failed. The silver bullet did not work—but there were lots of shiny pieces of shrapnel left lying on the ground after the big explosions. And legislators picked them up to make incremental reforms, sometimes taking years to finish the job.

Medical marijuana was finally legalized in 2007, and the criminal justice system changed with new laws limiting the seizure of assets before convictions and restricting the use of mandatory prison sentences for nonviolent crimes. Many pieces of Health Solutions were later adopted. The profits and overhead of insurance companies were limited, along with their ability to rescind policies or rate customers based on gender. And gradually legislators adopted restrictions on gifts and campaign contributions and financed some campaigns with public funds.

Perhaps none of these piecemeal reforms would have happened without the big packages. But had proponents insisted on an all-or-nothing approach they would have gone home empty handed.

Newly elected to the Senate in 1997, I, too, was in search of the Holy Grail—two Holy Grails, in fact: a Medicare-for-All health care reform that would use a single-payer system and public financing of all campaigns. But I found out it just wasn't that simple in a rural, risk-averse legislature. Sometimes if you pushed too hard for the perfect, or were unwilling to compromise, you lost the fight for the good. It's a lesson that many reformers, on both sides of the ideological spectrum, have not yet learned: Half a loaf is better than nothing.

One Person Can Make a Difference—and Perseverance Pays

I've told two stories here about the dedication of the women who sponsored landmark legislation to end the death penalty and cockfighting in New Mexico. It took them decades before their perseverance paid off. But they didn't give up, and each year they built a bigger coalition, educating the public, legislators, and anyone within listening range about their issue, until finally what seemed like a radical idea became acceptable. Ordinary citizens with a good idea have done the same—the push for medical marijuana started with Lynn Pierson, a cancer patient who haunted the halls of the legislature back in the 1970s. It continued with Erin Armstrong. Nadine Milford, whose daughter and grandchildren were killed in an alcohol-related crash in 1992, sat like a silent sentinel in the gallery for years, representing

Mothers Against Drunk Driving. Although her story is not covered here, her presence was a key factor in the passage of DWI legislation. Granny D's appearance at the capitol to join the struggle for campaign finance reform reminded us that one elderly woman in tennis shoes can make a big difference. Her determination boosted our spirits to continue to fight for public financing and limits on contributions, a never-ending struggle. Patty Jennings's fight for children with disabilities and, later, against breast cancer yielded results after many years.

"One hard working person can make the difference, particularly when paired with a committed bill sponsor," says Stuart Bluestone, who now lobbies for the attorney general's office.

Thinking back on the efforts of these advocates brought me back to a nineteenth-century German philosopher, Arthur Schopenhauer. I studied this man in college, and I found him extremely boring except for this one nugget, very relevant here: "All truth passes through three stages. First, it is ridiculed. Second, it is violently opposed. Third, it is accepted as being self-evident."

Know the Big Picture and Map the Personal Relationships

With a small population, a low per-capita income, and families who have roots stretching back generations, New Mexico runs on personal relationships. In the legislature, it's worth asking who is related to whom, or who grew up in the same neighborhood. Which legislators are best friends, and which are diehard enemies? Are there longstanding rivalries? Untangling the web of regional and personal loyalties between lobbyists, spouses, legislators, and staff may be the key to success, whether you are a legislator or an advocate.

"It's a big unruly family," lobbyist Gary Kilpatric told me. Until he understood that, he said, his effectiveness was limited. "At first I acted like a lawyer, and I lost." Kilpatric recalled the time when he was lobbying one committee chair to kill a bill and thought he had presented a pretty good case. "What do you think?" Kilpatric asked the chairman, who seemed somewhat evasive. "I'll have to check with the lobbyist on the other side," the chairman said. Kilpatric thought that sounded reasonable until someone told him that the other lobbyist had been the best man at the chairman's wedding.

Leanne Leith, a lobbyist for the Conservation Voters Alliance, knows the importance of friendships among legislators and tries to use them to good advantage. Asking the good friend of the president pro tem to sponsor a controversial bill, for example, may bring some help from on high. Choosing the wrong sponsor, someone who is not liked by the majority leader, may have dire consequences, even if the bill is not controversial.

I guess it's obvious, but often overlooked. Legislators want to vote with their friends. Just like anyone, they want to be liked by those they spend time with—so the opinions, the tastes, the loyalties of their buddies are important to understand. Notice that Sen. Tim Jennings and Stuart Ingle are always on the phone with each other; that they wear the same kind of plaid shirts, and have ties to the New Mexico Military Institute. And if you have a message to deliver to a legislator, pick the messenger carefully. Legislators usually dance with their partners, who can be identified by geographic proximity, contribution history, age, party, or common interests. It is important to take heed. For example, not understanding the depth of hostility between Jennings and Governor Richardson—based on a personal slight to Jennings's wife—cost me dearly during the health-care debate.

Understanding the big picture—the overriding issues of each session, the tensions between the executive and the legislature, and the budget situation—is also important. If you don't know what else is happening and only confine your efforts to one narrow issue, you will lose opportunities. Maybe your issue fits into a deal that must be made. Maybe it can be used as a bargaining chip, or it can serve as the second-best alternative. The bill to allow public financing of statewide judicial races was the least controversial item on a list of ethics bills that the Senate leadership did not want to consider during the 2007 special session. But I was there arguing for it as something to show for all our efforts. And it passed! During another special session called in the wake of the failure of Richardson's Health Solutions package, Senate leaders wanted to show some forward motion on addressing the issue of the rising number of uninsured New Mexicans, especially since they had just defeated Health Solutions. So, they expanded Medicaid for children, a fallback move that helped thousands of families.

Watch for Unlikely Allies and Helpful Lobbyists

If you are in it for the long run, it's important not to burn bridges with even the most hostile lobbyists or the legislators you distrust the most. Hundreds of votes and hundreds of issues arise during each session. Those who oppose your measure today may support another one of yours tomorrow. The lobbyists know this, too, and even if they told you that you were destroying their livelihood with your bill one session, they might team up with you next time. That's what happened when Pharma cut a deal with the trial lawyers. Although they had opposed my bill to allow patients to donate unused prescription drugs back to their doctors in 2009, they came around to it in 2011. With the two interest groups now holding hands, it passed unanimously in 2011.

When it came to health-care legislation, my colleague Rep. Ed Sandoval, the kind-hearted son of a janitor from the North Valley, put it best. "We've long realized it doesn't do us any good if the HMOs don't support it," Sandoval told one Albuquerque newspaper. "Without their support it won't have any chance of passing."[1] It took me a long time to realize that this didn't mean giving in to whatever the opponents wanted, but finding a few important items we could all support.

For me, having the support of unlikely allies like the pharmaceutical companies or HMOs was key in passing insurance reform and other health issues. Joining forces with potential opponents is not always possible in today's politically charged environment. But it was a key factor in my passage of a graduated drivers' license bill to train teenage drivers in 1999, a credit freeze to guard against identity theft in 2007, and a bill to restrict the use of all- terrain vehicles in rural New Mexico in 2005.

Never Underestimate the Power of a Good Story

If personal relationships are the coin of the realm at the legislature, personal stories are gold. They can seal the deal, allowing legislators—if just for a moment—to forget about partisan loyalty or sectional ties and trade on compassion, empathy, and humor.

A severely disabled young person making a well-prepared speech about opportunities he hopes for, or a young medical student testifying about the crushing debt he must repay, are more likely to affect hearts and minds than dry statistics on workforce shortages or disability rates. The tears of Essie DeBonet—and her seventy-eight-pound frame—did more to pass medical marijuana than the Department of Health. The stories of seniors riding a bus to Juárez, Mexico, to get low-cost medications, and those told by teenage mothers—with their crying babies in tow—about the support they received from the "Grads" educational program, made the difference in whether a program got funded or a law enacted. When the stories are spread in the media, even bigger changes are possible.

REFORMING THE ROUNDHOUSE FROM THE INSIDE

Fighting off special interests and focusing on public service would be a lot easier with some straightforward structural reforms, many of them long overdue in a legislature that does business much as it did one hundred years ago, when most senators were ranchers, the winter was the off season, and the total population of New Mexico was only about 330,000. Here are a few proposals:

Enter the Modern Era, but Keep the Potato Song

"The answers are obvious to everyone," Allen Sánchez, lobbyist for the Catholic bishops, told me emphatically. "We need longer sessions. . . . and legislators need to be paid."

The plea for longer sessions is echoed annually by dozens of legislators and citizens whose bills die on the final day of either the thirty- or sixty-day sessions prescribed by the 1912 constitution. It has now gotten to the point where 1,500 to 2,000 bills, memorials, and resolutions are introduced each year, with only 200 to 300 passing.[2] There is huge disappointment at the end of each session.

"A short session is an impediment to good policy," says lobbyist Gary Kilpatric. Sometimes items hastily considered during the thirty-day session have to be fixed later on, or a financial problem becomes exponentially worse before it can be resolved during the next session. Federal deadlines for state action come and go. Of course, more conservative proponents of limited government, like Sen. Tim Jennings and Sen. Stuart Ingle, are not in favor of this change, since they see it opening the door to more regulation. But others favor the change, and they have introduced proposals to have sixty-day sessions each year, or at least lengthen the short session to forty-five days—without success. The 2006 Legislative Structure and Process Task Force recommended that short sessions be lengthened to forty-five days and the long session to seventy-five days. The change would require a constitutional amendment.[3]

New Mexico's legislative sessions are among the shortest in the nation,[4] and while interim committees meet between sessions to formulate the next year's budget and propose legislation, they can take no action in times of fiscal crisis or emergency. Hence, in the past twenty years, scores of "special sessions" have been called to act on unfinished business such as health care or ethics reform, tobacco taxes, and other matters covered earlier. The sessions cost taxpayers a premium to restart committees, hire staff, and turn on the lights, and they are unpopular with legislators who must change plans, take time off from their businesses, and drive to Santa Fe from afar. Some simply do not show up.

Every year, senators complain about the extraneous celebrations, the mariachis, or the dancers who perform in the chambers. They complain about the time we waste debating the state necklace (the squash blossom, of course), the official state cowboy song, or declaring March 2, 2011, "Las Esperanzas Day" in the Senate. Many of the introductions have been eliminated and the celebrations streamlined in recent years. And they should be. But it would be sad for the Senate to eliminate some colorful rituals like Senator Pinto's annual Potato Song, sung in Navajo, or the daily pledge to the Zia symbol of perfect harmony among united cultures. They are essential ingredients of our unique legislative culture. They draw us together.

Another key premise of New Mexico's part-time citizen legislature is also showing signs of age. It is the system of compensating senators and representatives through per-diem payments (daily allowances to cover expenses) and mileage reimbursements alone. New Mexico is the only remaining state that does not pay its legislators an annual salary—even a token one that recognizes that the job of a legislator is year round, requiring attention to constituents, community, and policy outside the regular sessions. Traditionally, New Mexicans have been unwilling to recognize this fact of life, somehow believing that legislative sessions are just ceremonial gatherings in Santa Fe where the honor of attending makes the sacrifice worthwhile. Voters have regularly turned back constitutional amendments to even increase per diem. From 1911–1952 the payment remained $10 per day, with voters approving a hike to $20 in 1953, $40 in 1971, $75 in 1982, and finally to jibe with the federal level in 1996. It is now approximately $154 per day, which sounds good until you think of the lost professional opportunities because of meetings or caucuses and the high cost of hotels and meals in Santa Fe.

Politically, it is hard to propose a constitutional amendment to institute a salary for legislators. Most legislators desperately want one, but they don't have the courage to vote to even put it on the ballot since opponents will surely decry the move.

Yet the lack of salary has discouraged many from running for office, especially if they do not have access to some way of subsidizing their public service, through a pension, an inheritance, or a spouse whose income can make it possible. For the Senate, that has meant an older group, people who have retired from their primary occupation or who are consultants, independent business owners, or agents. The teachers, the hourly wage earners, the healthcare workers—these are few and far between.[5]

"You get what you pay for," lobbyist Leanne Leith says simply.

Another problem is that legislators have no full-time staff to help with constituent services and no expense account to help defer the cost of contacting their constituents by phone, mail, computer, or through personal visits. This has led legislators to dip into their campaign accounts for legitimate government expenses or to rely on lobbyists to pay for meals or even solve constituent problems for them.

The 2007 Ethics Task Force proposed to reimburse legislators up to $10,000 each year for legitimate constituent expenses such as surveys, district offices, secretarial services, postage, or interactive websites. At the same time legislators would be required to follow tighter restrictions on the uses of campaign funds. I introduced two companion bills to achieve these goals in 2012, but they didn't go far. One would have required a constitutional amendment; the other was a regular bill.

The other alternative is to simply bite the bullet and pay legislators the same way we pay county commissioners or other local officials. Realistically, this constitutional amendment would have to come from a legislative compensation commission or some other arms-length group.

"New Mexico is on the verge of entering the modern era," Heather Ferguson, a lobbyist for the Animal Protection Voters concluded when, after decades of efforts, cockfighting was finally outlawed in 2007. The comment applies to more than cockfighting.

A modern, more professional era in the New Mexico legislature is long overdue. But let's keep the potato song.

Give Good People Trapped in a Flawed System a Way Out

Even though I knew what I was in for when I ran for the unpaid position of senator, I often felt trapped in the endless rounds of fundraising, the meetings with advocates or constituents, and the rat race of interim committee hearings. With no staff except during the legislative session, I did most of my research myself. Sometimes interns or friends would pitch in—voluntarily. I could not offer them a stipend, and working with the various colleges and universities was sometimes a distraction. I could have used my campaign funds—but I wasn't sure whether it looked right. Other legislators have been pilloried in the media for using their campaign funds to pay for a 1955 Chevy pickup truck (Sen. Phil Griego said he used it only for parades and campaign events), massages (Rep. Miguel Garcia says his sciatica kicks up whenever he goes door to door), and even septic services (Rep. Ray Begaye didn't give an explanation for this one, but perhaps his volunteers needed a bathroom).

Clearly, legislators would benefit from some bright lines drawn in these gray areas. An independent ethics commission could educate public officials on the legalities, enforce existing laws, and hold them accountable. The present system is not working. But as you now know, there's plenty of resistance to the idea in the Senate, unless it's constructed to protect legislators from arbitrary accusations. Unfortunately the resistance contributes to the impression that senators hold themselves above the law—not a great message for restoring public trust.

Voluntary public financing of legislative campaigns would give legislators a way out of constant "call time" and remove the burden of fundraising large amounts from friends, associates, and, you guessed it, lobbyists and those with vested interests. The system now in place for the Public Regulation Commission, statewide courts, and the cities of Albuquerque and Santa Fe requires candidates to collect $5 contributions from a small percentage of voters in the district, forcing voter contact and allowing ordinary people to pitch in without being marginalized by big contributors. Our public financing system is in need of repair to address legal concerns Republicans have raised in the courts. But that can be done through legislation—if there is a will to get out of the cash-and-carry system and try something that would solve a number of problems.

Give Citizens a Way In

It's taken over a decade, but in 2009 the Senate finally acquiesced to open conference committees. After heated discussion and fancy foot dragging by the leadership, Senate sessions and committees are now webcast. Citizens can access information about state contracts and salaries through a "sunshine portal" on the state website. But there are still doors to open. Interim committees should be funded more fully to travel to remote communities around the state, and public comment should always be a part of the agenda. Some of the most valuable input on redistricting and on water and taxes has come from ordinary citizens who don't have an ax to grind but just a good idea to offer. We should be all ears.

Constituent surveys, whether online or sent through the mail, are underutilized by legislators who simply do not have the time or the money to do them. But along with town halls, surveys are a great way to engage citizens and strengthen democracy. Provide legislators with a few thousand dollars to accomplish the task, or some staff to help, and there would be more surveys. Constituents would immediately benefit and so would legislators, who would find out what their constituents are really thinking beyond the more general polls reported in the media. The debate just might change.

Hold Down Partisan Strife

Dream on, you might say. The divide has been widening in recent years, not narrowing. This is especially true at the national level, but in the New Mexico Senate, practical necessity—and compassion—have brought together Republicans and Democrats to share sacrifices during a period of recession, to legalize medical marijuana, to ban indoor smoking, and to pass important, incremental health care reforms. The partisan divide is at its height, naturally, during election season, when out-of-state interests spend big money (often independently and anonymously, thanks to the *Citizens United* Supreme Court decision) to help local candidates and state parties. Partisanship is also at the center of redrawing the lines for the legislative and congressional districts, which is done by the legislature every ten years.

One modest proposal to take some of the hyper-partisanship out of the system would be to use a nonpartisan, independent redistricting commission to draw district lines, rather than use legislators themselves. The two redistricting sessions in which I participated (2001 and 2011) were failures. With one exception (the Senate redistricting plan passed in 2002) the plans drawn by the legislature were vetoed by the governor and decided by judges. A redistricting commission would remove the incumbent-protection bias of current mapmakers, and maybe even more accurately reflect population shifts, now often minimized to make way for "deals" between the two parties. California, New Jersey, Washington, Montana, Arizona, Alaska, and Hawaii now use some variant of a redistricting commission. Politics does not end at the commission's door, however, and the selection of members and the finality of the maps drawn have become new sources of conflict. But it's worth a try.

I made another stab at impartiality during the 2009 and 2012 sessions when I introduced constitutional amendments to take the administration of elections out of the hands of a super-partisan official, the secretary of state (SOS), and put it in the hands of an elections commission. The idea was raised in the 2006 Ethics Task Force, but it was never pursued. It should be. In the past six years, one SOS (Rebecca Vigil Giron) has been indicted for alleged misuse of federal funds, and another has been criticized for incompetent election administration. The current SOS, Dianna Duran, the first Republican to serve in decades, has pushed the legislature for voter identification and, when that failed, used regulations that Democrats say will suppress voter turnout. Duran, an ex-senator and county clerk from Alamogordo, also eliminated straight ticket voting by fiat—something she had not been able to pass in the legislature.

The SOS is supposed to administer and enforce the elections in a nonpartisan fashion, but the fact that she (it's almost always been a she) is elected in a partisan election is a contradiction. Legislative and gubernatorial oversight of the secretary of state is difficult, because the officeholder is an independent executive who cannot be fired. The only controls come from the legislature's budget authority and the attorney general, who also is charged with enforcing election laws and who has been called in increasingly to settle partisan disputes. A nonpartisan elections committee would restore public confidence that elections will be run fairly and votes will be counted accurately.[6]

Reduce the Influence of Special Interests and Lobbyists

The legislature has made some progress in this area, enacting a gift act in 2007, requiring disclosure of campaign contributions from those who bid on state business, and limiting campaign contributions to candidates and PACs from organizations and individuals. But we have not gone far enough, and there are constant efforts to roll back or make exceptions to the laws on the books. The leeway enjoyed by lobbyists in New Mexico's relationship-based legislative culture has enhanced their influence, sometimes for the best, often for the worst. Lobbyists should disclose their salaries and clients. It is not an outrageous infringement on their freedom as some legislators have said. In New Mexico, where legislators lack personal staff, lobbyists play a large role in shaping public policy. In other states, they are subject to more restrictions, including bans on direct lobbying by wives, sons, daughters, business partners, and other family members of current legislators—common practice here. We ought to consider such a ban here, or at least get an ethics commission to draw better guidelines.

Finally, we need to close the revolving door whereby legislators leave service only to reemerge immediately as high-paid lobbyists. Sen. Kent Cravens, who resigned to become a lobbyist for the Oil and Gas Association in 2011, has been an embarrassment. It's hard not to see his transfer as an immediate cash-in on the contacts and insider knowledge he gained as an unpaid senator. Numerous bills (three had my name on them) have been introduced to end this practice or at least provide a decent interval—but none have moved very far. Twenty-six other states require cooling off periods of one or two years before legislators can lobby their former colleagues. I hope Gov. Susana Martinez continues to join with progressive Democrats to push this reform over the finish line. Let's tell the truth: relatives and former colleagues naturally have special access to legislators —and that's a bad message to ordinary citizens who may be reluctant to compete with the insiders.

THE BEST LITTLE CHORIZO LAB IN NEW MEXICO

Just about any political science textbook will use two images to describe state legislatures. One is that of a sausage factory, where it is better to just appreciate the taste of the sausages (i.e., the laws) than know exactly how they were made and what went into them. The other is that of a laboratory—a laboratory of democracy where states try out various solutions to problems, which may later be adopted or modified on a national level.

Both ideas apply to New Mexico, with a local flavor, where the sausage is chorizo and the lab is a decidedly unscientific place where people are smudging up the equipment with their fingerprints, delaying the results, and affecting the outcome in unforeseen ways. Sometimes the sausage needs to be recalled. I've often been frustrated by the process, the lack of professionalism, the control of special interests, and the slow pace of sausage making. But every time I've despaired, there have been reasons to hope.

The same Senate that resists an ethics commission and supports a culture based on lobbyists and contributions has risen to the occasion repeatedly to solve problems and even break new ground. Asked to describe the "finest hours" of the legislature in recent times, participants I interviewed for this book cited the Workers Compensation reforms, hammered out in a special session in 1991 with bipartisan cooperation under the leadership of former Sen. Marty Chavez, of Albuquerque, and former Rep. Fred Peralta, of Taos. Others cited gains made in the 1990s. Throughout the 1990s, lawmakers acted to expand access and insurance coverage for low-income children, people with disabilities and mental illness, and patients who needed protection from insurance companies. And at the end of the decade the legislature took the farsighted step of putting the proceeds of its tobacco settlement into a permanent fund, where it could grow and feed health programs for decades.[7] In 1997 we led the nation with a "harm reduction" bill that allowed the distribution of clean needles to addicts to reduce the spread of AIDS. It's a measure that would have made the hair on the heads of Republican legislators in other states stand on end. But it was passed with only two dissenting votes in the New Mexico Senate.

Another key moment was the historic extraordinary session in 2004 when legislators joined together to veto Governor Johnson's budget. Calling themselves back to Santa Fe, they fulfilled the legislature's basic job: coming up with a responsible budget. This task has become more challenging as budgets have shrunk, needs have increased, and the partisan divide has widened. Just doing it every year, without a total breakdown such as we've seen in our nation's capital, makes every year the budget passes overwhelmingly its finest hour, according to some observers.

Previous chapters in this book detail other hard-fought, unexpected victories in a basically conservative body, victories rooted in compassion and courage—the long delayed end of cockfighting, the bipartisan repeal of the death penalty, and legalization of medical marijuana. Usually, the same people who fell in line behind the NRA and the fireworks lobby voted for these measures—a testament to the independence of legislators who can, if given the right cues, move forward together.

The New Mexico legislature is like a little United Nations, says lobbyist Gary Kilpatric. "It's a deliberative body, which can be difficult with all the diverse viewpoints and backgrounds," he says. "There's too little time and too little information. But as dysfunctional as it sometimes is, there is just no alternative."

For all its warts, Bill Fulginiti, a longtime lobbyist for the New Mexico Municipal League, says he wouldn't trade it for anything else. "It's the most open and accessible legislature I've seen," says Fulginiti, who used to lobby the Pennsylvania legislature in Harrisburg. "There, a bill wouldn't even get out of the filing cabinet—even if you represented a powerful group. You would have to beg to get it heard," he said.

Consider the alternative, both lobbyists say: a dictatorship—in this case an all-powerful governor—who might be more efficient but less deliberate and restrained.

So for now, I guess, we'll make do with our own chorizo lab. With a new economy shifting its foundations and new technology cracking open the windows to see what goes on there, the public can judge whether repairs are in order. For reformers like me who want to restore public trust in representative democracy, there are hopeful signs on the horizon. Foremost among them is a new crop of citizen activists who are savvy in media mobilization and social networking and still believe democracy is more than an insider's game.

Notes

CHAPTER I

1. Dan Boyd and Deb Baker, "State Races Awash in Super-Pac Cash," *Albuquerque Journal*, November 2, 2012, A1–A2.
2. In 2013, the number of women in the Senate was down to six.
3. Project New West poll for the Democratic Party of New Mexico, presented January 25, 2012, to the Senate Democratic Caucus. Poll data also showed 60 percent believed state government was corrupt.
4. Polling data from the 2000 *Albuquerque Journal* poll quoted in "Approval Ratings Fall for Johnson, Lawmakers," *Amarillo Globe-News*, March 23, 2000, http://amarillo.com/stories/2000/03/23/usn_ratings.shtml (accessed June 9, 2013); 2006 poll results e-mailed by Matt Hughes, of Research and Polling, Inc., to author, June 22, 2011.
5. Lilliard Richardson, David Konisky, and Jeffrey Milyo, "Public Approval of State Legislatures," *Legislative Studies Quarterly* 37, no. 1:99–116.
6. Project New West poll for the Democratic Party of New Mexico, presented January 25, 2012, to the Senate Democratic Caucus.
7. Like many bills passed by state legislators, my do-not-call bill, along with similar laws in other states, became the basis of a federal law passed by Congress a few years later.

CHAPTER 2

1. Figures were found using the Political Contribution Logarithmic Scatterplot Profile (or PULSE) tool on the National Institute on Money in State Politics website, http://www.followthemoney.org. The PULSE charts demonstrate the relationship between money, incumbency, and winning. See http://www.follow themoney.org/database/graphs/meta/meta.phtml (accessed December 18, 2012).
2. Thomas J. Cole, "Donation Limits Outweighed by Super-PACs," *Albuquerque Journal*, November 10, 2012, A1.
3. Figures were found using the PULSE tool on followthemoney.org.
4. Figures were found using the industry influence tool on followthemoney.org.

5. Contributions from dairy, agricultural services, construction, oil and gas, and in-surance industries to Republicans running for the state senate in 2008 were found using the industry influence tool on followthemoney.org. Contributions to Democratic candidates from lawyers, lobbyists, and labor were found there as well. See http://www.followthemoney.org/database/IndustryTotals.phtml (accessed June 11, 2013).

6. Common Cause New Mexico, *Connecting the Dots: The Role of Campaign Contributions in New Mexico Health Policy*, May 2012, 13–19, http://www. commoncause.org/atf/cf/{FB3C17E2-CDD1-4DF6-92BE-BD4429893665}/ Connecting%20the%20Dots%20--%20CCNM%20May%202012.pdf (accessed June 11, 2013).

7. Bruce King, *Cowboy in the Roundhouse* (Santa Fe: Sunstone Press, 1998), 349.

8. Dan Boyd and Deb Baker, "State Races Awash in Super-PAC Cash," *Albuquerque Journal*, November 2, 2012, A1–A2.

9. Thomas J. Cole, "Donation Limits Outweighed by Super-PACs," *Albuquerque Journal*, November 10, 2012, A1.

CHAPTER 3

1. Craig Fritz, photo for "GOP Talks Bills to Death," *Santa Fe New Mexican*, March 23, 1997, A1.

2. John Robertson, "King of the Senate," *Albuquerque Journal*, March 17, 1997, A1–A2.

3. Tim Archuleta, "Speaking his Mind," *Albuquerque Tribune*, January 29, 1998, 1 and 3.

4. Robertson, "King of the Senate," A2.

5. In an act of high political theater, Manny introduced a bill to abolish the park and give jurisdiction back to the Middle Rio Grande Conservancy District. It was a feint to get the City of Albuquerque to put more money into the park areas in his district, although he never told us what he was doing.

6. Editorial, "Senate Leader Out of Control," *Albuquerque Journal*, March 23, 1997, B2.

7. Christopher Ketcham, "The Albany Handshake," *Harpers Magazine*, May 2010, 60.

8. Deb Baker, "Powerful Ex-Lawmaker Dunn Dies," *Albuquerque Journal*, August 25, 2012, C2.

9. Common Cause New Mexico, *Connecting the Dots*, (accessed October 29, 2012).

10. Steve Terrell and Ben Neary, "NM Senator Blasts Governor's 'Bullying,'" *Santa Fe New Mexican*, February 6, 2004, A1 and A8.

11. Ibid.

12. Heath Haussaman, "In session's final days, all eyes are on Sanchez," *NMPolitics. net*, March 17, 2011, http://www.nmpolitics.net/index/2011/03/in-session's-final-days-all-eyes-are-on-sanchez (accessed June 12, 2013).

13. Common Cause New Mexico, *Connecting the Dots*, 36 (accessed October 29, 2012).

CHAPTER 4

1. This belief persists. Nationally, in 2011, a CNN poll indicated that 86 percent of those surveyed felt Washington politicians are mostly influenced by pressures from major campaign contributors rather than what is in the best interest of the country. See CNN Opinion Research Poll, June 3–7, 2011, http://i2.cdn.turner. com/cnn/2011/images/06/14/rel10d.pdf (accessed June 12, 2013).

2. New Mexico Secretary of State Lobbyist Reports, as of August 2012.

3. Steve Terrell, "Lobbyists Help Lawmakers 'Mingle' Over a Free Meal," *Santa Fe New Mexican*, March 1, 2011, A10.

4. Lawrence Lessing, *Republic, Lost* (New York: Twelve Books, 2011).

5. Terrell, "Lobbyists Help Lawmakers," *Santa Fe New Mexican*, March 1, 2011, A10.

6. New Mexico Secretary of State Lobbyist Reports, as of August 2012.

7. Thomas Cole, "Politics 'Infiltrated' with Money," *Albuquerque Journal*, February 25, 2009, A1–A2.

8. http://www.followthemoney.org/database/state_overview.phtml?y=2008&s=NM (accessed June 12, 2013).

9. This list includes contributions of cash or goods and services. It excludes contributions of less than $250, candidate self-financing, contributions from political party groups, and candidate committees. In a December 19, 2012, *Albuquerque Journal* article on the 2012 election, Thomas Cole did a similar analysis, finding that the pattern had changed a little. Energy companies, utilities, business interests, doctors, lawyers, bankers, and unions still dominated the list of large donors. But PACs and corporations accounted for 63 percent of legislative contributions.

10. Thomas Cole, "Clients of Lobby Team Gave $333K," *Albuquerque Journal*, March 14, 2009, A1.

11. Cole, "Politics 'Infiltrated' with Money," A1–A2.

12. Ibid.

13. Common Cause New Mexico has published seven *Connect the Dots* reports on various industries, including oil and gas, tobacco, real estate, and health care since 2003. See http://www.commoncause.org/site/pp.asp?c=dkLNK1MQIwG&b=4847985 (accessed June 12, 2013).

14. Thomas Cole "Lobbyists and Clients Give Big to Lawmakers," *Albuquerque Journal*, February 14, 2009, A1–A2.

15. Trip Jennings, "Senate OKs Limit on Gifts to Officials," *Albuquerque Journal*, March 13, 2007, A4.

CHAPTER 5

1. "Lobbyist: Trujillo, Anthony (T.J)," New Mexico Secretary of State Campaign Finance Information System, https://cfis.state.nm.us/media/ReportLobbyist Details.aspx?id=523&na=Trujillo,%20Anthony%20%28T.J.%29 (accessed October 30, 2012).

2. Steve Terrell, "Fireworks Measure Fizzles," *Santa Fe New Mexican*, March 6, 2012, A1, A4.

3. Ibid.

4. "Lobbyist: Otero, Luke," New Mexico Secretary of State Campaign Finance Information System, https://cfis.state.nm.us/media/ReportLobbyistDetails. aspx?id=191&na=Otero,%20Luke (accessed October 30, 2012).

5. Terrell, "Fireworks Measure Fizzles," A1, A4.

6. "Contributor: Occidental Oil & Gas, Co.," New Mexico Secretary of State Campaign Finance Information System, https://cfis.state.nm.us/media/Report DetailsContributorsC.aspx?cn=Occidental+Oil+%26+Gas+Co.&add=604+West+1 4th+Street&ct=Austin&st=TX&z=78701 (accessed October 30, 2012).

7. "Lobbyist: Trujillo, Anthony (T. J.)," New Mexico Secretary of State Campaign Finance Information System, https://cfis.state.nm.us/media/ReportLobbyist

Details.aspx?id=523&na=Trujillo,%20Anthony%20%28T.J.%29 (accessed October 30, 2012).

CHAPTER 6

1. Janet Lundy, "Prescription Drug Trends," *A Report of the Kaiser Family Foundation*, May 2010, 3. http://kaiserfamilyfoundation.files.wordpress.com/2013/01/3057-08. pdf (accessed June 6, 2013).
2. Mark Hummels, "Lawmakers Tackle Cost of Prescriptions," *Santa Fe New Mexican*, January 20, 2001, A1.
3. Robert Pear, "Drug Companies Increase Spending to Lobby Congress and Governments," *The New York Times*, June 1, 2003, http://www.nytimes.com/2003/06/01/us/drug-companies-increase-spending-on-efforts-to-lobby-congress-and-governments.html?pagewanted=all&src=pm (accessed June 12, 2013). Lundy, "Prescription Drug Trends," 4, also describes the profitability of the industry.
4. Robert Pear, "Drug Companies Increase Spending," *New York Times*, June 1, 2003.
5. *State Health Notes*, National Conference of State Legislatures, February 11, 2002. For more information on how states can save money on Medicaid through prescription drug strategies go to the National Conference of State Legislature's online health archive at http://www.ncsl.org/issues-research/health/medicaid-pharmaceutical-laws-and-policies.aspx (accessed June 6, 2013).
6. Tom Hamburger, "Drug Industry Steps Up Campaign to Boost Image Ahead of Elections," *The Wall Street Journal*, September 17, 2002, http://online.wsj.com/article/SB1032130597939650835.html (accessed June 6, 2013).
7. Follow the Money, "Bill Richardson," http://www.followthemoney.org/database/uniquecandidate.phtml?uc=4138 (accessed October 29, 2012).
8. Ibid.
9. Common Cause New Mexico, *Connecting the Dots* (accessed October 29, 2012).
10. Harry Chen, M.D., "States Tackle Pharmaceutical Marketing and Costs," presentation to the Health and Human Services Committee of the New Mexico legislature, Santa Fe, NM, December 8, 2008.
11. Follow the Money, "Tim Jennings," http://www.followthemoney.org/database/uniquecandidate.phtml?uc=1322 (accessed October 29, 2012).
12. Follow the Money, report on the pharmaceutical and health products industry's contributions to New Mexico senators in 2009–2010, http://www.followthemoney.org/database/StateGlance/contributor_details.phtml?s=NM&y=2010&i=68&f=S (accessed June 5, 2013).
13. Common Cause New Mexico, *Connecting the Dots,* 36 (accessed October 29, 2012).
14. ProPublica, "Payments to New Mexico Health Care Practitioners," http://projects.propublica.org/docdollars/states/new-mexico?order=amount (accessed October 29, 2012).

CHAPTER 7

1. "The Toll of Tobacco in New Mexico," Campaign for Tobacco-Free Kids, http://www.tobaccofreekids.org/facts_issues/toll_us/new_mexico (accessed December 10, 2012).
2. "Preventing Tobacco Use Among Youth and Young Adults: Report of the Surgeon General, 2012: Fact Sheet," website for Surgeon General Regina M. Benjamin,

http://www.surgeongeneral.gov/library/reports/preventing-youth-tobacco-use/factsheet.html (accessed December 10, 2012).

3. *Tobacco Price Promotion*, a publication of the Center for Public Health and Tobacco Policy, October 2011, 2–5. Boston Mass quotes these industry remarks and has an extensive discussion of price sensitivity, http://www.tobaccopolicycenter.org/documents/Tobacco%20Price%20Promotion%20Complete%20Report.pdf (accessed June 6, 2013).

4. Numerous studies are cited in the *2012 Surgeon General's Report*, "Preventing Tobacco Use Among Youth and Young Adults," 809–10, http://www.surgeongeneral.gov/library/reports/preventing-youth-tobacco-use/sgr_chapt6.pdf (accessed June 6, 2013).

5. "New Mexico Tobacco Industry Documents," TobaccoFreedom.org, http://tobaccofreedom.org/issues/documents/new_mexico (accessed December 10, 2012).

6. "The Toll of Tobacco in New Mexico," Campaign for Tobacco-Free Kids, http://www.tobaccofreekids.org/facts_issues/toll_us/new_mexico (accessed December 10, 2012).

7. Jackie Jadrnak, "Coalition to Push Bigger Cigarette Tax," *Albuquerque Journal*, August 22, 2002, D2.

8. Barry Massey, "Lobbyists Give Almost $1 Million to Politicians," *Albuquerque Journal*, January 26, 2003, B5.

9. Mike Surrusco, *New Mexico: The Campaign Contributions and Lobbying Expenditures of the Tobacco Industry and Its Allies*, Draft Common Cause Education Fund, June 2006, http://www.commoncause.org/atf/cf/%7Bfb3c17e2-cdd1-4df6-92be-bd4429893665%7D/Tobacco%20ctd.pdf (accessed June 8, 2013).

10. Ibid.

11. Ibid.

12. Common Cause New Mexico, *Connecting the Dots*, 22–27 (accessed June 12, 2013).

CHAPTER 8

1. Elected in 1996 as Gail Chasey Beam, Gail changed her name to Gail Chasey in 2005, following the death of her father and before she entered law school.

2. Bill Jordan, "Talking Points for the Children and Firearm Safety Act and the Child Access Prevention Act," New Mexico Advocates for Children and Families, Fact Sheet, 2001, archives of New Mexico Voices for Children, Albuquerque, NM.

3. David Espo and Nancy Benac, "Gun Control Calls Go Unanswered," *Albuquerque Journal*, July 22, 2012, A6. The article cites a 1990 Gallup poll where 78 percent of those surveyed said laws covering the sale of firearms should be stricter, while 19 percent said they should remain the same or be loosened. By the fall of 2004, support for tougher laws had dropped to 54 percent. In a 2011 opinion poll, 43 percent said laws should be stricter and 55 percent said they should stay the same or be made more lenient.

4. Barry Massey, "Senate Approves Trigger-Lock Measure," *Albuquerque Journal*, February 22, 2001, A8.

5. Mark Hummels, "House Passes Concealed-Gun Measure 43–20," *Santa Fe New Mexican*, March 14, 2001, A1, A2.

6. Mark Hummels, "Democrat Revives Concealed-Firearm Issue," *Santa Fe New Mexican*, February 11, 2001, A1.

7. Hummels, "House Passes Concealed-Gun Measure 43–20."

8. Loie Fecteau, "Senate OKs Gun Measure," *Albuquerque Journal*, March 16, 2001, A1, A6.

9. Steve Terrell, "Senate Passes Concealed-Gun Measure Despite Controversy," *Santa Fe New Mexican*, March 16, 2001, A5.

10. NRA contributions to federal candidates have decreased from $1.6 million in 1994 to $1.14 million in 2010. In 2008, individual contributions to endorsed candidates were dwarfed by the NRA's independent expenditures—$17.9 million used in opposition or support of candidates. Ninety-nine percent of the contributions supported Republicans. See the Center for Responsive Politics website, http://www.opensecrets.org/news/2011/01/ideologically-confused-corporations.html (accessed July 19, 2012). At the state level in 2008, the NRA donated $11,000 to legislative candidates (Thom Cole, "UpFront," *Albuquerque Journal*, February 25, 2009, A1).

11. Associated Press, "Boy Shoots Toddler with Father's Pistol," *Lubbock Avalanche Journal*, March 5th, 2002, http://lubbockonline.com/stories/030502/nat_030502060.shtml (accessed July 9, 2012).

12. Deborah Baker, "Court Backs Concealed-Gun Law," *Albuquerque Journal*, January 6, 2004, A1, A4.

13. As a presidential candidate in 2008, Richardson got the support of the NRA through an independent expenditure of $15,180. See OpenSecrets.org, http://www.opensecrets.org/pres08/indexp_indiv.php?cid=N00024821&cycle=2008 (accessed June 7, 2013).

14. Jill Lepore, "Battleground America," *The New Yorker*, April 23, 2012, 38–47.

15. Gov. Susana Martinez, Twitter, August 2011. Martinez also reminisced about her gun during her speech at the 2012 Republican Convention in Tampa.

16. Statistics cited in Bill Moyers video posted to the *Huffington Post*, August 23, 2012, http://www.huffingtonpost.com/2012/07/23/bill-moyers-nra-enabler-of-death-colorado-shootings_n_1695658.html?utm_hp_ref=media (accessed June 7, 2013).

17. Statistic cited by Joline Gutierrez Krueger, "Add Common Sense to Gun Law Arsenal," *Albuquerque Journal*, July 27, 2012, A1.

18. Michael Landen, New Mexico Department of Health, Department of Injury Prevention, e-mail messages and charts sent to the author, June 19 and 25, 2012.

CHAPTER 9

1. Matt Brix and Bill Wiese, *The Role of the Health Care Industry in New Mexico State Politics*, Common Cause New Mexico, August 2008, 6–7. The complete report is available in the research section of Common Cause's website, http://www.commoncause.org/site/pp.asp?c=dkLNK1MQIwG&b=4847593 (accessed June 7, 2013).

2. Tim Archuleta, "Push Is on to Get State to Police 'HMOs,'" *Albuquerque Tribune*, January 9, 1998, A1, A8.

3. Cathy Schoen, Kristof Stremikis, Sabrina K. H. How, and Sara R. Collins, "State Trends in Premiums and Deductibles, 2003–2009: How Building on the Affordable Care Act Will Help Stem the Tide of Rising Costs and Eroding Benefits," The Commonwealth Fund, December 2, 2010. Vol. 104, http://www.commonwealthfund.org/Publications/Issue-Briefs/2010/Dec/State-Trends-Premiums-and-Deductibles.aspx (accessed June 7, 2013).

4. James McKinley Jr. and Michael Haederle, "Inquiry Highlights New Mexico's Few Ethics Laws," *New York Times*, January 11, 2009, http://www.nytimes.com/2009/01/11/us/11newmexico.html?pagewanted=all&_r=0] (accessed June 7, 2013).

5. Brix and Wiese, *The Role of the Health Care Industry*, 8–9. The complete report is available in the research section of Common Cause's website, http://www.commoncause.org/site/pp.asp?c=dkLNK1MQIwG&b=4847593 (accessed June 7, 2013).

6. Winthrop Quigley, "Health Care Gives Gov. a Booster Shot," *Albuquerque Journal*, May 22, 2006, http://www.abqjournal.com/news/state/462193nm05-22-06.htm (accessed June 7, 2013). Campaign contributions from COLTS contractors were also revealed in testimony before the Health and Human Services Committee, September 2007. Dave Contarino, Richardson's former campaign manager and chief of staff, became a lobbyist for Value Options and longtime political advisor Richard Stratton was hired by United Health Care.

7. Trip Jennings, "Health Insurance Companies Give Big to NM politicians," *New Mexico Independent*, August 16, 2010. Legislators themselves received hefty contributions during this period with $67,500 going to key legislative leaders—including me. I received $9,150 during this period. Presbyterian Health Services alone contributed more than $250,000 to New Mexico elected officials from 2004 to 2008.

8. Trip Jennings, "Friends of Bill Find it Pays to Play," *New Mexico Independent*, January 12, 2009.

9. Winthrop Quigley, "House Panel Passes State Health Care Bill," *Albuquerque Journal*, February 1, 2008, A1, A5.

10. Trip Jennings, "Governor Blasts Senate 'Gridlock,'" *Albuquerque Journal*, February 15, 2008, A1, A6.

11. Quoted in Molly Ivins, *Nothing but Good Times Ahead* (New York: Random House, 1993), 76.

CHAPTER 10

1. Bill Wiese, *Final Report on Senate Memorial 18*, New Mexico Drug Policy Task Force, Fall 2011, 5. A summary of this report can be found on the legislative website at http://www.nmlegis.gov/lcs/handouts/BHS%20081911%20SM%2018%20New%20Mexico%20Drug%20Policy%20Task%20Force.PDF. The full report is in the Legislative Council Service library in the state capitol building and the library at the Robert Wood Johnson Foundation Center for Health Policy at the University of New Mexico.

2. Deborah Baker, "Medical Marijuana Bill Signed Into Law," *Albuquerque Journal*, April 3, 2007, C1, C3.

3. Ibid.

4. Deborah Baker, "Guv Ready for Medical Pot Flak," *Albuquerque Tribune*, March 16, 2007, A1.

5. Deborah Baker, "Richardson Signs Medical Marijuana Bill," *Santa Fe New Mexican*, April 3, 2007, C1, C3.

6. Jacob Sullum, "General Consternation," *Reason*, December 1999, http://reason.com/archives/1999/12/01/general-consternation (accessed December 2012).

7. Steve Terrell, "House Narrowly OKs Medical Marijuana," *Santa Fe New Mexican*, March 13, 2001, A1, A2.

8. Ibid.

9. Jonathan McDonald, "Republicans Feud Over Drug-Reform Legislation," *Santa Fe New Mexican*, February 6, 2002, A4.

10. V. B. Price, "It's Possible to Do the Right Thing in 30 Days," *Albuquerque Tribune*, January 25, 2002, D1.

11. Ellick, "A Ban on Cockfighting, but Tradition Lives On."

12. "Medical Marijuana Bill Takes Step," *Albuquerque Tribune*, February 21, 2003, A6.

13. Barry Massey, "Pleas Made to OK Pot for Pain," *Albuquerque Journal*, February 8, 2005, A4.

14. Todd Eric Lovato, "Grace Under Fire," *Albuquerque Journal*, April 13, 2007, C1, C3.

15. Deborah Baker, "Panel OKs Medical Marijuana Over Drug Czar's Opposition," *Clovis News Journal*, January 28, 2006, 18.

16. "Medical Marijuana Bill Overwhelmingly Passes the Senate Judiciary Committee," news release, Drug Policy Alliance, January 27, 2006, available in the archives of the New Mexico Drug Policy Alliance, Santa Fe, NM.

17. Heather Clark, "Panel Shelves Medical Marijuana Bill," *Albuquerque Journal*, February 12, 2006. B1, B5.

18. Erin Armstrong, Letter to Honorable Speaker Ben Lujan, February 14, 2006, available in the archives of the New Mexico Drug Policy Alliance, Santa Fe, NM.

19. Associated Press, "House Rejects Medical Marijuana Bill," *Gallup Independent*, March 9, 2007, 5.

20. Tom Moody, "Malaga Man Victim of Conflicting Marijuana Laws," *The Carlsbad Current-Argus*, September 2, 2007, 1A, 10A.

CHAPTER 11

1. Mary Jane Garcia, "Cockfighting's All About Gambling, Not N.M. Culture," *Albuquerque Journal*, January 24, 2007, A11. The op ed also appeared in the *Las Cruces Sun-Times* and the *Alamagordo News*.

2. Christopher Cooper, "How a Tradition Ends in New Mexico," *Wall Street Journal*, February 13, 2007, A8.

3. Russell Max Simon, "Fight to the Death," *Albuquerque Journal*, January 21, 2007, A1, A4.

4. Ibid.

5. Adam B. Ellick, "A Ban on Cockfighting, but Tradition Lives On," *New York Times*, July 6, 2008, http://www.nytimes.com/2008/07/06/us/06fight.html?pagewanted=all&_r=0 (accessed June 8, 2013).

6. Staff and wire reports, "Per Diem: Roundhouse Report—Endangered Roosters," *Albuquerque Tribune*, February 26, 2007, A3.

7. Garcia, "Cockfighting's All About Gambling."

8. David Miles, "Cockfighting Ban Clears House, Returns to Senate," *Santa Fe New Mexican*, March 9, 2007, A4.

9. David Miles, "Cockfighters Lose Major Battle," *Santa Fe New Mexican*, February 2, 2007, A1, A5.

10. Danielle Bays, "Cockfighting's Death Knell in New Mexico?" *PETroglyphs*, Spring 2007, http://www.petroglyphsnm.org/covers/cockfightban.html (accessed June 8, 2013).

11. Ellick, "A Ban on Cockfighting, but Tradition Lives On."

CHAPTER 12

1. Elected in 1996 as Gail Chasey Beam, Gail changed her name to Gail Chasey in 2005, following the death of her father and before she entered law school.
2. Steve Terrell, "Decades of Doubt," *Santa Fe New Mexican*, March 13, 2009, A1, A4.
3. Jack Kutz, *The Wild West Never Died* (Corrales, NM: Rhombus Publishing, 2012), 78.
4. Barry Massey, "As the 2002 Legislature Convenes, Gov. Gary Johnson Says He Will Consider Repeal of the Death Penalty," *Santa Fe New Mexican*, January 16, 2002, A1. Johnson allowed the item on the agenda during the short 2002 session and later said he would have signed a bill if it reached his desk.
5. Loie Fecteau, "House to Weigh Death Penalty Repeal," *Albuquerque Journal*, February 25, 1999, A8.
6. Steve Terrell, "Capital Punishment Repeal is Unlikely," *Santa Fe New Mexican*, February 1, 2001, A1.
7. Jason Auslander, "Police Back Plan to Reverse Ban," *Santa Fe New Mexican*, March 21, 2009, C1, C4.
8. Steve Terrell, "Death Penalty Goes to Judiciary Panel," *Las Cruces Sun News*, March 4, 2009, http://www.lcsun-news.com/ci_11830961 (accessed June 8, 2013).
9. Deborah Baker, "Old Issue, New Argument," *Santa Fe New Mexican*, February 13, 2009, A8.
10. Kate Nelson, "Death Penalty Vote Brings Rep to Tears," *Albuquerque Tribune*, February 14, 2003, A1.
11. Steve Terrell, "Senate Backs Death Penalty Repeal," *The Santa Fe New Mexican*, March 14, 2009, A1, A6.
12. Dan Boyd, "Death Penalty's Final Hour?" *The Albuquerque Journal*, March 14, 2009, A1, A5.
13. Ibid.
14. Gov. Bill Richardson, Official Statement, March 18, 2009, http://votesmart.org/public-statement/413351/governor-bill-richardson-signs-repeal-of-the-death-penalty#.UbOoGOBh4QI (accessed June 8, 2013).
15. Dan Boyd, "Repealed," *Albuquerque Journal*, March 19, 2009, A1, A4.
16. Joanne Ford, "New Mexico Honored at Colosseum," *L'Osservatore Romano*, April 22, 2009.

CHAPTER 13

1. Dan Vukelich, "Lawmaker Survives Attempt to Expel Him from House," *Albuquerque Tribune*, February 18, 1992, A1, A6.
2. John Yaeger, "House Censures Olguin, Votes Against Ouster," *Albuquerque Journal*, February 18, 1992, A3.
3. Vukelich, "Lawmaker Survives," *Albuquerque Tribune*, February 18, 1992, A6.
4. Senate Rules 26–1-A, New Mexico Legislature's website, http://www.nmlegis.gov/lcs/lcsdocs/handbook/Senaterules.pdf (accessed June 9, 2013).
5. Colleen Heild, "Money Scrum: UNM Think Tank Cash Diverted to Rugby Club," *Albuquerque Journal*, January 13, 2008, A1–A3.
6. Lobbyists often help legislators run interference for their constituents when they need help from the lobbyists' clients, whether they are hospitals, health plans, or restaurants. I also depended on constituent and campaign contributions to put

out a constituent questionnaire each year. Without that support I would have paid approximately $2,500 each year to provide this service.

7. Editorial, "Public Wants Reform; Will Santa Fe Listen?," *Albuquerque Journal*, September 12, 2006, A7.

8. Editorial, "Senate Must See the Big Picture on Ethics," *Albuquerque Journal*, March 4, 2007, B2.

9. Ibid.

10. Felicia Fonseca, "Gov. Considers Ethics Special Session," *Albuquerque Journal*, April 1, 2007, B1, B5.

11. Sen. Michael Sanchez, "Changing How New Mexico Does Business," *New Mexico Politics* (blog), March 19, 2009, http://www.nmpolitics.net/index/2009/03/changing-how-new-mexico-does-business (accessed June 9, 2013).

12. Editorial, "State Senators Should Work, Not Whine," *Albuquerque Tribune*, April 2, 2007, B3.

13. "Public Wants Reform," *Albuquerque Journal*, September 12, 2006, A7.

14. "Pay to Play Insider Deals, No-bid Contracts . . . Are Those Days coming Back?" Reform New Mexico election flyer, October 16, 2012, from the author's personal collection of campaign literature.

15. Peggy Kerns and Ginger Sampson, "Do Ethics Laws Work?" *State Legislatures Magazine*, July/August 2003, 40.

16. John Robertson, "New Mexico Identity Linked to Corruption," *Albuquerque Journal*, August 7, 2011, A1–A2.

CHAPTER 14

1. New Mexico Open Meetings Act, *New Mexico Statues Annotated, 1978* (1974), §10–15–1(A).

2. Lago, LLC, an oil and gas company, gave that amount to candidate Rory McMinn in a 2008 Republican Senate primary. The contribution constituted over 44 percent of McMinn's funding. "McMinn, Rory: Follow The Money," *National Institute on Money in State Politics*, http://www.followthemoney.org/database/StateGlance/candidate.phtml?c=101303 (accessed October 23, 2012).

3. Deborah Baker, "Panel's Work May Become Public," *Albuquerque Journal*, February 4, 2006, A6.

4. Tripp Jennings, "Senate Votes to Keep Secret Meetings Secret," *Albuquerque Journal*, February 11, 2006, http://www.albuquerquejournal.com/cgi-bin/print_it.pl?page=/xgr/432508xgr02-11-06.htm (accessed June 9, 2013).

5. "Per Diem Roundhouse Report," *Albuquerque Tribune*, February 11, 2006, A4.

6. Editorial, "Open Last Sanctum of Roundhouse Secrecy," *Albuquerque Journal*, March 1, 2007.

7. Walt Rubel, "Papen Corrects Gaff," *Las Cruces Sun News*, February 28, 2007, http://www.lcsun-news.com/ci_5319308 (accessed June 9, 2013).

8. Kate Nash, "Ethics Trouble? Blame the Press," *Albuquerque Tribune*, March 1, 2007, A1, A7.

9. Heath Haussamen, "Senators Won't Allow Open Conference Committees," *New Mexico Politics*, February 15, 2007, http://www.nmpolitics.net/index/2007/02/senators-wont-allow-open-conference-committees (accessed June 9, 2013).

10. The Campaign Disclosure Project, *Grading State Disclosure 2007; Evaluating*

States' Efforts to Bring Sunlight to Political Money, http://campaigndisclosure.org/gradingstate2007/gsd07_elecfinal.pdf (accessed October 23, 2011).

11. Eli Young Lee, "Transparency Watch: NM State Senate Proves Irony is Not Dead," Center for Civic Policy, February 4, 2009, http://civicpolicy.com/3/ (accessed June 9, 2013).

12. Heath Haussamen, "Open Conference Committees are Good After All!" *New Mexico Politics*, March 23, 2009, http://www.nmpolitics.net/index/2009/03/open-conference-committees-are-good-after-all/ (accessed June 9, 2013).

13. Kate Nash, "House Speaker Clashes with Senator," *The New Mexican*, March 22, 2009, http://www.sfnewmexican.com/LocalNews/House-speaker-clashes-with-senator#.UbT8_-Bh4QI (accessed June 9, 2013).

14. 2011 State of the State Address, http://www.governor.state.nm.us/ (accessed Oct. 23, 2012).

15. In late May, 2013, Jamie Estrada, former campaign manager for Susana Martinez, was indicted for allegedly intercepting the administration's private e-mail.

CHAPTER 15

1. Mark Oswald, "Campaign Reform Dies Again," *Santa Fe New Mexican*, March 19, 1997, A4.

2. Arizona Gov. Janet Napolitano was also elected using public financing.

3. The poll was conducted on January 18 and 25, 1999, by Research and Polling Inc. for Re-Visioning New Mexico using a random sample of 416 registered voters, with results quoted in a New Mexicans for Campaign Reform Fact Sheet, "59% of New Mexicans Favor Public Financing of Elections!!" The full report is in the files of Research and Polling Inc., Albuquerque, NM.

4. Barry Massey, "Campaign Funding Targeted," *Albuquerque Journal*, January 23, 2001, A4.

5. Steve Terrell, "Activist Speaks in Capitol," *Santa Fe New Mexican*, January 18, 2001, A5.

6. A number of candidates for the PRC have used the system successfully. A court case nullified the matching provision in 2012, but several candidates, including the winner in the Albuquerque area, used it.

7. Editorial, "Lack of Ethics Reform Is Not One Bit Funny," *Albuquerque Tribune*, March 3, 2007, C2.

8. Editorial, "What Will It Take To Get Ethics Reform?" *Albuquerque Journal*, April 2, 2007, A8.

CONCLUSION

1. Tim Archuleta, "Push Is on to Get State to Police 'HMOs,'" *Albuquerque Tribune*, January 9, 1998, A1, A8.

2. In 2011, my last long session, 1,523 measures were introduced, a low number due largely to diminished expectations from a recession. Of these, 284 were passed, with Governor Martinez vetoing ninety-eight or 34.5 percent of them, the largest proportion since Gov. Gary Johnson in 1996. See *2011 Highlights*, New Mexico Legislative Council Services, http://www.nmlegis.gov/lcs/misc/2011_highlights.pdf (accessed December 19, 2012).

3. Other proposed reforms have included limiting the number of interim

committees, prefiling bills and prioritizing legislation, shortening the bill intro-
duction period, and establishing deadlines for the passage of bills in each house.
See *Final Report, New Mexico State Legislative Structure and Process Study Task
Force*, http://nmlegis.gov/lcs/fileExists/interimreports/LSPS07.pdf (accessed
December 19, 2012).

4. Only South Dakota and Wyoming have shorter sessions, with Arkansas, Kansas,
   Kentucky, Montana, Virginia, Utah, and New Hampshire meeting the same number of days over a two-year period. See National Conference of State Legislatures,
   http://www.ncsl.org/legislatures-elections/legislatures/legislative-session-length.
   aspx (accessed December 19, 2012).

5. In 2012 controversy over whether Albuquerque Public Schools should compen-
   sate—or even allow—employees to serve in the legislature erupted in the media.
   It may have discouraged Albuquerque teachers from running for office. With very
   few exceptions most of the "educators" in Santa Fe are not classroom teachers.
   They are either retired or are administrators of one sort or another.

6. Rep. Brian Egolf introduced a bill in 2013 to form a combined ethics and elections
   commission. It died in the Senate Rules Committee. Sen. Howie Morales introduced a constitutional amendment for an elections commission. It died in the
   same committee.

7. With repeated raids by subsequent legislatures, the Tobacco Fund became a sort
   of semipermanent fund that did not garner as much interest as hoped.

Glossary

acequia: A ditch carrying irrigation water from the river to the fields.

ALEC: A national conservative alliance of state legislators funded by corporations.

amendment: A change or addition to any bill made in committee or on the floor; it must be passed by a majority considering the bill.

attorney general's opinion: Can be requested by legislators to find out whether a bill or policy is constitutional or legal. It is an opinion only and does not have the force of law.

blast a bill out of committee: When a bill has been tabled or has been held up in a committee, a member may make a motion to remove the bill from the committee and bring it down to the floor or refer it to another committee. The body must consent unanimously or by majority vote.

Call of the Senate: When seven senators request it, all members of the Senate must be in the chambers, at their seats and voting.

capital outlay: Money appropriated for brick-and-mortar projects based on the issuance of bonds.

COLTS: A program started in the Richardson administration to coordinate long-term services for seniors and people with disabilities using private HMOs.

Committee on Committees: A Senate committee appointed by the president pro tem that appoints committee chairmen and members and makes decisions on the operation of the Senate.

competitive district: A legislative district in which past election results indicate a fairly even number of Republican and Democratic voters.

concurrence calendar: Contains a list of bills that the other chamber has passed in an amended form. The Senate (or House) must agree to the bill in its amended form. If not, the bill goes to a conference committee to iron out differences.

conference committee: A temporary committee composed of House and Senate members appointed by the pro tem and Speaker to iron out differences between bills.

cowboy coalition: A conservative coalition in the House during the 1980s.

drive-up liquor window: Until 1998 you could drive your car up to a liquor establishment, purchase alcohol through a carry-out window, and drive away.

DWI: Driving while intoxicated.

e-blast: Notices, newsletters, or information sent to groups of constituents or voters via e-mail.

extraordinary session: Called by three-fifths of legislators themselves; has only been done once.

filibuster: A delaying tactic used to make it difficult to conduct business or pass bills because one person is speaking continuously; a filibuster in the Senate is limited to two hours.

fiscal impact report (FIR): FIRs are analyses of the financial implications of each bill for government and taxpayers.

germane: Relevant to a short session either by decree of the Committee on Committees or by receiving a written message from the governor to the Senate. Only bills that are deemed germane may be heard during a short session.

GRIP: Governor Richardson's Improvement Package to build and repair roads and state highways—and the New Mexico Rail Runner train.

harm reduction: A public health philosophy that says if you cannot completely eliminate harms like drug addiction or AIDS, you can at least minimize the damage by the legal provision of clean needles, for example, or the use of antidotes by nonprofessionals to prevent drug overdoses.

Health and Human Services Committee: A joint interim committee set up in the 1990s to consider these issues; it became the locus for many reforms throughout the decades. Sometimes called the misery and suffering committee.

HMOs: Health Maintenance Organizations are insurance companies that manage the care for their subscribers by providing it through a network of local hospitals, doctors, and other providers.

hybrid judicial selection system: New Mexico uses a selection system that is half election and half appointment. The governor may appoint judges when there is a vacancy; however, these judges and all judicial candidates must stand in a partisan election at least once. After they are elected they then stand in election for retention or rejection.

initiative: A measure placed on the ballot by petition from the citizens. The New Mexico constitution does not provide this opportunity.

interim committee: Meets during the summer and fall when the legislature is not in session; composed of House and Senate members.

Legislative Council Service: Permanent staff of the legislature that writes bills and does research.

Legislative Finance Committee: An important interim committee composed of House and Senate members that takes testimony during the interim and writes a proposed budget.

line item veto: The governor's power to cross out words and lines in the budget and other appropriations bills.

long session: The sixty-day meeting of the legislature prescribed by the New Mexico constitution to start in January every odd numbered year; a thirty-day short session meets in even numbered years.

managed care: A system that became popular in the 1990s to cut costs and provide care. In New Mexico, Medicaid services are managed by insurance companies using this model, but elsewhere Medicaid programs contract directly with medical-provider groups and nonprofits to deliver care.

Master Settlement Agreement: A legal settlement that was made between the attorneys general of the states and the tobacco companies in 1998 after a huge lawsuit. Companies had to pay states in perpetuity for costs of tobacco-related illnesses.

Medicaid: A federal-state program to provide health insurance for children under the poverty line, seniors in nursing homes, and people with disabilities.

memorial: A measure passed by the legislature that does not have the force of law but that recommends studies or task forces, or makes statements to other branches of government.

movida: A political move designed to accomplish a certain end, sometimes in secret.

PACs: Political Action Committees, used to raise funds and contribute them to candidates. Usually affiliated with corporations, unions, or political groups.

parciente: Someone who gets irrigation water from a ditch association and participates in the local governing body.

pass with no recommendation: In committee, bills can pass, get tabled, or pass with no recommendation. Unless tabled or held back by the committee chair, they go on to the next committee or the floor.

patrón politics: Patróns are local leaders who deliver votes for candidates, have loyal followers, and try to use their influence to help members of their group get jobs and other benefits.

pay-to-play: When applicants for state contracts or jobs give money, gifts, or campaign contributions in order to get the job.

per diem: Reimbursement for a day's service during the legislative session or interim.

permanent funds: The New Mexico constitution set up several accounts composed of revenue from energy taxes, rents, and royalties on state land that are separate from the general budget and used only for specific purposes. A constitutional amendment is needed to break into the huge treasure chests—a rare occurrence.

Pharma: The array of lobbyists, lawyers, and groups that push for favorable treatment for pharmaceutical companies through direct marketing, lobbying, and campaign contributions on both the state and federal level.

PhRMA: The trade association representing pharmaceutical companies.

pork: Colloquial term for capital-outlay funds used for brick-and-mortar projects around the state. In New Mexico, pork is allocated by individual legislators for projects they choose and can be used to reward friends.

pro tem: Short for president pro tempore of the Senate. The Latin phrase means he who presides for a time (temporarily). The lieutenant governor is nominally the president of the Senate, and the pro tem presides in his (or her) absence.

reconsideration: A parliamentary move used to revote on a certain bill. In order to reconsider a measure that has passed (or failed), a reconsideration motion must be made by a person who voted in the majority within a day of the original vote. If this passes, another vote is then taken on the measure.

redistricting: Redrawing of district lines to accommodate changes in population described by the census. It happens in a special session every ten years. The legislature draws the lines for itself, the U.S. Congress, the state school board, and the Public Regulation Commission.

referendum: When an issue is put to a popular vote. In New Mexico, the only state referendum we have is on a constitutional amendment, which is formulated by the legislature, passed by an extraordinary majority, and then placed on the ballot in the next election.

robo calls: Automated electronic calls made on behalf of candidates or marketers.

sergeant at arms: An elected position in each house; he or she has a staff of attendants that help with mundane but important details of bills and committees.

short session: Thirty-day session held every other year for budget and taxation purposes only—unless the governor asks for consideration of other specific issues.

sine die: To adjourn without a day—permanently, without returning. The last motion made in each session is to adjourn sine die.

SOS: Secretary of state, an elected office in charge of running elections.

special session: Called by the governor to handle matters when the regular session is over.

sponge bond: Bonds that are issued by the state to generate cash and that are to be paid off in a short time—days or months—with severance taxes.

sponsor: A prime sponsor is the legislator who signs and designs a bill, then guides it though the process. Co-sponsors also sign and help in its passage.

standing committee: Meets during the session only.

substitute bill: Bills introduced by legislators can be amended. When the changes are so many or substantial, or when a number of bills are combined into one, a substitute is often drawn up in committee or on the floor. The substitute replaces the original bill.

sunset clause: Attached at the end of a bill to end the provisions after a certain number of years and thus require reauthorization.

sunshine portal: A website that contains information about state government.

super PACs: PACs that are unrestrained in spending. Super PACs were created by the 2009 *Citizens United* Supreme Court ruling. Some do not have to reveal their contributors; most use negative TV and direct-mail advertisements to vilify the opposing candidates and their records.

table a bill: A majority of those present at a committee meeting or on the floor of the Senate can lay a bill on the table, meaning that no further action will be taken unless a person who voted to table it requests that it be brought up again for a vote. Sometimes bills are temporarily tabled pending the preparation of an amendment or further negotiations and then revived. More often it is a way of preventing them from moving forward, or "killing" them.

tax increment development district: TIDDs are special districts where taxes are reduced or rearranged in order to encourage development.

term limits: A limitation on the number of terms a legislator may serve. It is usually set by the constitution, voters, or by law passed by the legislature. New Mexico has none. Senators can serve as many four-year terms and House members as many two-year terms as they can, provided voters reelect them.

waiver: The federal government may allow a state to modify the Medicaid program by approving a waiver. Medicaid waivers usually require budget neutrality; that is, the new practice should not cost the feds more than the old one did.

walk: Avoid voting by not being physically present when the vote is taken.

walk list: Used by candidates and volunteers to solicit voters when walking door to door.

Index

Page numbers in italic text indicate illustrations.